# The Winds
## of Freedom

# Dean Rusk

Dean Rusk was born on a small farm in Cherokee County, Georgia, on February 9, 1909. His father had been trained as a Presbyterian minister but a throat ailment compelled him to turn to other work, and he was, in turn, a small farmer and a mail-carrier. His mother had been a teacher. He attended public schools in Atlanta and, with some scholarship aid, he earned his way through Davidson College. A Rhodes Scholarship enabled him to study for three years at Oxford, where he received the Honours Degree in Philosophy, Politics and Economics. He gave special attention to international affairs and wrote an essay which won the Cecil Peace Prize. In this same period he spent considerable time at German universities.

On returning to the United States in 1934, Mr. Rusk became associate professor of government and international relations at Mills College. He taught there for approximately six years, becoming dean of the faculty. An Infantry Reserve Officer since 1931, he was called to active duty in December 1940. After nearly a year with the Third Division, he was assigned to military intelligence. In 1943 he was transferred to the China-Burma-India Theater, where he rose to the position of Deputy Chief of Staff. In June 1945, he returned to the War Department to serve in the Operations Division of the General Staff.

Demobilized in early 1946, he entered the Department of State as Assistant Director of the Division of International Security Affairs. After a few months he was recalled to the Pentagon as Special Assistant to the Secretary of War. In February 1947, he returned to the State Department as Director of the Office of Special Political Affairs. Subsequently he served as Assistant Secretary for United Nations Affairs, Deputy Under Secretary, and Assistant Secretary for Far Eastern Affairs.

From 1952 to 1960 he was President of the Rockefeller Foundation. He kept in touch with international affairs not only through the Rockefeller Foundation's activities overseas but as a member of various study groups, including the Rockefeller Brothers Fund panels. He first met John F. Kennedy after the 1960 election, when the President-elect invited him to Washington for a talk. Shortly thereafter Mr. Kennedy invited him to a second talk and offered him the post of Secretary of State.

# *The Winds of Freedom*

Selections from the Speeches and Statements of
SECRETARY OF STATE DEAN RUSK
January 1961—August 1962

Edited and with an Introduction by
ERNEST K. LINDLEY
Special Assistant to the Secretary

BEACON PRESS    BOSTON

First published in 1963 by Beacon Press
Copyright © 1963 by Beacon Press
Library of Congress catalog card number: 63-10139
*All rights reserved*
Published simultaneously in Canada by
S. J. Reginald Saunders and Co., Ltd., Toronto
Printed in the United States of America

# Contents

INTRODUCTION BY THE EDITOR     ix

I. THE WINDS OF FREEDOM     1

II. THE NATURE OF THE WORLD STRUGGLE     11
    *Coercion Versus Free Choice* 11
    *The Cause of the Cold War* 19
    *The Shaping of History* 27

III. OUR POSITIVE STRATEGY     41

IV. MEN, ADMINISTRATION AND PUBLIC SERVICE     61
    *The Making and Execution of Foreign Policy* 61
    *The Role of the Foreign Service* 70
    *Strengthening Our Public Service* 80
    *Quality and Gallantry in the Foreign Service* 83

V. TRADE AND THE ATLANTIC PARTNERSHIP     85
    *Trade and Aid—Essentials of Free World Leadership* 85
    *The Trade Expansion Act of 1962* 97
    *Trade, the Commonwealth and the United States* 102

VI. FOREIGN AID     107
    *Charting a New Course in Foreign Aid* 107
    *The Foreign Aid Program for Fiscal Year 1963* 115

VII. CUBA, THE WESTERN HEMISPHERE AND THE
ALLIANCE FOR PROGRESS     127
    *The Communist Offensive in the Western Hemisphere* 127
    *Closing Statement at Punta del Este Conference* 142
    *Report to the Nation on the Punta del Este Conference* 144
    *The Alliance for Progress in the Context of World Affairs* 149

VIII. BERLIN, GERMANY AND NATO          159

    *The Soviets Cannot Extinguish Western Rights* 161
    *We Stand Firm But Are Willing To Talk* 163
    *The Berlin Wall* 167
    *Exploratory Talks* 168
    *The Future of Germany* 171
    *Strengthening the Western Alliance* 174

IX. SOUTHEAST ASIA          177

    *The Importance of SEATO* 177
    *The Neutralization of Laos* 182
    *The Aggression Against Viet-Nam* 194

X. THE FAR EAST AND THE PACIFIC          197

    *The Importance of ANZUS* 197
    *Our Duties in the Pacific* 205
    *The Importance of Japan* 212
    *Our Continuing Interest in Korea* 215
    *China and the United Nations* 216
    *No Settlement in Sight* 218

XI. AFRICA, THE MIDDLE EAST AND SOUTH ASIA          221

    *Our Policy in Regard to the Congo* 221
    *Our Purposes in Africa* 226
    *Our Interest in CENTO* 228
    *Our Stake in India* 233

XII. TRADE AND EXCHANGES WITH THE COMMUNIST STATES          235

XIII. DISARMAMENT, A NUCLEAR TEST BAN AND SPACE          257

    *Why We Seek Disarmament and Arms Control* 257
    *Disarmament—the U. S. Position and Some New Proposals* 267
    *The U. S. Still Hopes for a Nuclear Test Ban Agreement* 277
    *A Safe Total Environment* 288
    *New Frontiers of Science, Space and Foreign Policy* 289
    *A Call for Action* 294

XIV. THE UNITED NATION     301

     *Why We Support the United Nations 301*
     *The Troika 305*
     *The Succession to Dag Hammarskjold 307*

XV. EDUCATION, INFORMATION AND CULTURAL AFFAIRS     315

     *The Community of Science and Scholarship 315*
     *Education and Development 318*
     *Education—Do It Right 320*
     *On Knowing What America Stands For 321*
     *The Voice of America 324*

XVI. TOASTS AND TRIBUTES     327

     *Bataan and Corregidor 327*
     *To the President of the Republic of China 329*
     *To the Shah of Iran 331*
     *To the President of the Republic of the Ivory Coast 332*
     *To John Foster Dulles 335*
     *To Diplomacy 339*

XVII. OUR GOAL: A WORLDWIDE VICTORY FOR FREEDOM     341

     INDEX     353

# Introduction

The Secretary of State is the President's principal adviser in formulating foreign policy and his principal agent in conducting it. He is also the President's chief deputy in explaining it—to Congress and the American people, to the governments and peoples of more than forty allies and of more than that many other non-Communist nations, and, indeed, to our Communist adversaries.

In simpler days when we felt secure in isolation and our foreign relations were largely formal and passive, the Secretary of State's responsibility for spreading understanding of our policies was of limited importance. Now, when the United States, as the leader of a struggle to preserve and spread freedom, is heavily engaged in action on every continent and confronts unprecedented complexities and dangers, the support of the American people is indispensable. This support depends upon understanding. So does the cooperation of our allies and of all the other nations which would not survive in independence if American policy were to fail or falter.

This volume represents primarily Dean Rusk's activity as an expounder of American policy during his first nineteen months as Secretary of State under President John F. Kennedy—January 1961-August 1962. A full compilation of his public utterances during this period would require three or four volumes of this size. The editor has chosen representative items which seemed to help give an intelligent reader a firm understanding of the main lines of American policy. To the same end, the selections are grouped according to subject, beginning with the more fundamental expressions.

The period covered by this book has been one of crises. These have exacted the urgent attention of the President and the Secretary of State. But they have not arrested or deflected the development of constructive, coordinated policies. These rest on the foundations laid during the Truman and Eisenhower Administrations. But they have been revised, amplified and, in some respects, sharpened in the light of experience and changing conditions.

In this book may be found a central philosophy rooted in American history and ideals; analyses of the nature of the world struggle; a set of objectives designed to protect and enhance the security of the United States and all free peoples; a grand strategy for pursuing those objectives; and the application of grand strategy to many concrete problems. The reader may see the relationship of the parts to the whole and that (as is underlined in the last chapter) the ultimate goal of American policy is a world-wide victory for freedom.

In a volume of this length, it is not feasible to set forth our specific policies regarding every problem and every nation. At the same time it seemed unnecessary to reiterate our fundamental purposes and strategy as often as Secretary Rusk has reiterated them in different places and different times. The editor has not deleted all duplications of theme, however. To have done so would have devitalized and distorted the harmony of Secretary Rusk's thinking. The book ends on the same theme with which it begins, and this theme permeates all that lies between.

Although this volume chiefly reflects Secretary Rusk as an expositor of American policy, it contains glimpses of some of his other major activities. It includes his views on the methods of formulating and conducting foreign policy. It brings out, implicitly at least, that diplomacy is no longer a thing apart, that the waging of this global contest requires the coordination of all instruments—military, economic, technical, educational, informational and cultural—as well as diplomatic. The Secretary of

State is the President's first deputy in maintaining such coordination.

Some of the selections show the Secretary of State engaged in the intricate and time-consuming, but essential, business of managing our relations with our allies. Others concern the gravest of his responsibilities: negotiations with the Soviet Union, particularly on Laos, disarmament, an atomic test ban and Berlin.

Another of the Secretary of State's duties—to entertain as well as to confer with distinguished visitors—is indicated by the inclusion of a few of some forty toasts at state dinners and luncheons. These, too, are part of the stuff of diplomacy. The few chosen are purely illustrative: to have published them all would have lengthened this volume unduly.

Like an iceberg, the Secretary of State's work is mostly beneath the surface. Secretary Rusk is a strong believer in quiet diplomacy, which is another reason why little or nothing about certain problems and our relations with the countries involved in them appears in this volume. Much else that is important—such as his advice to the President, his personal role in formulating policy, his relations with his colleagues and his direction of the State Department and our overseas missions—must await the biographers and the historians.

It can be asserted without danger of contradiction that Secretary Rusk has been a busy man. In the nineteen months covered by this book he traveled more than 185,000 miles, nearly 161,000 of them on foreign missions—somewhat more than John Foster Dulles traveled in the first nineteen months he was Secretary of State. He attended fifteen major international conferences, and held innumerable bilateral talks with chiefs of state, heads of government, foreign ministers and ambassadors— abroad, at the United Nations and in Washington. He testified before Congressional committees forty-seven times, held forty press conferences and appeared on twenty-three television and radio programs in the U.S., plus others abroad. In addition, he held many background briefings for important groups. His normal work week has been seven days and his normal workday from 8:30 A.M. to well into the night. In the nineteen months covered by this book he took no vacation, and was away from his job only eleven days—two Saturdays, eight Sundays, and Christmas—plus a few Saturday and Sunday afternoons.

Exceptional energy and stamina are essentials for a Secretary of State in these times. Other qualities are even more important. Among them are immense knowledge of the world; understanding of the often intricate relationships of one problem to other problems; a steady capacity for clear analysis and for arriving, often quickly, at decisions. They include skill, firmness and persistence in negotiation, gifts of persuasion, the ability to lead and to direct or to guide the work of others, and the candor, consistency and integrity which build confidence. Not least in the thermonuclear age, they include prudent judgment. These qualities may be seen, I think, in the ensuing pages.

I hope that the reader may sense also some of Dean Rusk's warmer characteristics: his sense of humor, his courteousness, his generosity toward his colleagues (his word for his subordinates), his modesty and his selfless dedication to the national interest and the cause of freedom. To his associates he exemplifies the motto: "Suaviter in modo—fortiter in re."

For help in assembling and editing these papers and preparing explanatory notes, I am obliged to several members of the Secretary's personal staff, of the Executive Secretariat and of various bureaus of the Department. I am indebted particularly to Marion L. Terrell, Karen L. Johnston, and Anne C. Boehringer of the Bureau of Public Affairs and, above all, to my secretary, Christine A. Stavrou. I appreciate also helpful suggestions from the Beacon Press, which proposed this book and is expediting its publication. The responsibility for choosing, arranging and editing the material, and for wording the explanatory notes—thus for whatever shortcomings this volume may have—has been, however, exclusively mine.

ERNEST K. LINDLEY

*Special Assistant to the Secretary of State and member of the Policy Planning Council, Department of State.*

*Washington, September 28, 1962*

*The Winds*
*of Freedom*

# I. THE WINDS OF FREEDOM

*In this article for the Saturday Evening Post (June 30-July 7 issue, 1962), Secretary Rusk summarized his basic political philosophy.*

The Fourth of July is an especially appropriate time to reflect on our political heritage and its meaning in our times. Seventeen months' experience as Secretary of State has strengthened my conviction that the ideas which inspired the American Revolution and have guided our national development are the most powerful forces at work in the world today.

These ideas were stated simply but eloquently in certain of the great lines of our Declaration of Independence: "that all men are created equal, that they are endowed by their Creator with certain unalienable Rights, that among these are Life, Liberty and the pursuit of Happiness. That to secure these rights, Governments are instituted among Men, deriving their just powers from the consent of the governed."

We were born as a nation out of a commitment to government by "the consent of the governed" and the proposition that man has certain unalienable rights. We adopted and have preserved a Constitution, with its Bill of Rights, to give form to these ideas and to protect them. At home as well as on the world scene these general commitments have, in the end, governed our policy as a nation.

Over the generations we have struggled to improve the application of these principles. We have fought to defend them. And we have the means and the will to defend them today.

As President Kennedy said in his Inaugural Address: "Let every nation know, whether it wishes us well or ill, that we shall pay any price, bear any burden, meet any hardship, support any friend, oppose any foe to assure the survival and the success of liberty."

### IDEAS OF UNIVERSAL APPEAL

We have become the strongest nation in the world and achieved the highest level of wellbeing for the average citizen that mankind has known. But that is not, I think, the primary reason why these ideas are the most powerful force at work in the world today. It is because the ideas themselves have proved universal in their appeal, because the truths which the Declaration of Independence called "self-evident" have seized, or are seizing, the minds of men everywhere.

These universal ideas gave rise to the democracies of Western Europe. They inspired the liberators of Latin America. They guided the development of the British Commonwealth. Since the Second World War they have led to the creation of more than forty independent nations in Asia and Africa. We welcome these new nations with open arms to "the separate and equal station to which the Laws of Nature and of Nature's God entitle them."

Thomas Jefferson and John Adams and the others who helped to frame or subscribed to the Declaration would not have been surprised by this. Quite the contrary. They did not pretend to have invented anything new. The burden of complaint in the Declaration was that a tyrannical king was depriving the people of the American colonies of rights and liberties they had long enjoyed. Such opposition was in the British tradition. The British people had been building their liberties bit by bit, in no small part by contending that certain rights had previously existed. Magna Charta, the Petition of Right, the Declaration of Rights, among other great documents in the growth of the British Constitution, demanded what their claimants insisted was already the law of the land. The common-law judges who, sometimes at the risk of their own lives, put their arms around a prisoner at the bar and said to the king, "No, you cannot do that to this man," were strengthening traditional rights. Old rights were gradually expanded and improved. Thus slowly evolved both the Common Law and British institutions of democratic government.

### DEPARTURE FROM BRITISH PATTERN

The larger principles stated in our Declaration of Independence were a departure from the British pattern. They were not articulated as the special historic rights and liberties of the British people or of the inhabitants of the British colonies on the eastern edges of the North American continent. But neither were they set forth as novel doctrine. They were presented as universal truths, arising out of a discourse on the nature and purpose of man which had begun more than 2000 years earlier in Greece.

Likewise the French Declaration of the Rights of Man of 1789 was presented as a manifesto not just for the Frenchmen of that day, but for all men and all time.

From North America and Western Europe these ideas have spread over the world. Their strength and the willingness of men to fight for them have brought down one despotism after another. They are challenged today by the Communist tyrannies. But even the Communists seem to recognize the appeal of the notions of liberty and democracy. They call their governments "republics" or "people's republics" or "democratic republics," although not one of them is a republic, not one rests on the consent of the governed tested in free elections. They are fond of such words as "democracy" and "freedom," although they invariably use them to mean the precise opposite. Likewise they apply the label "wars of liberation" to their efforts to impose their system on others by force. Their so-called "war of liberation" in South Viet-nam is in reality a gangster war of assassination and terror against the common people of that country.

### NEW NATIONS CHERISH OUR PRINCIPLES

Some people—too many—have fallen under the control of Communist regimes; but nowhere is communism as a creed deeply rooted. Communists have signally failed in their efforts to capture control of the independence movements in Asia and Africa. With partial exceptions for North Korea and North Vietnam, the new nations have come into being under the impulse of Western ideas and, in the main, under the leadership of men educated in Western universities or in local universities or mission schools where the concepts and practices of democracy, law and liberty were taught.

As Secretary of State I have talked with many of the leaders of these new nations. It has been thrilling and reassuring to hear so many of them advocate the great principles we have so long cherished—and with an understanding of their meaning which is the same as ours. What the Great Seal of the United States calls the "new order of the ages" is the example which most of the people of the world seek to follow.

As Robert Frost put it in his special poem for President Kennedy's inauguration:

> *New order of the ages did they say?*
> *The newest thing in which they led the way*
> *Is in our very papers of the day.*

But we of the West, and particularly we Americans, should not overstate our contribution. We have done our share in formulating and advocating these principles and in protecting their practice. We can glory in having been among the first to endeavor systematically to apply them. Had we failed, the cause of freedom would have been set back for a long time. In his first inaugural Washington said that "the preservation of the sacred fire of liberty and the destiny of the republican model of government are justly considered as deeply, perhaps as finally, staked on the

experiment intrusted to the hands of the American people."
(The underlining was Washington's.)

But I do not believe that these ideas and the institutions
which seek to translate them into a way of life would have spread
over the world if they were not, as the authors of the Declaration
of Independence believed, rooted in the aspirations of men everywhere. In plain fact, these concepts are not exclusively Western.
They were articulated in ancient philosophies and various re-
ligions. They appeared in rudimentary form in the traditional
autonomy of villages in many lands, and even in the taboos of
primitive societies.

The idea that men should be free to speak their minds is
certainly not peculiar to us or to the West. The idea that raw
power must be curbed, that men are entitled to justice under
law, is not peculiar to us or to the West. Nor does the West have
an exclusive patent on the notion of consent of the governed or,
as Lincoln put it more affirmatively, "government of the people,
by the people, for the people."

As President Kennedy said on July fifth of last year at the
ceremonies which marked the 150th anniversary of Venezuelan
independence, the revolution whose principles were clarioned in
our own Declaration of Independence is a "great world revolution . . . a revolution so flexible it answers the needs of all countries, of all races, of all cultures."

### FREEDOM NOT A WESTERN MONOPOLY

I have heard it contended that the failure of some of the
new nations to achieve or maintain fully democratic governments proves that democracy is unsuited to the peoples of Asia
and Africa. I reject that contention. It is true that democracy
cannot be created overnight. It is the most difficult form of
government to operate. It requires an enlightened citizenry, a
wide consensus on national purposes, forbearance and much
skill. Only a few nations have thus far been successful in making
democracy work continuously. And none, including ourselves,
can claim to operate it perfectly.

But peoples keep turning and returning to democracy, because it is the system which harmonizes with human dignity and the abiding impulse of men to organize their societies in ways which protect that dignity. We have seen that happen in every continent. I have no doubt that we shall see it happen in still other countries where democracy has momentarily broken down or not yet been fully achieved. The exact forms of democratic institutions may vary from country to country. Perhaps some of the new nations erred in trying to copy exactly the parliamentary systems of the former colonial powers. There are many conceivable forms of democratic institutions. Ours have changed in some respects over the years. I am confident that the new nations which have not yet found the way to make democratic institutions work will succeed eventually. For I believe that the basic motivations and aspirations of men are essentially the same, regardless of the color of their skin or the continent or island on which they live. The human race is one.

### THE MANDARIN AND THE PEASANT

A traditional Vietnamese story bears on this proposition. In the words of Hoang Van Chi (in his article "Collectivization and Rice Production," in *The China Quarterly,* January-March, 1962, issue) it runs this way:

There was once a peasant who grew such excellent fruit that his fame spread far and wide throughout the land. The governor of the district in which the man lived made a special journey to visit him and to inquire about the methods he employed to produce such magnificent fruit.

The peasant was a little overawed by the presence of such a great mandarin, but he did his best to reply to the latter's questions. "To tell you the truth," he said, "I haven't any special method at all. Whenever I plant a fruit tree, I provide it with as much manure as I can, set it upright in the hole, tamp the earth back firmly around the trunk, and then I leave it to itself. I never prune it, or train its branches, or chop its roots like the other people do, and it provides me with plenty of fine fruit."

The mandarin nodded his head in approval and then put another question to the peasant. "You seem to be able to manage your fruit trees admirably. Can you give me any advice about how to manage men, about how to govern a district?"

The unexpected question surprised the peasant, so he was obliged to pause for a few moments and to think before he eventually replied. "Administration," he said, "has never been my profession, so I have never really devoted much thought to it, but it is my opinion that men are like fruit trees. If you provide them with the conditions in which they can live and work, and keep a fatherly eye upon them from time to time, they will be prosperous, happy and will cause you no trouble. If, however, you summon them daily to your office and order them to do this or forbid them to do that, they will prove to be a constant source of trouble, disorder, and unhappiness."

As Mr. Hoang Van Chi pointed out, "The moral of this story is based upon centuries of experience, but the Vietnamese Communists are attempting to do just the reverse and are reaping the inevitable consequences. Man, having a mind and soul, is capable of being terrorized into submission, but only to a limited extent and for a limited time."

I share that conviction. I do not believe that even the modern police state, with all of its elaborate apparatus for repression, can permanently terrorize men into submission. I do not believe that any iron or bamboo curtain can permanently insulate large numbers of people against the great ideas of freedom and human dignity.

Today, even within the Soviet Union, there are signs that men and women want more freedom to state their views, greater scope to express the uniqueness and integrity born into them. Pasternak is dead, but his poems and great novel live. And some younger Soviet writers, reaching back into the rich and long Russian tradition, are choosing to focus their thoughts on the meaning of man and the worth of the individual. These stirrings may seem feeble to us, who have so long enjoyed liberty. But they are evidence that the Communists have not succeeded in turning men into robots. The themes of young writers and poets tell much of the direction societies will take; and in the Soviet Union these writers of the new generation are the beginning of what I believe will be a continuing trend—a slow trend perhaps, but one leading inexorably toward freedom.

I turn to another aspect of the struggle between freedom and coercion: the relative capacities of the two systems to improve the material wellbeing of men. The Soviets have made substantial progress in developing their physical resources. That is not especially surprising. They inherited a vast domain, with immense and varied natural riches, a very considerable industrial establishment and a talented and industrious people. The Communists claim to have invented a quick way of modernizing an economy. Although I cannot prove it, I believe that their economy could have been modernized faster under a political system which would have given full scope to individual initiatives and incentives. But any of us can muster ample evidence to repudiate the Communist claim that our economic development has been slow here at home.

All Americans of my generation know firsthand of the amazing economic and social advance of our own country in our own lifetimes. Many, like myself, were born in underdeveloped parts of the United States. Our society in rural Georgia when I was growing up was prescientific, pretechnical, premedical, prepublic health, preeducation—by present-day standards.

FREE SYSTEMS SURPASS SOVIETS

Forty years ago only two American farms out of one hundred had any electric power; today ninety-eight out of one hundred have power for dozens of chores. Consider what has been done to lighten the burdens of the mother and housewife, to improve health and living conditions, within the past thirty-five years, and even within the past ten. Since the Bolshevik revolution we have added to our national production more than the entire present production of the Soviet Union.

Look at the amazing economic progress of Western Europe

and Japan under free systems. Compare East Germany with West Germany, or Eastern Europe with Western Europe. Compare Communist China with almost any country you would care to name. The "great leap forward" has come down bottom side up. The vaunted "shortcut to the future" has proved to be the shortcut to misery.

Those who are responsible for what is happening all the way from East Germany to North Viet-Nam have not found the answer to the central problem to which they claim to have addressed themselves—the problem of economic and social satisfaction. They have not solved even the elementary problems of food production.

So when we say to our friends in the developing countries that the Communists have not found a magic formula and that the proved way of rapid development is through free institutions, devised by each nation in the light of its own history, we speak on the basis of the solid lessons of long human experience.

The economic and social performance of the industrialized free nations has knocked the bottom out of Marxist dogma. Marx predicted that the poor would become more numerous and ever poorer and that the rich would become fewer and ever richer. The precise opposite has occurred. The advanced nations of the free world devised means of directing the flow of income and of using their resources to improve the life of the ordinary man. It is in them that one sees the highest levels of wellbeing most equitably distributed.

POWER OF THE HUMAN SPIRIT

Marx predicted also a chain of recurring and ever deepening economic crises. But the advanced free nations have devised means of curbing economic cycles and stimulating economic growth. Marx failed to reckon with the mind and spirit of men, their compassion and political ingenuity, their capacity to use free institutions to advance their lot.

It is not for us to fear the great winds of change that are

blowing today. They are the winds we have long known and sailed with, the winds which have carried man on his unending journey, the winds of freedom.

We don't have to argue with people in other parts of the world about what we are really after and what they are really after. Have you ever been able to find anyone who would rather be ignorant than educated? Or hungry than fed? Or sick than healthy? Or gagged instead of free to speak his mind? Or shut up behind a wall or barbed wire instead of free to move about? Or who relished the knock on the door at midnight which means terror?

These simple ideas I have been writing about are the great power of the human spirit. Because they are central to our purposes, America at her best is admired and trusted; and America is at her best when she is true to the commitments we made to ourselves and to history in the Declaration of Independence. These are the ideas and ideals which give us allies, spoken or silent, among men and women in every corner of the earth. They are part of the unfinished business which is a part of our story. This is the basis of our confidence; this is the scope of our task.

The revolution of freedom, which we have so proudly nurtured and fought for in the past and to which we pledge today, as in 1776, "our Lives, our Fortunes and our Sacred Honor," is the true, enduring revolution, because it springs from the deepest, most persistent aspirations of men. History says this revolution will not fail.

# II.  THE NATURE
## OF THE WORLD STRUGGLE

*Coercion Versus Free Choice*

*This was the most fundamental of Mr. Rusk's early speeches as Secretary of State. His definition of the central issue of the world crisis stands as basic doctrine.*

Last year, as a private citizen, I had the temerity to give three lectures on the conduct of our foreign relations. They dealt with the roles of the President, the Secretary of State and the Congress. The first was published; the other two, happily, were not. The three were to make up a thin book—how thin I did not then appreciate. One matter which I underestimated was the problem of explaining foreign policy in a vigorous democracy, a democracy closely associated with more than forty allies and in friendly relations with more than fifty so-called "uncommitted

Address at the National Press Club, Washington, D. C., July 10, 1961.

11

nations," with, in the background, those also listening who would like to bring our democracy down.

Public officials are engaged in "inservice training," and I am grateful to many of you for your help—intended and unintended —with my education during these first months of office. I deeply believe that the public should be fully informed about the world situation and our courses of action to deal with it. In no other way can we mobilize both the necessary effort of a people who act through consent and the unity which is critically necessary in hazardous times. I believe, as well, that responsible public officials should in their statements seek to serve the public interest and not merely its passing curiosity. The public has a right to know, including the right to know that its serious business is being handled in a responsible fashion. For example, if there are differences between us and friendly nations about one or another aspect of the passing parade of events, these are more likely to be resolved by quiet conversation than by a public quarrel. If two of our friends find themselves in difficulty with each other, it is not always conducive to agreement for it to be publicly known that we have been offering friendly counsel.

And again, if a matter arises which is of deep concern to our allies and where unity among allies is critical to the sound handling of the issues involved, it is not always easy for the United States to sound off prematurely without consultation with those whose vital interests are also at stake.

But our policies are public, our purposes are those which the Nation itself enjoins upon its government; in the main, our acts are public, because that is the way a democracy moves. But diplomacy cannot always be so, or else it would be little more than debate, adding its fuel to the very fires it hopes to quench.

The press and public officials have a common problem in presenting foreign policy issues to the American people. It is the problem of context. It arises in part because of the limitations of space and time limitations imposed upon both those who offer information and those who read or listen to it. It is almost never possible to give a complete story on each of the events which arouse public interest. You and we share the difficulty of reducing complexities to manageable proportions and of using accurately and economically the moments of attention we get from a busy and preoccupied nation.

We are accustomed to think of our foreign relations as a series of large or small crises. To do so is itself to distort out of context, for it overlooks the mass of constructive relationships which are steadily building across national frontiers and does not convey the sense of the persistent underlying crisis under which the world has lived since World War II.

### BUILDING A DECENT WORLD ORDER

. . . I should like to comment on this underlying crisis from which many—but not all—of the troubles which attract our attention are derived.

Let us start from where we ourselves are and what we in this country should like to achieve in our relations with the rest of the world. Since World War II we have had more than one so-called great debate about foreign policy. Actually, the greatest debate of all occurred during that war, and the most eloquent voice was the war itself. Before the fighting was over we had concluded as a nation that we must throw ourselves into the building of a decent world order in which such conflagrations could not occur.

The nature of that world order was set forth succinctly in the charter of the United Nations, a charter backed by an overwhelming majority of the Senate and supported by an overwhelming majority of the Nation. It called for a community of independent nations, each free to work out its own institutions as it saw fit but cooperating effectively and loyally with other nations on matters of common interest and concern. The inevitable disputes were to be settled by peaceful means; and let us not forget that the charter supposed that the tried processes of negotiation, mediation and adjudication were to be preferred over violent or fruitless debate. But parties in serious dispute were to seek the help of the broader international community in order that disinterested judgments could be brought to bear upon sensitive or inflamed issues.

As such a world order grew in strength and effectiveness, the limitation and reduction of arms would become possible, cooperation on economic and social problems would improve the lot of man, human rights would be strengthened, and the role of law would steadily take over from the law of the jungle. On matters of political arrangements, the underlying thesis was that the people themselves should play the decisive role as the principle of self-determination was brought to bear. It was then, and remains, our hope that man can take up once again the ancient aspirations of the race and move to free himself from the burdens of war, tyranny and misery.

With deference to our shortcomings, I think it can be properly said that the United States threw itself with honesty and diligence into this great effort. It rapidly demobilized—more rapidly than events proved wise. It offered its atomic weapons to international control. It committed vast resources to the reconstruction of war-torn nations. It cooperated both in the large and in detail with the great cooperative ventures of the community of nations. Most important of all, it turned aside from the ambitions and appetites which have historically been associated with great power and conformed its national aims to those I have just described.

WHAT HAS GONE WRONG?

What has gone wrong? Why, after fifteen years, is there so much tension and danger in a world which had hoped for so much just yesterday? To be fair, let us not suppose that all of our problems are traceable to a single source. Under the best of conditions, the surging tides of nationalism and the insistent demands for economic and social improvement would have required great skill and understanding to handle the inevitable changes which were bound to come in our postwar world. But these were manageable, and there is no reason to suppose that they could not be accommodated in the processes of peaceful change.

The underlying crisis of our generation arises from the fact that the Soviet Union did not join the United Nations in fact, as well as in form, and lend itself to the commitments they and the rest of us made in the midst of a great war. The possession of power was transformed once more to ambition for more power. The capacity to defy law became a contempt for law. Doctrines were revised and adapted to promote an imperialism as old as the tragic history of man. An entire people was sealed off from the rest of the world, and secrecy became a prime strategic weapon. The institutions of the international community were either ignored or undermined from within. The Soviet Union has just cast its ninety-fifth veto in the Security Council of the United Nations.

In the process the very language of international intercourse became distorted and contrived. "Peace" has become a word to describe whatever condition would promote their world revolution. "Aggression" is whatever stands in its way. "People's Democracy" is a term applied to regimes no one of which has been chosen by free election. Self-determination is loudly espoused but only in areas not under Communist control.

The normally attractive word "negotiation" is used as a weapon, for the only subjects to be negotiated are further concessions to Communist appetite. Agreements are offered but against the background of a long and sobering list of broken promises; an agreement is apparently a rest camp, where one pauses and refits for a further advance. New assurances are offered in the very act of withdrawing those earlier given. Law, as one of their spokesmen put it, "is like the tongue of a wagon—it goes in the direction in which it is pointed." And the gains of lawlessness are cited as the "new conditions" which justify new invasions of the rights of others.

Neutrality is temporary, a pasture growing green for future grazing. On January 6, Mr. Khrushchev said, "The revolutionary emergence of more and more peoples into the world arena creates exceptionally favorable conditions for an unprecedented broadening of the sphere of influence of Marxism-Leninism. The time is not far away when Marxism-Leninism will possess the minds of the majority of the world's population." Apparently, according to one of his homely maxims, "Every vegetable has its season."

### CENTRAL ISSUE OF THE CRISIS

The underlying crisis is not an ideological conflict between nineteenth-century capitalism and nineteenth-century Marxism. It does not result from a bilateral conflict between the Soviet Union and the United States.

The central issue of the crisis is the announced determination to impose a world of coercion upon those not already subjected to it. If this seems exaggerated simplicity, let us not be misled by our own reluctance to believe what they say, for on this point they have proved that they mean it. At stake is the survival and growth of the world of free choice and of the free cooperation pledged in the charter. There is no "troika" on this issue—it is posed between the Sino-Soviet empire and all the rest, whether allied or neutral; and it is now posed in every continent.

The underlying crisis has shown itself in many forms—from the cynical disregard of the pledges on liberated areas, made at Yalta, to the latest threats to West Berlin. The calendar of conflict between these two dates is filled with unceasing attempts to expand an empire—some successful but many repelled by those determined to be free.

### STRENGTHENING WESTERN SOLIDARITY

President Kennedy has taken up his great task with a deep awareness of the nature of the crisis and of the actions required by the continuing struggle for freedom.

It is essential to get on with the building of the world community designed by the charter. This we would do in any event; but it is here that the breadth and depth of the crisis are fully revealed, and it is here that those who would not be coerced can act together for a world of peace. We speak of uncommitted nations, and we usually mean those who are committed to neither of the principal blocs on the present scene. But all nations have commitments arising out of their own interests and out of their own hopes for the future. In the United Nations commitments to the charter can weave the fabric of common interest which, by reaching beyond the cold war, may determine its outcome.

No less essential is the strengthening of the solidarity of NATO and of the Western community—possessed of enormous capacity to shape the course of events. The political, economic and military strengthening of the Western community is an urgent matter to which the administration is giving full attention. The President has also seen that the Western World must recapture the leadership of its own revolution of political freedom. It is a revolution which the West itself has taken into every continent and which continues to stir men to action. This struggle for freedom in the West itself was not painless; nor will it be in other places in our own time. But we dare not yield its leadership to those who would seize it, subvert it, and use it to destroy us.

The President is also asking us, and other economically advanced free nations, to reassert our leadership of the revolution of economic and social progress. The world of coercion is offering tempting bait for those who are determined to shake off their misery and want. We believe that freedom and progress are historic partners and that the alleged choice between rapid progress and free institutions is false. But this we must prove. This is the meaning of the President's Alliance for Progress, which is stirring the hopes and the hard thinking of the nations of our own hemisphere. This is the meaning of the rapidly growing effort of the Western community to throw substantial resources behind the economic and social development of less favored nations. This is why the President is asking for thoughtful planning, effective leadership, and determined self-help from those who need external assistance for national growth. And this is why the President is asking the Congress for aid legislation and appropriations which will put us in a position to help generate the momentum of development—aid which must be provided, in association with others, in the amounts and for the periods of time required to achieve enduring and satisfying results.

During these first months the President has established direct contact with the leadership of many nations in order to give us as quickly as possible an accurate understanding of their interests and views. In his own discussions with them, through the Vice President, Ambassador Stevenson and others, he has been able to lay the basis for the greater unity of our several alliances and the greater effort which will be required to deal with the continuing crisis.

The President has recognized the changes which are occurring in the strategic problems which we and our allies must face and is moving, in consultation with other governments, to bring the free world's capabilities up to the needs of the variety of dangers which have to be confronted.

### EFFORT TO RELIEVE ARMS RACE

Despite the continuing crisis, we have felt it necessary to work diligently and realistically at the possibilities of disarmament. Even though the political atmosphere is not encouraging, an imaginative effort must be made to relieve the tensions arising from the arms race itself. We cannot understand how the Soviet Union, which has expended so much eloquence on disarmament, could have rejected the reasonable and workable treaty for the ban of nuclear testing which was tabled at Geneva this spring. "General and complete disarmament" are apparently among those words given a special meaning in the glossary of their world revolution. For reasonable people would suppose that the way to get there is to start and that the steps along the way must be such as to leave no one, in Aristide Briand's words, as "dupes or victims." Nevertheless our work goes forward, and we earnestly hope that the Congress will support the recent proposals of the President to make it effective.

Let me conclude by saying that the agenda of our foreign relations is filled with problems requiring and getting urgent attention. If there are those looking for still waters, we are not yet there. We can move on with confidence if we are prepared to do what has to be done. The free world has enormous strength, including the inner strength of purposes which are deeply rooted in the nature of man.

The world of coercion has its problems too. Dissensions

within its ranks, national resistance to this modern imperialism, and a growing demand for freedom are among them. It has learned that economic aid does not buy puppets, that intimidation awakens its own resistance, that the United Nations is tougher than it thought, and that those who set out to "possess the minds" of man have set themselves against the course of history.

Our democracy must have its turbulent debate. Free nations will, of course, differ among themselves as they move to build a common interest out of disparate circumstances and varied responsibility. But the underlying crisis is becoming more widely understood, and out of it will come the responses which men must make when their freedom is at stake.

## The Cause of the Cold War

*Another basic speech, delivered after President Kennedy had made it plain that the United States, with its Allies, would defend the vital interests they share with the people of West Berlin.*

I have been a member of this Association for a number of years—in sentiment and interest longer than you might think. As a boy of twelve, I began my Army training in high school ROTC in Atlanta, Georgia, and have greatly valued my lifelong

Portion of address at the George C. Marshall Memorial Dinner given by the Association of the United States Army in honor of John J. McCloy, September 8, 1961. (Then the President's Adviser on Disarmament, Mr. McCloy had been Assistant Secretary of War during World War II, President of the International Bank and United States High Commissioner in Germany.)

ties with the Army. Indeed, Secretary Marshall, some fourteen years ago, summoned me to the Department of State just three days before I was to take the oath of office as an officer of the Regular Army.

It is not easy for me to speak in measured tones about George Catlett Marshall—a rigorous and accomplished soldier who was, at the same time, one of the greatest civilians of his day. Few men have had such profound influence upon all who served with him; he brought to living reality, for all around him, such simple notions as duty, justice, integrity and love of country. He left his associates a rich legacy of practical wisdom, not in polished essays but in countless fleeting comments in the course of daily business. "Don't ask me a question," he would say, "without bringing me your proposed answer." "Don't wait for me to tell you what you ought to be doing—you tell me what I ought to be doing." Or—"Gentlemen, let's not talk about this matter too much in military terms; to do so might make it a military problem."

You could have found no more suitable recipient for the George C. Marshall Award than John J. McCloy. He has served his country well in distinguished posts but none calling for more imagination, clarity of thought and persistence than the one he now holds as the President's Adviser on Disarmament. A man with less courage would abandon the task; a man with less humor would find it intolerable; a man with less hope for the future of man would give up in despair. The necessity for his effort is simply explained: We shall not find our way through the troubled world of today unless we keep working toward the world which must come into being if man is to survive.

Others have shown interest in the fact that General Marshall, Army Chief of Staff during the greatest war in our history, also earned the Nobel Peace Prize. So, too, that a former Assistant Secretary of War now heads our work on disarmament. We in America do not find this odd. For in their own lives these men remind us of both the olive branch and the arrows in our Great Seal, the symbols of a people who love peace but who take their liberties seriously in a dangerous world.

I wish to speak briefly this evening about danger and some

of the simple truths which moments of crisis clarify. If what I say is not new, it is because our commitment to freedom is as old as our Republic. We ourselves must try to be clear if others are to understand—at a time when the world cannot afford misunderstanding. We must find ways to make it clear that our desire to live in peace is not weakness—and to make it clear that our readiness to fight for freedom is not belligerence.

The forces of aggression in the world are trying to sow confusion, as have other aggressors in other decades. "All we want is a peace treaty," they say, but a peace treaty which threatens the peace. "All we want is a free city of Berlin," but the freedom they have in mind can be seen across the walls and through the barbed wire which divide that city. "Settle Berlin, and the way will be open for a period of peace and relaxation," they say. "Just once more" is a familiar phrase we have heard before, the nerve gas to prepare the way for endless appetite and ambition.

Their hope must be that we and the rest of the world will have short memories about this postwar world. Though we have all lived through it, we ourselves sometimes forget.

The United States emerged from World War II at a pinnacle of power never before achieved by any nation. Our productive facilities were incomparable and, alone among the larger industrialized nations, were unscathed by bomb or shell. We had a great army and the mightiest sea and air forces the world had ever seen. These were deployed around the globe on every sea and continent. We had developed a fantastic weapon, and we alone had it.

One thinks of Lord Acton's thought that "Power tends to corrupt; absolute power corrupts absolutely." It has been refuted by the course pursued by the United States in the last sixteen years.

DEDICATION TO U.N. PRINCIPLES

It is not a small thing in the history of the world that a nation with supreme, well-nigh unchallengeable power turned away from the exploitation of that power, from the corrupting policies which power could entail. We committed ourselves whole-heartedly to building a peaceful world order based on the principles which were written into the United Nations Charter. We took a leading role in creating the United Nations. I know of no better statement of the enduring purposes of the foreign policy of the American people than articles one and two of that charter.

Every nation which joined the United Nations joined in solemn commitments to renounce and suppress aggression and to settle disputes by peaceful means. Machinery was established to facilitate peaceful settlements—the Security Council, the General Assembly, the International Court. The members pledged themselves to use not only these bodies but the traditional processes of negotiation, conciliation, mediation and arbitration.

When one thinks of that great document, one remembers the hopes that went into its drafting. In the vernacular of the GI, it looked as if "man almost had it made."

We not only abided by the principles of the United Nations and dedicated ourselves to constructing the sort of world envisioned by the charter. We also moved to dismantle our own military power. In fact, we disarmed unilaterally and precipitously. By the end of 1946 we had no single Army division and no Air Force group ready for combat.

We still had an atomic monopoly. But we proposed to divest ourselves of atomic weapons, too. I was on the General Staff when Hiroshima occurred. I remember a remark of a colleague: "War has turned upon and devoured itself, for no human purpose can be achieved by war under these conditions." We as a nation believed that. We presented a plan for the international control of atomic energy, to assure that it would be used only for the peaceful benefit of all the peoples of the world and to avoid the kind of nuclear arms race which is subjecting the world to terror today. We most earnestly endeavored to get the United Nations to put that plan into effect. Our efforts were frustrated by one member: the Soviet Union.

We also sought to activate article forty-seven of the charter, providing for establishment of a United Nations force to be available to the Security Council itself, assisted by a Military Staff Committee—a force to be used in keeping the peace.

And, not least, we repeatedly have tried to give effect to the provisions of articles twenty-six and forty-seven for establishing a system for the regulation of armaments.

### HOPES FOR PEACE FRUSTRATED BY SOVIET UNION

Why have these hopes, which we are convinced are the hopes of most of mankind, been frustrated? Why have all our efforts borne so little fruit? The central reason is that one government refused to join with the rest in building the kind of world the United Nations Charter envisioned and, instead, embarked upon a course of aggression.

The Soviet Union contemptuously reneged on its wartime pledges to permit self-determination in Eastern Europe. It supported an aggression against Greece, thinly disguised as a "civil war." It tried to intimidate Turkey into yielding concessions which would have jeopardized the independence of Turkey and exposed other nations in the eastern Mediterranean and beyond to aggression.

Counting on economic chaos as its ally, the Soviet Union sought to extend its dominion into Western Europe. In 1948, in violation of its agreements with the Western allies, it blockaded Berlin, denounced the quadripartite control machinery for Germany, and set about making the part of Germany which it occupied a political and social segment of the Soviet Union itself. Then came the aggression in Korea. A little later came the ruthless suppression of Hungary.

One incident after another has made it quite clear that the Soviet Union will not tolerate self-determination by any people over whom it can extend its sway. One incident after another has demonstrated that it is not prepared to work toward a world of law. As one Soviet representative put it: "The law is like the tongue of a wagon: It goes in the direction in which it is pointed." Or, as other representatives have put it: "The Soviet Union will not submit its interests to decision by anyone else." Such a policy—and its corollary, the "troika," which would paralyze the executive functions of the United Nations—torpedoes the possibility of law, of adjudication, of mediation, of peaceful settlement, peaceful adjustment of conflicting interests.

That declared policy of noncooperation, plus modern weapons—plus the Soviets' terroristic threats to employ those weapons—gives dramatic content to the words used by Thomas Hobbes in describing the law of the jungle: "nasty, brutish, and short."

Against this background, the meaning of the cold war becomes clearer. We did not declare it; we ourselves cannot end it. The cold war is the direct expression of the announced determination of the Sino-Soviet bloc to extend their "historically inevitable" world revolution by every available means. It is a program of action, which they sometimes try to disguise as a scientific principle. They speak of the irresistible spread of ideas—but have failed to show a single instance of a people who have voluntarily embraced communism through free elections. The cold war will end when those who declared it decide to abandon it. Otherwise, it cannot end so long as peoples throughout the world are determined to be free, to decide their own institutions, to control their own destinies.

### THE CHALLENGE TO SOVIET LEADERSHIP

The Soviet leaders do have in their hands a revolutionary potential more dramatic than anything we have yet seen. That lies in their capacity to transform the world in which we live by a simple decision to live at peace with it. One can experience no more startling a reflection than to imagine what could be within the grasp of mankind if the principles of the United Nations Charter were deeply established as the rule of conduct of all nations, including the Soviet Union. We are familiar with the capacity of law to enlarge the areas of individual freedom by simple arrangements for protecting each against the undue intrusion of the others. We have made great progress in applying a rule of law across national frontiers in arranging the countless daily transactions of the world's work. Already, throughout most of the world there are in progress every day throughout the year acts of cooperation which support what Raymond Fosdick has called "the infinity of threads which bind peace together." But a large, important and powerful part of the world has not joined this effort and, indeed, seeks to disrupt it. This is the great challenge to Soviet leadership; this is the direction in which they can move to write brilliant chapters in the history of man. If they are in another world, it is their own choice; in the world we know, there is room for all who are prepared to join in carrying forward the promise which lies within the grasp of man.

In the field of disarmament Soviet leaders hold in their hands another crucial key. It is not difficult to disarm the United States; we are a people who would prefer to turn our resources to other purposes. The most effective way to disarm is to begin by keeping the peace—to demonstrate over time that they will leave their neighbors alone. If the United States is spending for arms today almost four times what we spent in the immediate postwar years, it is not because we prefer it that way, or because economic prosperity depends upon it. We do so reluctantly as a harsh necessity. Without the clear necessity, the American people could not be compelled to sustain so heavy a burden for arms.

Obviously, what I have suggested would take time—time which we may not have. The arms race produces its own tension. If we could find a way to limit that race before broad political issues are resolved, we should make the effort. Here, again, the key is not in our hands. Important steps could be taken promptly if those involved would abandon the fetish of secrecy. Disarmament cannot occur if those who are prepared to act in good faith and with full public knowledge are to become what Aristide Briand called "dupes or victims." We must continue our own effort to achieve reasonable and practical proposals; present tensions make the effort more and not less essential. This is why we hope very much that the Congress will complete action at this session on President Kennedy's proposals for a Disarmament Agency.

### THE ISSUE OF BERLIN

The months ahead will be critical months and much will turn on the issue of Berlin. President Kennedy has called it "the great testing place of Western courage and will, a focal point where our solemn commitments, stretching back over the years since 1945, and Soviet ambitions now meet in basic confrontation." He has called upon our own people and upon our allies to undertake fresh sacrifices to give the free world the additional strength we shall need to keep the peace or to meet the dangers which might arise. . . .

At the very time he called for greater strength, President Kennedy said,

> . . . we shall always be prepared to discuss international problems with any and all nations that are willing to talk—and listen—with reason. . . . If they seek genuine understanding, not concessions of our rights, we shall meet with them. . . . We cannot negotiate with those who say, "What's mine is mine and what's yours is negotiable."

We expect negotiations on Berlin as soon as it is apparent that negotiations of a serious and constructive character can occur. We cannot believe that any power could press so dangerous an issue without full exploration with all whose interests and pledges are involved. There are channels of communication available between Moscow and the West; they are not being neglected. The problem is whether channels can lead to a meeting of minds, whether peace is a common purpose, whether there are arrangements, in the President's words, "consistent with the maintenance of peace and freedom and with the legitimate security interests of all nations."

If peaceful processes are to succeed, they must be given their chance. This means that unilateral action taken against the vital interests of the free world in West Berlin could only court disaster. There have been threats and implied threats of such action in recent weeks, with particular regard to allied air traffic into Berlin. These threats have been rejected promptly and in the most solemn terms by the Western Powers. I spoke earlier of clarity. It is possible for those who do not understand democracy to make a mistake about these matters—by listening only to the voices they wish to hear, by confusing debate with disunity, by reading a desire for peace as a willingness to yield. These are mistakes which Moscow cannot afford and which mankind cannot afford.

## The Shaping of History

*A third basic speech, which answers some searching questions.*

I accepted your invitation to speak on this occasion with genuine satisfaction but with an appreciation of the exacting demands imposed by the nature of my audience. Indeed, I find myself with an assignment which you yourselves have set, more particularly in the excellent presidential address delivered by Professor Bemis [Samuel Flagg Bemis, president of the American Historical Association] last evening—an address notable both for its lucid review of the course we have traveled and for the sharpness and relevance of the questions it posed for us today.

The community of historians and a Secretary of State are linked by a common task—that of finding and articulating the scarlet threads of meaning and direction in the flow of tumultuous events. Their approach may differ both in time and in purpose because of their differing responsibilities. What to the historian becomes a swirling blizzard of papers is for a Secretary of State an unrelenting parade of precise day-to-day business. The historian has a slight advantage in that he knows a bit more about how the story came out; a Secretary has the stimulation which comes from a commitment, as the President's adviser, to try to shape the story toward a tolerable conclusion.

Both historian and Secretary must wrestle with the problem of complexity, each in his own way. At no point in our history has this been more exigent than now, and it would be naive to

Address before the American Historical Association at Washington, D. C., December 30, 1961.

hope that we are moving toward simplicity. It was not until 1823 that John Quincy Adams established our tenth diplomatic mission abroad, not until a century later that Charles Evans Hughes established our fiftieth, and only forty years later that Christian Herter established our hundredth. Before World War II less than ten capitals disposed of the foreign relations of the vast continent of Africa; today the number is over thirty. With 104 members in the United Nations and approximately one hundred items on the agenda of the recent General Assembly, some 10,000 primary votes were cast in which the United States had a larger or lesser interest. Our missions in a number of capitals exchange some 10,000 telegrams with the Department in the course of a year. How grateful we become to those capitals which are never responsible for a telephone call past midnight! When Thomas Jefferson or John Marshall bade God-speed to an American ambassador departing for his post, they knew that it might be months before they would hear from him again. How tempting it now is to say to his modern colleague, "If I don't hear from you for the first year, you would please me very much."

There is a widespread illusion that modern communications have degraded the role of the ambassador—that cable, telephone and radio have made him merely the messenger boy of impulses from his capital. The trouble with this notion is that it overlooks the breathtaking acceleration of the flow of events, brought about largely by these same communications and the latest modes of travel and transport. The man on the spot is more just exactly that than ever before, and every week brings instances of the critical responsibility of the ambassador abroad.

This question of pace is perhaps more difficult for a Secretary than for the historian, who can make certain choices. For a Secretary lives with the spurs of time upon him. His is not the luxury of a leisurely conclusion but the pressures of inescapable decisions, for he knows that both action and inaction are decisions where the United States is concerned. He is conscious of the decisions made, but he is haunted by the limitless possibilities of the decisions which are taken by not being made—the decisions which tantalize and often escape the view of the historian.

It occurred to me that it would be appropriate for me to

comment on the larger issues of contemporary history posed at the close of Professor Bemis's address and to relate these to my daily tasks.

### CLARITY OF PURPOSE A BASIS OF PEACE

First is this searching question: Does our comfortable democracy have the nerve and will to protect its essential interests and the frontiers of freedom in the face of potential enemies who command nuclear weapons and the capacity to deliver them against our homeland?

This is not a rhetorical issue, and we must clearly understand its grim reality. There are several paths to nuclear war. It could happen if one side or the other deliberately sets out to provoke one. I am inclined to believe that the irrationality of such a course makes it relatively unlikely. Another would be a situation in which two sides confront each other, each utterly convinced that under no circumstances would the other resort to nuclear war, each therefore tempted to press its demands across the threshold of disaster. A third path lies in simple confusion about essential interests, misapprehensions about the tolerable limits of conduct.

We confront a direct challenge, in Berlin, to the vital interests of the United States and the West. The challenge takes the form of the assertion that our presence there, on the basis of well-established rights, and access to Berlin from the West, can be radically altered or extinguished by the unilateral act of the other side and that this act would require us to petition the authorities in East Germany for the privilege of maintaining the freedom of West Berlin.

Before the President spoke to the American people on July 25th, he and other Western leaders decided that vital interests and commitments in West Berlin, crucial to our own security, must be defended at whatever cost. That decision remains the basis on which we intend to explore the possibilities of a peaceful resolution of the Berlin crisis. If peace depends on clarity, the other side must not be allowed any dangerous illusion.

This clarity is the basis of an assurance to our own and other peoples that the possibilities of patient diplomacy will be exhausted to insure that vital interests are protected and that the other side will not be permitted to make a fatal mistake. We regard it as essential that our negotiators—wherever they may sit—work with measured confidence, knowing that behind them there exist well-balanced, flexible and highly mobile military strength and a government and people prepared to use that strength if vital interests are threatened.

Since George Washington first enjoined the American people to recognize a connection between the maintenance of adequate military strength and the maintenance of the peace, our history has underlined that the danger of war is greatest when potential enemies are in doubt about the capacity of nations to defend their vital interests, about their will to defend them, or about how they define those vital interests. All three of those conditions for a peaceful resolution of differences are heightened in a world where the use of nuclear weapons may quickly come into play once conflict begins at any level.

I believe the American people, and other free peoples with whom we are allied, have long memories and understand that unlimited appetite grows in the act of devouring and, as President Kennedy has put it, ". . . if there is one path above all others to war, it is the path of weakness and disunity." I believe free peoples understood him when he said,

> We do not want to fight, but we have fought before. And others in earlier times have made the same dangerous mistake of assuming that the West was too selfish and too soft and too divided to resist invasions of freedom in other lands.

The answer to Professor Bemis's first question is and must be "Yes," because the other answer would make war inevitable.

### DEALING WITH TECHNIQUES OF COMMUNIST POWER

A second question with which Professor Bemis confronts us is this: Do the United States, its allies and other non-Communist

nations have the capacity to deal with the techniques of Communist power now being applied to Asia, the Middle East, Africa and Latin America?

In the two years preceding this administration's assumption of responsibility four significant holes had been punched in the truce lines which had emerged after the Second World War: Pathet Lao forces in Laos had moved out of the two northern provinces which had been identified by the Geneva Agreement of 1954; the authorities in Hanoi, building on foundations which they had maintained in the south since 1954, systematically expanded the guerrilla forces in South Viet-Nam from something like 2,000 in 1959 to more than 16,000 at present, in a purposeful and organized act of international aggression; in the Congo, amidst the confusion which followed the end of colonialism, the Communists were rigorously seeking to establish a central African base; in Cuba a Communist regime was installed, having seized and successfully subverted what appeared to be a broad-based national movement to escape an intolerable dictatorship. These limited break-throughs carried with them serious threats to the security of southeast Asia, to Africa and to Latin America.

It has been a first charge on our energies to find ways to deal with these problems. I shall not detail here the policies we have adopted in each case, for they are undoubtedly familiar to you. In different ways, however, they all pose for us the test of learning to deal with what is called, in the inverted language of communism, "wars of national liberation." Behind this concept is the notion that the safest way to extend Communist power and influence in the contemporary world is to exploit the inevitable turbulence which accompanies the revolutionary movement toward modernization, by building a political base rooted in local frustrations, painful memories and unfulfilled aspirations, and by mounting, on that base, insurrectional activity aided from outside the country. The objective is, of course, not national liberation but entrapment within the Communist bloc. This method, from the Communist point of view, is designed to bypass American nuclear strength, to bypass the conventional strength that we have helped build with our allies, and to tear down institutions not under their own control.

Over the past year we have given increased attention to this form of mixed political and military aggression, and in South Viet-Nam we—and the whole world community—are up against a formidable problem: mounting from outside an independent nation of a guerrilla war with men trained, infiltered, supplied and directed from day to day across international boundaries. The free world must recognize this familiar form of aggression and act accordingly.

I cannot report to you that we have fully solved these problems which were waiting for us in January of this year. I do believe that we have made some headway, but they remain on the list of unfinished business. We can draw confidence from the long list of failures in other and somewhat similar Communist efforts to expand their empire. And we can be encouraged to note that the large numbers of new nations which have become independent since World War II have shown a stubborn resistance to the imposition of Communist rule.

But the points of crisis which dominate the headlines do not reflect adequately all that is going forward in the underdeveloped areas in the southern half of the world.

Our objective in these regions of revolution is simple. We wish to see emerge out of the powerful ferment of modernization a community of independent nations. We wish them to modernize, not in our image but in the image they themselves formulate out of their own unique histories, cultures and aspirations. We are confident that if, in this crucial transitional process, they maintain their independence, they will fashion societies which, in one way or another, will move in the direction of consent.

Democracy is not an absolute; and the conditions for democracy are complex. It requires not merely a literate population but a sense of national direction and of consensus, a linkage of urban and rural peoples, the existence of rules and institutions of law, a civil service and armed forces dedicated to nationhood and not to faction. And in the end political freedom requires a citizenry which assumes substantial individual responsibility for the fate of the community.

All this takes time. Our first objective, therefore, is to help preserve the independence of the modernization process, meanwhile working to help build the conditions which will make consent increasingly a reality and to encourage those who would remain steadfast to their own version of the democratic objective.

How should we assess our chances? What are the possibilities of seeing emerge in the southern half of the world an environment of independent and increasingly democratic states which would permit our own society to maintain and develop its humane and open character?

The task ahead is long, but I am basically optimistic. The impulse of these peoples and governments to remain independent is strong. I sense that there is a new generation emerging, dedicated to modernizing their societies with vigor and imagination. I sense that the word is spreading that the pragmatic and apparently diffuse methods of free men are more effective than the illusory efficiency of totalitarianism.

The issue is not yet fully decided. There are certain to be frustrations and setbacks; but I would doubt that the Communist leadership, assessing recent developments and trends, believes with confidence that communism is the wave of the future in the underdeveloped areas of the free world. It is our assessment that the wave of the future will lie with those who struggle for their independence, face their problems pragmatically, and maintain loyalty to the long-run goal of political and social democracy.

It is in this sober but confident spirit that we are going forward with the Alliance for Progress, with our programs of long-term economic development elsewhere, and with other measures of authentic partnership with the new nations who are entering the world community.

### COMPLEXITIES OF ALLIANCE POLICY

Professor Bemis, in his concluding pages, puts to us a third question, which I might rephrase as follows: Can a free-world system, based on a loose alliance of sovereign nations, stand up against the outward thrust of a highly centralized Communist bloc? Can an international democracy of nations deal with disciplined and purposeful totalitarian adversaries?

No Secretary of State can be unmindful of the complexities of alliance policy in a period when our allies number more than forty. The problem of clarifying a national policy within our own Federal Government is, in all conscience, complex enough; and to achieve common action within a large alliance is, as you well know, major business.

Nevertheless, having seen that business at close range, I can again report to you a mood of temperate optimism. Over the past year our Western allies have been subjected to an ugly threat: the threat of being held in nuclear hostage by the intermediate-range ballistic missiles which the Soviet Union now commands. They have stood firm against that threat, and I have no doubt but that the Soviet Union will find, in the response of the West, that this form of blackmail is counter-productive.

More than that, there is a wholesome ferment in Europe and throughout the Atlantic community, generating a debate which historians may well rank with the American constitutional debate of the 1780s. This ferment centers on the emergence and articulation of a new vision: the vision of a Europe moving toward unity and establishing, as it does so, a transatlantic partnership in all the affairs with which great powers must be concerned in the 1960s—the problems of defense in a nuclear age, the problems of sustained assistance to the underdeveloped areas, the problems of trade, the problems of using our international monetary reserves with economy and wisdom in the mutual support of each other's currencies, and problems of economic growth itself. This ferment has not yet yielded a resolution of all the complicated matters involved. But beneath the surface our alliance arrangements are moving into a new and rather grand phase.

In 1947 the American Government decided that it would link the recovery of Europe to efforts at European unification. We chose quite consciously not to play a balance-of-power game with the nations of Europe but to build toward a strong partnership in the affairs of the West. At that moment we joined forces with those Europeans who drew from the lessons of the Second

World War, and indeed from the longer history of Europe, the conclusion that the great European center of Western culture and strength could play its proper part on the world scene only if it transcended its national divisions and moved toward unity. The extraordinary resurgence in Europe of the 1950s now provides the base for a major move forward, and I am confident that we shall see the "grand design" unfold in coming months and years.

Our relations with the countries of Western Europe have, of course, been complicated from time to time since the Second World War by problems arising from the end of the colonial era. During the past year we have confronted several problems where there have been divergencies, in emphasis at least, with some of our European partners. These inevitable difficulties should not, however, obscure the larger pattern which is emerging—a pattern of constructive association among the whole of the northern half of the world, from Tokyo to Bonn, and with the new nations to the south—an association based on principles of partnership among equals, a shared interest in the economic development of the emerging nations, and, in the end, a shared commitment to the objectives of the United Nations Charter.

#### HISTORY HAS NOT STOPPED IN COMMUNIST WORLD

A fourth question posed by Professor Bemis is, in effect, whether we are wholly on the defensive. Must we look to a future in which we can, at best, hold the frontiers of freedom? Must we abandon hope that the principles of independence and democracy might emerge within what is now the Communist bloc?

It would not be prudent to close one's eyes to the capacity of totalitarian methods to maintain a surface of unity and order. It is infinitely harder, for example, for opposition to make itself felt in a police state than in an open society. Nor should we underestimate the capacity of a totalitarian system to produce striking results by mobilizing men and resources around high-priority objectives. But it is inaccurate to believe that history has stopped within the Communist world or that the currents of history are moving automatically to its advantage.

In Europe we have had, in the postwar years, a fundamental test of Western and Communist concepts as they apply to economic, social and political life. No one can question, I believe, the outcome of that test thus far. It is Western, and not Eastern, Europe that constitutes the more vital center.

Despite a Communist monopoly of education and propaganda, the peoples of Eastern Europe remain loyal to their culture and to their nationhood. In every field—from natural and social science to painting and music—they find ways to express their traditional association with Western civilization. And in time, as Communists know perhaps better than others, these tests of historical vitality count.

In free Asia there has been another test; and there, too, free men are doing vastly better than even the greatest optimists would have predicted only a few years ago. The economic progress of the new Japan—democratic and working in cooperation with other free nations—is one of the splendid achievements of the postwar era. In the Indian Peninsula, in southeast Asia, in Hong Kong, on Formosa and now in Korea, there is a resilience, a will to get on with the job, the emergence of a new, modern generation of men and women which promise well for the future. Meanwhile, in the areas controlled by communism the techniques of totalitarianism, applied in regions where three-fourths of the people live in the countryside, have been unable to deal with hunger and apathy. Every day it becomes clear that the Communist methods for modernizing an underdeveloped area are old-fashioned, reactionary and restrictive, quite aside from their simple inhumanity. And this, too, will count.

Finally, it is becoming clear that the same powerful forces which are diffusing power and influence within the free world—forces which our own political history and instinctive methods teach us how to weave together in new patterns of interdependence—are operating within the Communist world itself. We should take no cheap comfort from the deep schisms within the Communist bloc. On the other hand, we should be aware that the concept of independent nationhood, of national interest and of national culture are day to day asserting themselves strongly. And if we are wise, we can patiently find ways to pick up strands of overlapping national interest between Communist nations and the free world, moving toward a cushioning of the raw clash of power.

From Berlin to Laos, from the question of arms control and disarmament to the exchange of persons, we are prepared to look at each proposal and possibility on its merits and to look systematically toward a world which would permit us all to live easier on a planet shadowed by nuclear weapons. And we are prepared to do so not defensively, out of fear, but out of an inner confidence that, if we use time well, time is on the side of the forces making for independent nationhood, dignified interdependence and human freedom.

### TAKING OUR PART IN THE SHAPING OF HISTORY

What of the American base? Is ours a society really given to "loose social dalliance and crooning softness"? There is enough dalliance to merit our genuine concern, but my view of our condition is less somber than your President's.

Democracies have always given an appearance of some disarray and self-indulgence. As a student I knew well interwar Britain. It was a costly conclusion that Hitler and Mussolini— and perhaps Stalin—deduced from surface phenomena that Britain of those years had lost its fiber. I was present in the Oxford Union, for example, when the house resolved "not to fight for King and country." It was apparent to most of us present that the vote was a compliment to the entertaining brilliance of C. E. M. Joad rather than a verdict on the merits of the issue. Although the Union was not amused by a later effort to expunge the record, the record was set right, in fact, within a few short years by the gallantry of its members in fighting for King and country, and for freedom, in a great war.

I recall, too, the headshaking of many Americans about our youth in the twenties and thirties. In the twenties it was said that they were irresponsible, even decadent; in the thirties, that they lacked enterprise, yearned only for security, and neither wished nor knew how to work. Yet these were the generations which fought our greatest war, fashioned a remarkable achievement in our own society, and took up a worldwide responsibility we have never known before.

Moreover, I am not excessively concerned with the tendency of Americans to self-examination and self-criticism. Long ago Alexis de Tocqueville noted that we were a self-conscious people, compelled by our remarkable origins to measure our day-to-day performance against exceedingly high standards and the transcendent idealism built into our Declaration of Independence.

I am confident that we still have the will and the dedication required for the great tasks ahead. From the men in the Strategic Air Command, flying complex missions on endless alert, to the volunteers in the Peace Corps; from our special forces working side by side with soldiers in southeast Asian villages to our Berlin garrison; from our imaginative scientists to my devoted colleagues working long hours at the Department of State and abroad, there is solid reason for confidence—not for despair—in the fiber of our people in general and of our youth in particular.

Moreover, I believe I detect among our citizens a developing ability to live in this world of revolutionary change, of multiple crisis, and of nuclear threat with a poise supported by the endemic sense of humor which has always been a great solvent in our national life. We go about our business with a solid sense of a good and grave and resilient people behind us.

And so, as we deal with the day-to-day problems which are our lot, we are not merely counterpunching against crises. We are taking our part in the shaping of history. Step by step, cable by cable, we are trying to build a commonwealth of independent nations, each—including ourselves—trying to improve the degree to which we actually live by the high standards of democratic ideals. We are trying to pull together in new association the powerful, industrialized nations of the north; we are trying to build a new partnership between the north and the south. Against the background of an enlarged and increasingly flexible military strength, we are protecting the frontiers of freedom; and with confidence we are peering beyond for every constructive possibility of bringing the nations now under communism toward that commonwealth which the charter of the United Nations described in 1945.

Perhaps it is a profession of faith to believe that the human story continues to show the power and majesty of the notion of political freedom. But the historian can find the evidence, and many have done so. The future historian will assess what we in our generation are doing to write new chapters in that story and how we emerge from this climactic period in which we sense we now live. Our commitments are deeply rooted in our own history, a history which links us in aspiration to the great body of mankind. If we move ahead with these shared commitments, we shall not lack company, for men at their best are builders of free commonwealths and a peaceful world community.

# III.   OUR POSITIVE STRATEGY

*One of several major speeches setting forth the main components of United States policy.*

. . . . We live in an era when tremendous, often conflicting, forces are pressing for change. Among these is the force of scientific knowledge, expanding in a progression of endless and breathtaking momentum. We are learning at one and the same time the secrets of the more abundant life and of a more immediate destruction. For the first time in human history there is the possibility that the world can provide adequate resources to feed, house and educate its people and to maintain their health and welfare. Yet this same science has brought about a radical change in the destructive potential of military weapons—with the power of offensive nuclear weapons for the present far outstripping the defensive.

Against this background of scientific change there are at work three other forces of revolutionary power whose interplay determines that we live in an era of recurring crisis.

The first and oldest of these is the revolution of freedom. It

"America's Destiny in the Building of a World Community," major portion of address at third annual symposium on "Government and World Crisis" at the University of Tennessee, Knoxville, Tennessee, May 17, 1962.

is our own revolution. It is, I believe, without question the strongest political force in the world today.

Its concept is magnificently simple. It was stated by Thomas Jefferson with an eloquence which will never die:

> We hold these truths to be self-evident, that all men are created equal, that they are endowed by their Creator with certain unalienable Rights, that among these are Life, Liberty and the pursuit of Happiness. That to secure these rights, Governments are instituted among Men, *deriving their just powers from the consent of the governed.* That whenever any Form of Government becomes destructive of those ends, it is the Right of the People to alter or abolish it, and to institute a new Government, laying its foundations on such principles and organizing its powers *in such form, as to them* shall seem most likely to effect their Safety and Happiness.

These words declare the fundamental basis of the community of free nations. It is our belief that governments derive their just powers from the consent of the governed, that it is the right of each people, in establishing their government, to do so *in such form as to them* seems most likely to effect their safety and happiness.

Although Jefferson's language was in the mainstream of centuries of Western thought, aspiration, and experience, it has meaning in every quarter of the globe—on both sides of the Iron Curtain—and it converges with canons developed independently out of the history and culture of non-Western societies. We should never let ourselves believe that the thrust for human freedom is a peculiar creation and concern of the West.

The revolution of freedom confronts the second great force at work today—the counterrevolution of coercion. Its purpose is to destroy freedom. It does not concede the existence of unalienable rights. Its government is not based upon the consent of the governed but upon the will and force of the governing. It does not concede the right of each people to choose their own form of government but is determined to impose a monolithic form, based on a historical dogma enshrined as doctrine.

The leaders of international communism are not content to

rely on their faith in the inevitability of its victory. They know that what they want must be achieved against the will of the majority and that tight conspiratorial organization must substitute for popular support if they are to win.

In forty years they have expanded their power from a small revolutionary party in Russia to control by force of all or parts of eighteen nations with some one billion people, a third of the world's population.

I have emphasized "to control by force" for it is significant that not a single nation has installed the rule of communism by the free choice of its own people. In not one case have the masters of international communism allowed the people of any nation under their dominion to choose whether they wish to "institute a new Government . . . in such form, as *to them* shall seem most likely to effect their Safety and Happiness."

This is a matter which the peoples of scores of former colonies, given their freedom of choice by the Western nations, must have pondered, for not one of them has passed behind the curtain.

The third great revolution is the revolution of progress. It has long affected the Western world. The industrial revolution, when tempered by social reforms, has brought with it the sharp and increasing rise in Western standards of living; it is a revolution which now attracts the people of the developing nations of Asia, Africa and Latin America. The intensity of the desire for progress felt by the people of these nations springs from the poverty and misery of their lives. Their average per capita output is only about one-twentieth of ours. A third or fewer may be literate. Their average life expectancy is perhaps one-half our own. These peoples are determined to have economic progress for themselves and their children. They are also determined to have rapid social progress: opportunities for education, for health, for homes, for employment and for a more equitable share of the products of their labor. And they know that the dignity and status of their nations on the world scene depend ultimately on their capacity to absorb effectively into their societies the fruits of modern science and technology.

The converging forces of the desires for material progress,

social justice and modern nationhood are compelling. Yet the peoples involved do not in many cases yet have the technical and managerial skills or the capital to create the progress to which they understandably aspire. But they will not be denied. They are, therefore, turning to the more highly developed nations for help. The future of the world and our own peace and prosperity will almost certainly depend on the character of our response.

### AN ERA OF CRISES

I have referred to these revolutionary forces because I believe recognition of them helps us to understand more fully the era of crises in which we live.

These crises are not unrelated. They are the result of the internal stresses and the collisions of the revolutionary forces I have described. With one or two exceptions such as Berlin, the crises of the past decade have arisen in the newly independent or newly developing areas of the world. And the great majority are the result of the efforts of international communism to seize and direct the revolutions of independence and of progress in those nations. The Communists did not create the revolutionary forces at work in the less developed areas; but they aim to exploit them to the full. They aim to isolate, neutralize, subvert, and take over the less developed nations as opportunity and their own ingenuity permit. There is a time, they say, for every fruit to fall from the tree.

### TOWARD THE COMMUNITY OF FREE NATIONS

These then are the great revolutionary forces and the fundamental crises of our time. What is our policy to be? It must be to get on with our main task—to move forward, to build, protect and extend a community of free nations. In this task we will find common ground with allied, neutral and uncommitted nations alike. In this task also we will be true to our own heritage, to the most profound motivations of our history as a people.

Thomas Jefferson's declaration of the rights of all free peoples in 1776 was echoed by Woodrow Wilson, who said to the Nation in 1917:

. . . the right is more precious than peace, and we shall fight for the things which we have always carried nearest our hearts—for democracy, for the right of those who submit to authority to have a voice in their own Governments, for the rights and liberties of small nations, for a universal dominion of right by such a concert of free peoples as shall bring peace and safety to all nations and make the world itself at last free.

A generation later this fundamental declaration was re-echoed by Cordell Hull in the Charter of the United Nations. It called for a community of independent nations, each free to create its own form of government but all committed to work together for progress in peace. It looked toward the strengthening of human rights, the solution of economic and social problems by cooperative effort, the rule of law above the rule of force, and, by the limitation and reduction of arms, the freeing of mankind from its most costly burden. Our nation gladly accepted these principles with the support of an overwhelming majority of our people and a near unanimous vote of our Senate.

The declarations of Jefferson, of Wilson and of Hull are among the stars by which we chart our course. As President Kennedy said in his message on the state of the Union:

. . . our basic goal remains the same: a peaceful world community of free and independent states, free to choose their own future . . . so long as it does not threaten the freedom of others. . . . We can welcome diversity—the Communists cannot. For we offer a world of choice —they offer a world of coercion. And . . . freedom, not coercion, is the wave of the future.

The President thus calls upon us to resume our leadership in the revolution of freedom and to join with it our leadership in the revolution of economic and social progress.

This is a noble task, worthy of our people. It is the task of uniting the nations into one great family of man. It is the dream of the ages toward which, with energy and devotion, we may make true progress in our lifetimes.

How shall we work toward this goal?

To move forward toward this large objective we are pursuing six basic policies.

### MAINTAINING U.S. STRENGTH AND DETERMINATION

First, we must maintain the strength and determination of our own nation. "America, the hope of the world" was never an idle phrase. It is an image that every American generation must recreate by its own efforts and performance. It is an image which others will not confer upon us, except it be earned.

The world of coercion engages in a ceaseless drumfire of propaganda to convince the peoples of the newly developing nations that communism is the road to progress. The most effective response is to show those peoples what free peoples have achieved and are achieving in freedom and to work and learn with them how, in their societies, progress and freedom can go forward together.

The advances we have made here in the South, in my own lifetime since I was a boy on a Georgia farm, provide a most impressive example of the progress which can be made in freedom.

Only three decades ago, just before the Tennessee Valley Authority was created, our Southland had many of the characteristics of an underdeveloped area. In the deep depression year of 1933 the average per capita income here in the valley region was $168, or 45 per cent of the national average. Now it is $1,490—up to 65 per cent of the national average and still growing. In 1933 only three farms in a hundred had electricity—and for most of them this meant only electric lights. Now 98 per cent of the farms have electric service with all this means in terms of light, the convenience and sanitation of running water, refrigeration and its benefit to the family and the commercial storage of food, and farm shops and equipment with their aid to farm production—and I cannot forget some of the burdens which electricity has lifted from our women. In 1933 in malarious areas, one-third of the population was infected, with the consequent effects of misery and impaired ability to farm and work. Now, I understand, it has been over ten years since a single case of malaria of local origin has been found in the Tennessee Valley.

In this same period there has been a basic revolution in agriculture. The region has moved to a highly diversified agriculture. There has been a steady increase in acreage devoted to hay and pasture and the production of livestock and livestock products. Seedlings initially supplied by the TVA and now by the states—planted by the farmers to replace the thinned-out and rundown forests and to protect the watersheds—are now the source of a great and growing forest industry. There is a certain poignancy in the fact that unemployed CCC [Civilian Conservation Corps] boys in the thirties planted seedlings which today are producing new jobs. At the same time, employment in industry has risen from less than 190,000 to over 440,000.

This unfinished process carries lessons of great value to the leaders of scores of nations striving to guide the economic growth of their peoples. It is no wonder that some 3,000 visitors from foreign nations come to your Tennessee Valley region each year to see this process at work.

What they see is a fine example of the American system in action. The people of all our states, acting through the Federal Government, made this investment in the Tennessee Valley Authority to attack the basic problems of the area, particularly water, land, and forests. This was done under our Federal system in a way designed to encourage and strengthen the local governmental institutions and private enterprise in the area. The purpose was to enable them to have an increasing capacity to stand on their own feet and to contribute to the education, health and social progress of their own people and, through rising incomes and taxable revenues, to contribute strength to the whole nation and, indeed, to the free world.

We who have day-to-day responsibility in foreign policy count your performance in the Tennessee Valley a major national asset on the world scene.

And what has been done here is only illustrative of the nation. The increase in the national product of our country in these past thirty years is greater than the entire national product of the Soviet Union today.

We cannot, and I know we will not, rest where we now stand. It is imperative that we increase our present rate of growth, that we increase our productivity and our competitive position; for our world position rests on our ability to maintain a large surplus in our balance of payments to finance our expenses abroad in the defense of freedom.

### MAINTAINING WESTERN MILITARY STRENGTH

The second main policy we follow is to maintain our own military strength and that of allied and friendly nations abroad. As tragically wasteful as it is in manpower and resources, a defensive shield is necessary if we are to have freedom of action to move toward the community of free nations. No nation now free could long remain free if the military power and will of free nations, both allied and uncommitted, were not available to deter and counter aggression. On our own part we must maintain great and varied forces, capable of responding to a variety of challenges. We must have not only an effective and flexible nuclear striking force but also conventional forces of great power and mobility and a capability for helping other free nations defend themselves against guerrilla and other subversive attacks. For the Communist assaults against the free nations will continue to be carefully calculated to probe points of weakness— points remote from the centers of free-world power where local conditions hold open the opportunity of advantage to be gained by limited, often surreptitious, force.

We must not let ourselves be frozen in our choices so that, when these remote and varied attacks take place against a member of the free community, we are limited either to submission or to resort to forces of unlimited and uncontrollable destruction.

The defense of the free world should not, however, depend only upon our strength and our will. It must also depend upon the strength and the will of the nations whose freedom is directly threatened. It is essential, therefore, that the nations along the frontiers of freedom have forces trained, equipped and available on their own home soil at points where aggression—direct or concealed—may come.

Our foreign military assistance program is the principal means by which we help sustain our worldwide collective security systems and the strength and will of free nations. It is an essential part of our total U.S. defense. We should never underestimate the value of this program. The Chairman of the Joint Chiefs of Staff has declared that no amount of money spent on our own forces could give the United States a comparable asset of trained, well-equipped forces, familiar with the terrain and in a suitable position for immediate resistance to local aggression. I would add that, without the confidence which the people of nation after nation have developed from the presence of their own forces to which we have given arms and training, the existing structure of free and independent nations might well have crumbled long ago.

### CONSOLIDATING TIES OF INDUSTRIALIZED NATIONS

Third, we should press forward with our efforts to strengthen and consolidate the bonds between the already more highly industrialized nations, such as our allies of Western Europe, Canada and Japan.

In Europe, after the war, we have already taken one of the most daring steps in all history—the Marshall plan. The Marshall plan achieved its goal. It not only made possible the revival of a free and vigorous economy in Europe; it laid the foundation for evident and decisive progress toward realization of a centuries-old dream, a united Europe.

In 1957 six nations of Europe—France, Italy, Germany, Belgium, the Netherlands and Luxembourg—joined together in the Treaty of Rome, creating the European Economic Community. This was a solemn act of great political significance. Although we hear most of the customs union, which is rapidly taking shape under it, the community has far larger political implications. The main force behind the creation of the community was the desire to lay the groundwork for a unified Europe.

The treaty provides for the creation of an executive, a parliamentary body and a court of justice. It provides also for a wide range of common action covering all aspects of economic integration, including the free movement not only of goods, but of labor, capital, and services.

I stress these larger political implications of the European community because as it continues to progress, and if the negotiations initiated by Great Britain to join the community succeed, there will be created on the other side of the Atlantic a great community of states which will embrace a population of about a quarter of a billion people whose gross national products on the basis of the latest figures would approximate $350 billion —a unit larger in population and resources than the Soviet Union.

This new great center of power and commerce and we ourselves will remain deeply interdependent. If their strength is combined through close economic relations, there will be a consolidation of the strength of the great industrial powers of the free world which cannot be matched within the predictable future. We must see to it that trade shall not become a source of difference and discord between us but a cement to bind our policies more closely together.

This is the purpose of the trade expansion legislation which President Kennedy has proposed to the Congress. It is founded upon the same concepts which Cordell Hull declared as the great spokesman of reciprocal trade. Its enactment will provide the opportunity for the President to work out with the Common Market trading arrangements which will serve to consolidate the strength of our two great industrial complexes. It will afford market opportunities for American exporters of a kind unequaled in our history as a trading nation. It will open up to American producers mass markets of a kind hitherto known only in the United States.

On the other hand, if we fail to take advantage of this great political and economic opportunity, that failure can be disastrous. For we have to sell our products over the barrier of a common external tariff while the producers of the same goods within any of the Common Market countries will be able to sell in the entire Common Market without the equalizing tariffs which in many cases now exist. At the same time, we will have put in motion divisive processes which can lead to dangerous weakening of the free world's strength.

We look to cooperation with a united Europe not only in trade but in the other tasks essential to building and defending a free community. These tasks cannot be discharged by the United States alone or by Europe alone. We need a strong partner in a close partnership with us. The strong partner will be an integrated Europe. The close partnership will be an increasingly cohesive Atlantic community, within whose framework we and Europe can work closely together.

While we look to Europe for new strength, we cannot forget that we are a Pacific as well as an Atlantic power. In the Pacific are old and trusted friends—the Philippines, Australia, New Zealand and the people of free China. In the postwar world new ties have been woven with the peoples of Korea and Southeast Asia. And in Japan we have a close and vital partner which, after a period of substantial American aid, has achieved a dramatic economic revival and growth and which has joined with other industrialized nations of the Northern Hemisphere to aid the less developed areas of the world.

### LONG-TERM PARTNERSHIP WITH DEVELOPING NATIONS . .

The fourth component of our policy is a long-term partnership with the developing nations of Latin America, of Africa and Asia to assist them in their plans to carry forward the revolution of economic and social progress. This is a great task and an historic opportunity. It is also immensely complex; and it will take time.

These nations are at different stages along the road to self-sustaining growth. Each has its own special problems. But through them all there runs a determination that their nation shall have a place of dignity on the world scene and that they and their children shall have lives of greater opportunity. They know these large national and human objectives require that they modernize their economies and learn how to grow. It is our purpose to aid them in this massive and intricate historical process.

Many things are required, but this above all is true: our loans and technicians can only help them to the extent that they can use such help. They must set their targets in terms of their aspirations; they must devise their plans and projects; they must mobilize the administrators, foremen, workers to move the earth and build the structures required for a modern economy. At every step of the way we can help—but only marginally. No amount of American aid can substitute for self-help.

That is why we are shifting our aid program to a long-term development basis where our assistance will flow to those nations who demonstrate a capacity and a will to organize their own resources.

The job will be long—longer than the Marshall plan. Our working horizon should be the Decade of Development. By the end of a decade the job will not be done, but the bulk of the peoples in the underdeveloped areas should be well along the road to self-sustained growth. This is the purpose of our programs of foreign aid, of the Alliance for Progress and of the Peace Corps.

It is against this background of thought over a long period of time that the Congress last year gave the administration authority to enter into long-term aid programs and commitments —an essential feature if our resources are to be effectively used.

I would call to your attention one specific aspect of the development task: the role of education. In our own country we did not wait to become rich before we built our educational system. We created it, and our trained people were then better able to create our wealth. The more we learn about economic growth— in developed as well as underdeveloped societies—the greater the role of education appears to be.

You here at the University of Tennessee are particularly aware of this link. You and sixty-eight other land-grant institutions—along with the entire nation—are celebrating this year the one hundredth anniversary of the land-grant college system. It is almost impossible to exaggerate the effect which this system, originated in legislation offered by Senator Morrill and signed into law by President Lincoln in 1862, has had upon the economic and social progress of our country. It focused the educational system directly on the tasks of a developing nation; for we were at a stage then not very different from that of many nations we are aiding in various parts of the world.

The farm research and extension education conducted by our land-grant institutions has transformed American agriculture. When the program was inaugurated in 1862, 55 per cent of our population was engaged in agriculture and one farm worker could produce only enough food for four to five other persons. Today only 8 per cent work on our farms, and each worker is able to produce enough food for himself and some twenty-six other persons. We have been able to achieve in this peaceful agricultural revolution what the Communist system has not yet been able even to approach, with all the misery of their collectivist experiments.

Many lessons of development cannot be transplanted from one nation to another, but the achievements of the land-grant system and of our agricultural extension system carry a lesson of universal significance to the less developed nations.

In our aid to these newly developing nations we believe that we should be joined by all the industrialized nations of the free world. Some of those whom we have aided in the past are now thriving. We can take a large measure of satisfaction that the flow of assistance from our NATO allies and Japan is substantially increasing. They are now providing in the neighborhood of $2.3 billion per year. For some of them the portion of their gross national product which they contribute to this purpose is comparable to our own.

We believe also that the developing nations have and should use the opportunity to help each other. As they learn the lesson of development they may share their knowledge with others traveling the same road.

And finally we are determined that our aid program should be administered as efficiently as possible. The Agency for International Development (AID) in the Department of State in Washington has been reshaped and staffed with vigorous leaders determined to make each aid dollar obtain the greatest possible benefits.

President Kennedy has asked the Congress for the funds needed to carry forward our aid program for the coming fiscal year. These funds are essential to maintain economic stability and the gathering momentum for development. The funds he has requested for these economic purposes, together with the necessary military assistance, total $4,878 million, or less than 1 per cent of the gross national product of our country. They are less than 5 per cent of what the President is requesting for new obligational authority in his budget for the coming fiscal year, yet they are in the most literal sense vital to our security as a nation and to the future prosperity of our people. Without them we cannot carry forward the struggle for the independence of the underdeveloped areas and for progress in freedom.

This fundamental policy of aid to the developing nations is strongly bipartisan in its origins and rests on a firm basis of support by the leaders of both parties. Former President Eisenhower said of our aid program:

We cannot safely confine Government programs to our own domestic progress and our own military power. We could be the wealthiest and the most mighty Nation and still lose the battle of the world if we do not help our world neighbors protect their freedom and advance their social and economic progress. It is not the goal of the American people that the United States should be the richest Nation in the graveyard of history.

## TOWARD A FREE-WORLD PARTNERSHIP OF EQUALS

The fifth element in our basic policy is a new concentration on the task of building a widening partnership between ourselves, the other nations of the Northern Hemisphere, and the new nations to the south. The purpose here is to help draw the new nations into a true free-world partnership among equals, thus to strengthen even further the links which bind the free community together. We seek to fulfill this purpose through many organizations which join free nations of the north and south in the common defensive and constructive tasks.

In our own hemisphere its basis is well established in the Alliance for Progress and the Organization of American States. For the Far East we see the Colombo Plan organization and the United Nations ECAFE [Economic Commission for Asia and the Far East] in the economic field; we see SEATO [Southeast Asia Treaty Organization] and ANZUS [Australia–New Zealand–United States] in the defense field. In the Middle East, countries with a common concern in the defense of this vital area have come together in CENTO [Central Treaty Organization]. In Africa we look to a variety of regional and subregional organizations whose activities may transcend the presently Balkanized structure of this emerging continent. And in many of these areas the British Commonwealth and the French community join former colonies and metropoles on a new basis of mutual respect and dignity.

The same principle of common effort for common ends is reflected in a number of specialized agencies in which the problems facing the free community are effectively addressed. The International Bank and its affiliate, the International Development Association, is taking an effective lead in bringing free nations together in aid to less developed areas. The International Monetary Fund helps these areas through fiscal crises and helps to insure that the free community makes the most effective use of its total financial reserves. The General Agreement on Tariffs and Trade (GATT) is a useful forum for worldwide trade negotiation, in which the United States will continue to press for a reduction in artificial barriers to commerce.

Over and above these specialized agencies is the organization that Cordell Hull did so much to create: the United Nations. Its labors open new vistas of progress and greater stability for all mankind. We shall continue to sustain those labors with utmost determination. We will seek to strengthen the ways in which the U.N. contributes to economic development within the context of the United Nations Decade of Development. We will also make a particular effort to strengthen its peacekeeping machinery, including standby arrangements for the dispatch of U.N. observers or patrol forces to troubled areas.

In all these varied ways—and many that I have not mentioned—we seek to strengthen the organizational arrangements that bind the peoples of the Northern and Southern Hemispheres together in the free community. In these and many other ways the ties between the citizens of these new and old nations are becoming closer as they work together—under public auspices and in many private relationships—to fulfill the whole wide range of other ordinary human activities.

The task of working closely with many peoples to build an evolving community of nations is a relatively new experience in our national history. Yet of all nations ours is perhaps the one best adapted by its own national heritage for this task. We as a nation have received, absorbed in our national life, and lived peacefully with more people from more nations coming to our shores to seek freedom and opportunity than has any other nation of the world. I have no doubt that it lies within our power to apply to the world community the lesson of this unique national experience.

### POSITION TOWARD COMMUNIST-DOMINATED COUNTRIES

The sixth major element in our effort to build this community relates to our posture toward the countries under Communist rule, which have excluded themselves from its peaceful labors. We want to hold the community of nations open to all men and to seek to draw them into it, if they will abandon their efforts to disrupt it in favor of constructive cooperation.

We have no illusions about the present intentions of the leaders of the Communist bloc and their dedication to the ultimate destruction of the independence of nations and of the freedom of individuals as we understand them. They tell us this plainly, and we see it in practice year after year.

Yet the great ideals of human freedom and of national independence are not confined to the peoples of the nations now free. We know that they are alive in the men, women, and children in nations now part of the international Communist system. We have seen that East Germany had to build a wall to prevent its lifeblood of technicians, workers, farmers and ordinary people from flowing away to freedom into West Berlin. Yet we know that those people of East Germany, now behind barbed wire, still cherish their old cultural values, their aspirations and their hope of freedom.

The entire Communist bloc is now caught up in a slow-moving crisis. Power is being diffused from the center, for the desire of men for national independence is universal—and no respecter of the Iron Curtain. The results of this massive and glacial movement cannot be expected soon. But human liberty within nations and independence among nations is based on the diffusion of power.

We cannot tell when or by what means the peoples and the nations still held under Communist domination may move toward freedom. Yet we must always leave the lamp of freedom lighted for them. We recognize them as brothers in the human race, and we look to the day when they may join us in common existence in the community of free men.

Meanwhile, when we are able to find common interests which the free world and the Communist bloc share we must be prepared to talk and negotiate about ways of acting together to fulfill those interests—even if they are narrow. By this slow process we may move toward a dampening of such crises as Berlin, a continuation of our exchange programs with the U.S.S.R., and new ventures of common advantage, as in Antarctica, public health, and outer space.

It is on this basis also that we are pressing the Soviet leaders to talk seriously about the problems of disarmament. Last year the President asked for the establishment within the executive branch of a new Arms Control and Disarmament Agency. Its purpose is to concentrate under one head experts to develop practical and effective plans to bring under control the weapons which threaten the very destruction of mankind.

. . . . We also believe that the free world and the Soviets have a common interest in preventing the extension of the arms race into space and for the use of space for peaceful purposes. President Kennedy has therefore made serious proposals to Mr. Khrushchev that our nations work together on specified projects in meteorology, communications and other peaceful uses of outer space. The Soviet response to this proposal has been direct and encouraging. Negotiations are now in process, and we can hope that there is a real possibility of achieving a cooperative effort in this dramatic new sphere in which the two nations have shown such scientific skill and heroism.

We are also pressing for limited measures to reduce two key dangers resulting from an uncontrolled arms race. We are seeking such measures as a ban on nuclear testing and the cessation of production of fissionable materials for weapons purposes in order to reduce the risk of nuclear proliferation. And we have proposed such steps as advance notification of military movements and exchange of observation posts—along with establishment of an international commission in which the U.S. and U.S.S.R. could discuss still further measures to reduce the risk of war by accident and miscalculation.

These matters will not move easily. Clearly we do not have such a good chance of success that we can afford to relax our efforts in other directions. But our effort to build a community of free nations would be incomplete if it did not include some steady patient efforts to reduce the hostile confrontation between that community and those who have declared themselves for another kind of world.

OUR DESTINY IS STILL BEFORE US

These are our goals. I believe they are our destiny.

The basis for my confidence is nowhere better stated than in the final passage of Cordell Hull's memoirs, which are the essence of my message:

I conclude these Memoirs with the abiding faith that our destiny as a nation is still before us, not behind us. We have reached maturity, but at the same time we are a youthful nation in vigor and resource, and one of the oldest of the nations in the unbroken span of our form of government. The skill, the energy, the strength of purpose, and the natural wealth that made the United States great are still with us, augmented and heightened. If we are willing from time to time to stop and appreciate our past, appraise our present and prepare for our future, I am convinced that the horizons of achievement still stretch before us like the unending Plains. And no achievement can be higher than that of working in harmony with other nations so that the lash of war may be lifted from our backs and a peace of lasting friendship descend upon us.

# IV. MEN, ADMINISTRATION AND PUBLIC SERVICE

## The Making and Execution of Foreign Policy

*Secretary Rusk's charge to policy-making officers soon after taking office.*

I am happy to have a chance to talk with my new colleagues in the Department about some of the things that are on my mind as well as some of the things which may be on your minds early in the new administration. I suppose you are wondering what the significance of a new administration is. You haven't experienced a change of party administration since 1952, and before that not since 1932.

I think the principal point is that a change in administration gives us a chance to take a fresh look at a good many of our policies, to make fresh approaches, and to see whether we are going in the direction in which we as a nation really want to go. I'm reminded that Senator [John Sherman] Cooper of Ken-

Informal remarks to the policy-making officers of the Department of State, February 20, 1961.

tucky, when asked in 1952 whether he expected major new foreign policies from the then new administration, remarked that the world situation was still pretty much the same and that few major changes in policy were likely.

It is quite true that the central themes of American foreign policy are more or less constant. They derive from the kind of people we are in this country and from the shape of the world situation. It has been interesting over the years to see how, in our democratic society based on the consent of the governed, movements off the main path of the ideas and aspirations of the American people have tended to swing back to the main path as a result of the steady pressures of public opinion.

Nevertheless we are today in a highly revolutionary world situation. Change is its dominant theme. I suppose that the central question before us is how we can properly relate ourselves to these fundamental and far-reaching changes. We are seeing a world in turmoil, reshaping itself in a way which is at least as significant as the breakdown of the Concert of Europe, or as the emergence of the national states in the Western system, or as the explosion of Europe into other continents of the world some three centuries ago.

Older political forms have disintegrated. New international forms are coming into being. We are experiencing enormous pressures to achieve economic and social improvements in all parts of the world, as masses of people who have largely been isolated from currents of world opinion, knowledge and information are coming to realize that their miseries are not a part of an ordained environment about which nothing can be done.

We could be passive in relation to these changes and take our chances. I think the view of the new administration is that, were we to be passive, we could not expect the institutions of freedom to survive. We could undertake an active defense of the *status quo.* My own guess is that, were we to do that, we would be fighting a losing battle. We can, on the other hand, attempt to take a certain leadership in change itself; certainly the world is not as we should like to see it, and the world is not as peoples elsewhere find tolerable. Leadership of change is a theme which we will be wanting to talk with you about and to have you keep in mind as we go about our daily business. It may, indeed, prove to be impossible to win the so-called cold war unless we develop our thoughts, in collaboration with our friends abroad, about what kind of world we are reaching for beyond the cold war.

I think another important factor for us to consider as we move into a new period turns on the President and his attitude toward the conduct of foreign relations. We have a President with great interest in foreign affairs. We have a President who will rely heavily upon the Department of State for the conduct of our foreign relations. This will not be a passive reliance but an active expectation on his part that this Department will in fact take charge of foreign policy. The recent Executive order which abolished the Operations Coordinating Board bore witness to the fact that the Department of State is expected to assume the leadership of foreign policy. In consequence, an enormous responsibility falls upon us here not only in developing policies but in seeing that they are carried out.


FOREIGN POLICY IN ITS TOTAL CONTEXT

With this enlarged role in mind, I should like to make a few suggestions: What we in the United States do or do not do will make a very large difference in what happens in the rest of the world. We in this Department must think about foreign policy in its total context. We cannot regard foreign policy as something left over after defense policy or trade policy or fiscal policy has been extracted. Foreign policy is the total involvement of the American people with peoples and governments abroad. That means that, if we are to achieve a new standard of leadership, we must think in terms of the total context of our situation. It is the concern of the Department of State that the American people are safe and secure—defense is not a monopoly concern of the Department of Defense. It is also the concern of the Department of State that our trading relationships with the rest of the world are vigorous, profitable and active—this is not just a passing interest or a matter of concern only to the Department of Commerce. We can no longer rely on interdepartmental machinery "somewhere upstairs" to resolve differences between this and other departments. Assistant Secretaries of State will now carry an increased burden of active formulation and coordination of policies. Means must be found to enable us to keep in touch as regularly and as efficiently as possible with our colleagues in other departments concerned with foreign policy.

I think we need to concern ourselves also with the timeliness of action. Every policy officer cannot help but be a planning officer. Unless we keep our eyes on the horizon ahead, we shall fail to bring ourselves on target with the present. The movement of events is so fast, the pace so severe, that an attempt to peer into the future is essential if we are to think accurately about the present. If there is anything which we can do in the executive branch of the Government to speed up the processes by which we come to decisions on matters on which we must act promptly, that in itself would be a major contribution to the conduct of our affairs. Action taken today is often far more valuable than action taken several months later in response to a situation then out of control.

There will of course be times for delay and inaction. What I am suggesting is that when we delay, or when we fail to act, we do so intentionally and not through inadvertence or through bureaucratic or procedural difficulties.

I also hope that we can do something about reducing the infant mortality rate of ideas—an affliction of all bureaucracies. We want to stimulate ideas from the bottom to the top of the Department. We want to make sure that our junior colleagues realize that ideas are welcome, that initiative goes right down to the bottom and goes all the way to the top. I hope no one expects that only Presidential appointees are looked upon as sources of ideas. The responsibility for taking the initiative in generating ideas is that of every officer in the Department who has a policy function, regardless of rank.

Further, I would hope that we could pay attention to little things. While observing the operations of our Government in various parts of the world, I have felt that in many situations where our policies were good we have tended to ignore minor problems which spoiled our main effort. To cite only a few examples: The wrong man in the wrong position, perhaps even in a junior position abroad, can be a source of great harm to our policy; the attitudes of a U.N. delegate who experiences difficulty in finding adequate housing in New York City, or of a foreign diplomat in similar circumstances in our Capital, can easily be directed against the United States and all that it stands for. Dozens of seemingly small matters go wrong all over the world. Sometimes those who know about them are too far down the line to be able to do anything about them. I would hope that we could create the recognition in the Department and overseas that those who come across little things going wrong have the responsibility for bringing these to the attention of those who can do something about them.

If the Department of State is to take primary responsibility for foreign policy in Washington, it follows that the ambassador is expected to take charge overseas. This does not mean in a purely bureaucratic sense but in an active, operational, interested, responsible fashion. He is expected to know about what is going on among the representatives of other agencies who are stationed in his country. He is expected to supervise, to encourage, to direct, to assist in any way he can. If any official operation abroad begins to go wrong, we shall look to the ambassador to find out why and to get suggestions for remedial action.

### THE PROBLEMS OF A POLICY OFFICER

It occurred to me that you might be interested in some thoughts which I expressed privately in recent years, in the hope of clearing up a certain confusion in the public mind about what foreign policy is all about and what it means, and of developing a certain compassion for those who are carrying such responsibilities inside Government. I tried to do so by calling to their attention some of the problems that a senior departmental policy officer faces. This means practically everybody in this room. Whether it will strike home for you or not will be for you to determine.

The senior policy officer may be moved to think hard about

a problem by any of an infinite variety of stimuli: an idea in his own head, the suggestions of a colleague, a question from the Secretary or the President, a proposal by another department, a communication from a foreign government or an American ambassador abroad, the filing of an item for the agenda of the United Nations or of any other of dozens of international bodies, a news item read at the breakfast table, a question to the President or the Secretary at a news conference, a speech by a Senator or Congressman, an article in a periodical, a resolution from a national organization, a request for assistance from some private American interests abroad, et cetera, ad infinitum. The policy officer lives with his antennae alerted for the questions which fall within his range of responsibility.

His first thought is about the question itself: Is there a question here for American foreign policy, and, if so, what is it? For he knows that the first and sometimes most difficult job is to know what the question is—that when it is accurately identified it sometimes answers itself, and that the way in which it is posed frequently shapes the answer.

Chewing it over with his colleagues and in his own mind, he reaches a tentative identification of the question—tentative because it may change as he explores it further and because, if no tolerable answer can be found, it may have to be changed into one which can be answered.

Meanwhile he has been thinking about the facts surrounding the problem, facts which he knows can never be complete, and the general background, much of which has already been lost to history. He is appreciative of the expert help available to him and draws these resources into play, taking care to examine at least some of the raw material which underlies their frequently policy-oriented conclusions. He knows that he must give the expert his place, but he knows that he must also keep him in it.

He is already beginning to box the compass of alternative lines of action, including doing nothing. He knows that he is thinking about action in relation to a future which can be perceived but dimly through a merciful fog. But he takes his bearings from the great guidelines of policy, well-established precedents, the commitments of the United States under international charters and treaties, basic statutes and well-understood notions of the American people about how we are to conduct ourselves, in policy literature such as country papers and National Security Council papers accumulated in the Department.

He will not be surprised to find that general principles produce conflicting results in the factual situation with which he is confronted. He must think about which of these principles must take precedence. He will know that general policy papers written months before may not fit his problem because of crucial changes in circumstance. He is aware that every moderately important problem merges imperceptibly into every other problem. He must deal with the question of how to manage a part when it cannot be handled without relation to the whole—when the whole is too large to grasp.

He must think of others who have a stake in the question and in its answer. Who should be consulted among his colleagues in the Department or other departments and agencies of the Government? Which American ambassadors could provide helpful advice? Are private interests sufficiently involved to be consulted? What is the probable attitude of other governments, including those less directly involved? How and at what stage and in what sequence are other governments to be consulted?

If action is indicated, what kind of action is relevant to the problem? The selection of the wrong tools can mean waste, at best, and at worst an unwanted inflammation of the problem itself. Can the President or the Secretary act under existing authority, or will new legislation and new money be required? Should the action be unilateral or multilateral? Is the matter one for the United Nations or some other international body? For, if so, the path leads through a complex process of parliamentary diplomacy which adds still another dimension to the problem.

RESPECT FOR THE OPINIONS OF MANKIND

What type of action can hope to win public support, first in this country and then abroad? For the policy officer will know that action can almost never be secret and that in general the effectiveness of policy will be conditioned by the readiness of the country to sustain it. He is interested in public opinion for two reasons: first, because it is important in itself, and, second, because he knows that the American public cares about a decent respect for the opinions of mankind. And, given probable public attitudes—about which reasonably good estimates can be made —what action is called for to insure necessary support?

May I add a caution on this particular point? We do not want policy officers below the level of Presidential appointees to concern themselves too much with problems of domestic politics in recommending foreign policy action. In the first place our business is foreign policy, and it is the business of the Presidential leadership and his appointees in the Department to consider the domestic political aspects of a problem. Mr. Truman emphasized this point by saying, "You fellows in the Department of State don't know much about domestic politics."

This is an important consideration. If we sit here reading editorials and looking at public-opinion polls and other reports that cross our desks, we should realize that this is raw, undigested opinion expressed in the absence of leadership. What the American people will do turns in large degree on their leadership. We cannot test public opinion until the President and the leaders of the country have gone to the public to explain what is required and have asked them for support for the necessary action. I doubt, for example, that three months before the leadership began to talk about what came to be the Marshall plan, any public-opinion expert would have said that the country would have accepted such proposals.

The problem in the policy officer's mind thus begins to take shape as a galaxy of utterly complicated factors—political, military, economic, financial, legal, legislative, procedural, administrative—to be sorted out and handled within a political system which moves by consent in relation to an external environment which cannot be under control.

And the policy officer has the hounds of time snapping at his heels. He knows that there is a time to act and a time to wait. But which is it in this instance? Today is not yesterday and tomorrow will be something else, and his problem is changing while he and his colleagues are working on it. He may labor prodigiously to produce an answer to a question which no longer exists.

In any event he knows that an idea is not a policy and that the transformation of an idea into a policy is frequently an exhausting and frustrating process. He is aware of the difference between a conclusion and a decision. The professor, the commentator, the lecturer may indulge in conclusions, may defer them until all the evidence is in, may change them when facts so compel. But the policy officer must move from conclusion to decision and must be prepared to live with the results, for he does not have a chance to do it again. If he waits, he has already made a decision, sometimes the right one, but the white heat of responsibility is upon him and he cannot escape it, however strenuously he tries.

There is one type of study which I have not seen, which I hope we can do something about in the months ahead. The pilot of a jet aircraft has a check list of many dozen questions which he must answer satisfactorily before he takes off his plane on a flight. Would it not be interesting and revealing if we had a check list of questions which we should answer systematically before we take off on a policy?

Perhaps this is a point at which to inject another passing comment. The processes of government have sometimes been described as a struggle for power among those holding public office. I am convinced that this is true only in a certain formal and bureaucratic sense, having to do with appropriations, job descriptions, trappings of prestige, water bottles and things of that sort. There is another struggle of far more consequence, the effort to diffuse or avoid responsibility. Power gravitates to those who are willing to make decisions and live with the results, simply because there are so many who readily yield to the intrepid few who take their duties seriously.

On this particular point the Department of State is entering, I think, something of a new phase in its existence. We are expected to take charge. We shall be supported in taking charge, but it throws upon us an enormous responsibility to think broadly and deeply and in a timely fashion about how the United States shall conduct itself in this tumultuous world in which we live.

I want to transmit to you not only my own complete confidence but the confidence of the President in our determination to back you in one of the most onerous responsibilities in the country, and indeed in the world today, and ask you for your maximum help as we try to get on with this job in the months ahead.

I hope to be seeing you from time to time in your own offices. Both Mr. Bowles [Chester Bowles, then Under Secretary of State] and I will try to visit different sections of the Department in the weeks ahead. In the meantime you may be sure that we shall be vitally interested in how you see this job and in how you think the United States should move to take charge of its future, to do its part to shape the course of events—to make history which will cause those after us to call us "blessed."

## The Role of the Foreign Service

*In this talk to career officers of the Foreign Service, Secretary Rusk set forth his views on the making and execution of foreign policy. This transcript has not heretofore been published.*

At the risk of committing an indiscretion I hope today to talk quite personally and informally to the present and former members of the Foreign Service.

Remarks at luncheon of American Foreign Service Association, Washington, D. C., February 23, 1961.

A thoughtful staff did in fact prepare some remarks for me today, but I set these aside because I remembered a friend on the West Coast, a professor who used to give his speaking assignments to his graduate students for the preparation of his lectures. They eventually lost their patience. On one occasion, as he came to the platform, his speech was put in his hands just as he mounted the steps, and, after he had gotten about halfway through, he got to a blank page on which was written, "Improvise for five minutes, you son-of-a-gun!"

As I recall, I took the oath of office to be an Assistant Secretary of State on my fortieth birthday, and on the next day I got a letter from the National Junior Chamber of Commerce, which started out describing its annual program for awards to the ten outstanding young men of the year. And as it explained what they were doing, and as my chest began to swell, I finally came to the last paragraph which said, "Would you as one of our elder statesmen serve as one of our judges?"

I am delighted to see so many elder statesmen in the room today. Indeed, I might say that there are a considerable number in the room who have a certain personal stake in my performance in the chair which I now occupy, because, if I have learned anything about it, you have been my teachers, and so it is in your interest that I perform at least adequately.

One cannot meet the Foreign Service without expressing a word of great respect for the great traditions of the Service. For some reason, perhaps associated with the traditional isolationism of the American people over the years, the American public has not yet begun to appreciate what it means to serve the United States in diplomacy abroad, how utterly dependent we are upon insight, wisdom, judgment, patience, courage and indeed gallantry—gallantry not only on the part of the men who serve but of their wives and their families who serve with them.

Looking back over the years, for example, I can remember that Tom Wasson was killed by an assassin's bullet in Palestine; but the thing that the public does not know is that within hours there were many, many telegrams from all over the world from Foreign Service officers volunteering instantly to take his place.

I remember flying frequently, during the war, with John

Davies in the CBI theater. I was not with him on the occasion when he and Eric Sevareid and others parachuted in the Naga headhunters country. John Davies was something of a jinx as a companion on air travel because he almost always found airplane trouble when he flew. But about five or six weeks after that, what is not reported is that John Davies was over the same Naga headhunter country in another plane, and it, too, developed trouble. And since he had been the first one out of the plane the first time, he was climbing into his parachute, and with a smile he said, "Well, at least I know these people down here!"

One thinks of these incidents as being something in the past. But when you read today's papers, or yesterday's papers, and see the outbreak of cultivated riots in many parts involving American Embassies, one realizes that distances far from home are still far from home, that dangers are still dangers, and that courage remains courage.

When we hear that political prisoners held in Stanleyville have been summarily executed, it may occur to some that we ourselves should entertain or organize or stimulate counter riots in order to even the score. But that is not in the American style or the American tradition. It does illustrate, however, one of the glories of American policy and one of our short-range handicaps. Because we are the kind of people we are, because our purposes are what they are, and because of a tradition of decency in our policy, we are trying to help others build a tolerable, a viable and effective society in which men can be free under law, both domestic law and international law all over the world.

Our rivals, at least in areas which are not under their own control, are determined to tear down, and tearing down is much easier than building up. It is one thing to organize a riot. It is quite another thing to help someone build a viable society. . . .

So because we are the kind of people we are, we shall be continuing to try to build. We shall have our setbacks and our disappointments. We shall pick ourselves up and start all over again, with patience, and persistence and courage; but we shall not betray our basic purposes by being something we are not.

Now, that requires courage to a high degree, and patience almost to the intolerable point, and persistence over decades. But in the long run there is great strength in that point of view, because I deeply believe that we in this country, after two thousand years of discourse on the political consequences of the nature of man, share the most fundamental purposes with men and women in all parts of the world. We do not have to argue with any of them, the common people of the world, about what our common purposes are: we know them, they know them. And in the long run this community of interest must surely prevail.

I would also like in this informal way to explain my own deep personal confidence in the Foreign Service. Some of you may have seen some press comment—which is accurate—that I came into this office without any personal political constituency of my own. Indeed, I came—when I was told that I was to come into this chair I was as surprised as the rest of you were. I have been asked: Where are my own lieutenants? Where is my own personal staff? And my answer has been that my own constituency is in my friends in the Foreign Service, because they are the ones on whom I intend to rely to get this job done.

I mentioned that to Averell Harriman just before we sat down, and Averell, who is not without some experience in politics, looked around the turnout in this room and said, "Well, with this turnout you had better run for public office."

But I am grateful to you for coming, because, as I said in the first moment when I was told that this chair was my responsibility, I spoke with the affection that I felt for the Departmental and Foreign Service officers, and it was partly because we and they had occupied the same foxholes together.

I am somewhat limited today in some of the things that I might like to say, because on last Monday I called together the policy-making officers of the Department, to have a talk with them about some of the things that we felt in the new Administration about the responsibilities and the obligations of the Department and of the Foreign Service, and there undoubtedly are many here today who were there at that meeting on Monday. But for some who were not, let me just say that President Kennedy in his new Administration is taking a keen personal interest in foreign policy, that he intends to occupy fully the constitutional prerogatives of the President in this field and to give it his complete attention as President of the United States, and that he has taken steps to put the Department of State in a position to take the full leadership of the nation in the formulation and in the conduct of our foreign relations.

This is not simply a bureaucratic delegation on his part. This is a declaration of high expectations from all of us in the Department and in the Foreign Service. If we are to take the leadership, we must lead responsibly. If we are to give guidance on foreign policy to all of the agencies of Washington, we must ourselves be qualified to think about foreign policy in its total breadth, complexity and depth.

We can no longer rely upon inter-agency and inter-departmental machinery to inject things which we have forgotten. We can no longer leave to others "upstairs" the discovery of the fatal flaws in our recommendations. We can no longer diffuse, disguise and hide our responsibilities on any theory that in any event we do not have the capacity to act.

And if this falls upon the Department as a whole, it falls particularly upon the Assistant Secretaries of State, because there they receive two important currents: one current of policy directive from the President and the Secretary of State as a matter of administrative policy, and the other current of initiative and sense of responsibility from the most junior officers of the Department as these suggestions, proposals and recommendations make their way up in our system.

The Assistant Secretaries must be artists in foreign policy. When I occupied one of these ten chairs—[I believe the number now is perhaps eleven, if not more—I haven't counted—] it was my habit each month to make a list of the subjects that I thought I ought to be worried about—one line, one subject. And month after month this check list of anxieties would run to sixty-five or seventy items. And although it was my practice to throw the old one away when I made the new one, by some sort of accident I did once upon a time come across one of those lists that was a year old, and it was perfectly fascinating to see what had happened to the list of things to worry about over a twelve months' period, to see which sorts of things had become worse, which things had become better, and to notice that whether they had become worse or better did not necessarily turn upon whether you did something about them or not.

But it was interesting to see and also to have a chance to reflect upon the extent to which the leadership, the upper echelons in the Administration, were in a sense prisoners of the judgments made at this level, because it is at this level of office directors, assistant secretaries, that prophecy has to occur, that planning has to occur, that judgments have to be made about whether this problem out on the edge of the horizon needs present attention from those upstairs or from the Administration, or whether it is something that can be left to mature, or to wither away, because an Administration will not be able to take up everything all at once, and the art of policy is to know when to act, in what way to act, through whom to act, with what tools to act, for what purpose to act, in a timely fashion and with the most effective means at our disposal.

The notion that policy is something sent down from on high has the most severe limitations. When we are sending out hundreds of policy cables from the Department every day, it is obvious that junior officers in the Department of State today of necessity must be sending out cables which perhaps before World War II—as late as that—would have gone to the Secretary of State himself. The mass of business, the pace of business, the complexity of business is such that those of you who staff the Department on any policy desk have the responsibility and the corresponding power to ask yourself this question: What would I do if I were the President of the United States in this situation?

Because if the Department of State is to be—as it has been designated—the leader in our foreign relations, we can no longer think in terms of what the so-called foreign policy implications of a particular problem are. We must consider the total impact of policy upon a total situation both here and abroad. And the officer who wants to come to grips realistically with his problems has to try to imagine, to put himself in the position of those who must accept eventual responsibility, final responsibility for the act, and say: Is what I am recommending what I would do if I were holding final responsibility? Our feet are now being held to the fire of responsibility, and we cannot avoid it. We do not wish to avoid it, and we accept this challenge, this responsibility, gladly.

Now if that is true of us here in the Department, it is also true of our Ambassadors abroad. Our Ambassadors are being called upon to take charge of American official relations with countries all over the world. That does not mean in any bureaucratic sense. That means in fact that we expect them to be in charge of the totality of our official relationships, and indeed to serve as advisers and helpful assistants to an entire range of relationships both in the public and in the private field, for our official relations abroad are only a fraction of our total foreign relations of the American people.

One can think, for example, of the growth of vast international communities which are coming into being without official participation or action, the international communities of science and scholarship, of the arts, of sports, of recreation, of tourism, of commerce, where literally hundreds of thousands of men and women are reaching out across national frontiers to join hands with people in other countries to get on with the day-to-day work of mankind.

So our Ambassadors have the problem of accepting responsibility for official action, and nurturing, refreshing, stimulating, encouraging the growth of these great international communities which themselves are among the infinity of threads that bind people together.

It would be more comfortable if I were meeting with you to look backward and congratulate the Foreign Service on a job splendidly done. It *has* been splendidly done. But I think it is more in keeping with the necessities of our day if I should rather more emphasize . . . the nature of the task in front of us in the coming years. We are in a period of historic revolutionary change, perhaps more revolutionary than any that we have seen for perhaps centuries in the West. Older forms are disintegrating, new forms are coming into being. A Communist operation, which presumes to suppose that it is the historically inevitable movement of the future, is moving with great force, subtlety, sophistication and great resources and great effect.

We in the free world, perhaps they in their world, are facing a crisis of talent. There has never been a time when the old adage was more true than it is today, that there is plenty of room at the top, because there is no sector of our American society—itself one of the most developed of countries—that is not anxious about its share of our top talent for its particular enterprise, whether in government, the universities, law, medicine, business—whatever it might be. And great effort is being put in by all of those segments of our society to recruit more top talent into their ranks. If this is so for us in this country, how many more times is it so for much of the rest of the world?

A Congo becoming independent with—what is the number? —twelve college graduates in the entire country! . . . A crisis of talent!

What does that mean for us in the Foreign Service? This has little to do with the capacities, the dedication of those of us who are in this business. It has something to do with what is required of us out ahead. A university group not too long ago made a study . . . as to what would be good for a Foreign Service officer to know. I believe they listed twenty of the standard academic disciplines as being fields of knowledge which it would be important for the Foreign Service officer to have under his belt, ranging from history to nuclear physics. What we need to know is everything there is. What we need to know cannot be accomplished in a man's lifetime. But we need to delve deeply into many fields in order that we as policy makers can make policy with understanding.

We cannot rely on experts without understanding what experts are talking about. Otherwise, policy determination is yielded to the expert. Now, I do not wish to offend anyone who might be present, but my experience with experts is that they are not reluctant to assume responsibility for policy.

But the demands upon the Foreign Service in this country and abroad in terms of knowledge, in terms of an understanding of what our nation is all about, in terms of the forces which are reshaping the world in which we live, are larger than they have ever been in the past and will not shrink in the future. So that we have a great stake in doing everything that we can to strengthen the Foreign Service, to attract as much top talent into it as we can.

Coming back into the Department after several years in the pastures of private life, I have been greatly encouraged to see that the Foreign Service has a fine chance to select top talent among the thousands of young applicants who are seeking admission in these recent years. One can sympathize with those who must be disappointed, but the possibility of attracting top talent is beginning to make itself felt. And if we ever went through a period when the young people were quizzical or doubtful or hesitant about coming toward the Foreign Service, those days apparently are, we hope, forever gone.

I think there is great encouragement in the steps which have been taken in the last few years to strengthen the Foreign Service in terms of its present personnel. The active language program has shown remarkable progress. The figures are very stimulating, very encouraging—not because it would not be possible to communicate without these language skills, but because language is a vehicle of understanding other cultures and other peoples, and because the readiness to take on a language and try to master it is a sign of respect for these other peoples which too often has been missing in the general American approach to countries abroad.

We do hope to continue efforts to strengthen the Foreign Service, to make its service attractive, stimulating, rewarding, not only in the practical support of the jobs themselves, and of the families who are necessarily involved in these jobs, but in terms of the opportunities for service, for interesting service and responsible service both here and abroad.

I think it is possible that there may have been, in an attempt to unify our services, steps taken to inject the Foreign Service into too many places, at least a few places where the duties were not those which contributed to the development of a top Foreign Service officer. We may want to look at some of those to see whether we are guilty of diverting officers from their chief preoccupation in building an effective Foreign Service.

But we shall continue to call upon the Foreign Service to take leadership both in the Department and overseas—in the Department with a mixture, as you would expect, of political responsibility and professional experience, and overseas with a strengthening of our missions, with opportunities for able Foreign Service officers to go as far and as fast as their own abilities and as the needs of the Service permit.

There is an unlimited job ahead of us, because what happens in this next decade may be of vital importance for decades to come. I recognize that the historian—and if I were among scholars I would have to elaborate this—I recognize that the historian is likely to say that each generation feels that it is living in a special time. But that does not mean that every generation is wrong when it thinks so. And I would suspect that we ourselves are living in a special time, when the number of states promises to reach 120 or more, when these great revolutionary changes are occurring, when hundreds of millions of people all over the earth are discovering that disease and misery are not parts of the physical environment about which no one can do anything, when new opportunities for working out a tolerable world order are appearing, some in the dramatic form, many in the quiet, day-by-day business transacted across national frontiers. We have an opportunity to take charge of these changes with the help of our friends abroad who are able to assist in directing these changes.

For changes there will be. We cannot be passive to them, or we shall lose our freedom. We cannot defend the status quo, because not only we but others would find the status quo intolerable. Change there will be—but we must help to take charge of that change, to make some of the history which is there to be made.

Among other things we in this country must, it seems to me, re-establish a vibrant contact between the American nation and its own great revolutionary tradition. I have said before that it seems almost grotesque that one should go into the General Assembly of the United Nations and see there more than sixty independent nations sitting there as fully independent members, who were at one time or another a part of a Western political system, beginning with the United States, and to have a man like Khrushchev make some headway as the leader of nationalist revolutions at the expense of those of us who invented it. . . .

Well, it is on these things that I wanted to speak to you

about today. I need not elaborate my regard for the Foreign Service. Those of you who know me know of that regard. But what I do say is that we shall be called upon, you and I, for our very best, that we shall be fortunate if our best is good enough, but we can offer no less, and that the stakes are such that the game is well worth the playing, and we can hope that this great nation of ours will get on with the great dreams which have moved it from its beginning.

## Strengthening our Public Service

. . . . The need to strengthen our public service comes about because of a rapid increase in the number of jobs requiring the highest level of executive talent. When we look at the tasks which have been laid upon our great departments of Government and consider the impact of what we do and how we act on the world these days, the wide range and limitless responsibilities of our public service come into full view.

We need to fill our pipelines with talented young people to rise to leadership. We need to take into account the flexibility, the imagination, the vision, as Mr. Rockefeller put it, to recognize change and adapt swiftly to new environmental factors. No one can cling for long to outworn customs in this society of ours. Alfred North Whitehead in his *Adventures of Ideas* puts it this way:

. . . tradition is warped by the vicious assumption that each generation will substantially live amid the conditions governing the lives of its fathers and will transmit those conditions to mould with equal force the lives of its children. We are living in the first period of human history for which this assumption is false.

. . . in the past the time-span of important change was considerably longer than that of a single human life. . . .

Today this time-span is considerably shorter than that of human

Remarks at the Rockefeller Public Service Awards Luncheon, Washington, D. C., April 11, 1961.

life, and accordingly our training must prepare individuals to face a novelty of conditions.

One must suggest in this connection—and I suspect that it would be a comfortable and exciting thought for Princeton—that because of these time factors there is still room for the basic liberal education which enables men to adjust to change; for the accelerating rate of change in our industrial society brought about by scientific discovery, technical progress, and rapid mechanization requires the administrator and executive in Government and business to become better educated and intellectually prepared. Our age of science calls for less and less muscle and more and more mind to control both matter and men.

In all the complexities which confront us in our troubled world, we may find that if we use our wits we shall not need to use our weapons.

As we look toward strengthening our public service, we must, I think, take into account the fact that in our society the public service is recruited voluntarily. We do not draft men and women nor assign them by fiat. We must entice them, stimulate and attract them, and support them in Government service in such a way as to make such service a satisfying, lifetime career. One of the great pleasures in working with dedicated career servants is to see the quiet, sustained satisfaction which they derive from serving their country.

We must continue to encourage our educational institutions to acquaint the nation's youth with the opportunities which exist in the field of public service and public administration.

We must give greater attention to fair employment practices, of which government has always been a stout champion but not always an ardent practitioner.

We must in our service provide full opportunity for growth —the growth of individuals—for nothing is more disconcerting than to find men in service who have not grown with the years and with the opportunities. As we continue our programs of in-service training for Government employees and as we expand opportunities for career development, we shall be filling a larger percentage of those notches at the top with career men and women.

We can as citizens applaud, encourage and express our appreciation for institutions like the Woodrow Wilson School and individuals like John D. Rockefeller III for the attention which they themselves are giving to excellence in the public service. The Rockefeller Public Service Awards, recognizing and honoring civilians in the Federal Government for distinguished service, focus public attention on the enormous variety of opportunities and satisfactions in the public service and enable their distinguished recipients to pass on to others the knowledge which they have gained from their years of experience.

Some ten years ago I made the remark that it may well be that the most important single factor of the twentieth century is that the energy, wealth, power and imagination of the American people are devoted to peace, liberty and the economic well-being of ourselves and others. For us to keep this type of commitment in mind, we shall need dedicated public servants of the highest order. The world is moving much too fast for us to stand still or to smile in satisfaction at all that we have in possession.

So let us honor these unusual public servants for the reality of their hold on truth. Let us also remember, with Archibald MacLeish, that

Freedom is never an accomplished fact. It is always a process. Which is why the drafters of the Declaration spoke of the *pursuit* of happiness: They knew their Thucydides and therefore knew that "The secret of happiness is freedom, and the secret of freedom, courage."

And here we give our thanks and our appreciation to these great public servants.

## Quality and Gallantry
## in the Foreign Service

. . . I am proud of the competence of our men and women in the Department of State. Not long ago I was called on by a distinguished group of private citizens who had helped us in our several selection and promotion boards in the Department of State.

Unanimously they told me personally about their impressions of the high quality of personnel in our Department. One of them, Mr. Charles Lewis, of the American Tobacco Company, was quoted the other day as saying, having served on one of these committees, "that as the record unfolded I became simply flabbergasted at the quality of the young women and young men we were reviewing. Frankly, they were so much better quality people, in my judgment, than comparable people in business that it was hard to believe."

I want to say just a word about courage and gallantry in our service, because in peacetime we tend to forget it. We tend to overlook those seventy-two members of the Foreign Service whose names are on a tablet in the Department of State and who gave their lives in active service abroad.

We tend to forget that our men are serving in distant, difficult and frequently dangerous parts of the world: that one week an ambassador will have a grenade tossed at his car—which fortunately does not go off; that another week a man— (by the way, whose blank, before the promotion board, opposite the category called "courage", had inscribed on it "Nothing special to report") —that this man, the very week that the board was looking at that blank, . . . rescued certain United Nations people in the Congo, at the risk of his own life.

The courage and gallantry of our men and their wives, their families . . . is something that is deeply impressive. . .

Excerpt from talk at the 1962 Washington Conference of the Advertising Council, Inc., Washington, D. C., March 6, 1962.

# V. TRADE AND THE ATLANTIC PARTNERSHIP

*Trade and Aid—Essentials of Free-World Leadership*

*A basic speech on economic policies.*

. . . . The promotion of trade has been a major element in our foreign policy since before our Republic was born. From the time when Benjamin Franklin first went abroad to solicit aid and trade and political support for the American Colonies, our diplomacy has sought to enlarge our trade, insure the supply of those things we need and markets in which to sell to pay for them. Patterns in both trade and diplomacy have changed with the times, but in every foreign office throughout the world practical matters of trade are vital and sensitive parts of the daily business.

Trade is essentially restless, for there is no such thing as enough. We need not be surprised, therefore, that great trading partners who exchange vast quantities of goods and services are

Portions of address at the Chamber of Commerce of Charlotte, North Carolina, February 21, 1962.

nevertheless constantly engaged in negotiations to handle the lesser frictions which inevitably accompany so vigorous and dynamic a relationship.

The changes in the world about us raise new challenges both for the businessman and for diplomacy. For a decade and a half after World War II the United States was relatively comfortable in its trading position. It had no difficulty in selling what it could produce. Competition abroad was negligible because recovery from the damage of war was incomplete. The Departments of State and Commerce were not compelled to seek out trading opportunities because their problems had more to do with allocating goods in short supply to a world in desperate need of them. Now, with the vigorous recovery of other industrial nations, the scene has changed. Competition is there to be met, salesmanship is an art to be revived, and questions of price, quality, delivery, service and credits have resumed their historical importance.

We in government are moving, as well, to adjust our actions and habits of mind to changing circumstances. Trade promotion is a central task; our ability to find markets for our products— industrial and agricultural—is critical to our ability to buy what we need to sustain a vigorous growth in our own economy. And we must sell more than we buy in order to sustain our defense, aid, and other commitments abroad as our part in the struggle for freedom. . . .

EUROPE'S 20TH-CENTURY RENAISSANCE

Let me speak first of the Trade Expansion Act of 1962, a legislative proposal which the President sent to Congress only a month ago. This measure was designed to take account of one of the great constructive undertakings of our time—Europe's twentieth-century renaissance. For a thousand years the homeland and base of Western civilization has been rent by division and devastated by war. Now, virtually for the first time since the breakup of Charlemagne's empire, millions of inhabitants of that historic peninsula called Europe are translating the dream of European unity into a reality. The European Economic Community, or Common Market, is bringing together by their own voluntary act millions of gifted and resourceful people commanding vast resources of skill and productive capacity.

The implications of this extraordinary development for the confrontation between the free world and the Communist bloc are unmistakable. In the curious new physics of political unity the whole not only can be, but almost always is, greater than the sum of its parts. Compared to the coming into its own of Western Europe such successes as the Communists have managed to obtain in the past dozen years are peripheral and—we may hope—destined to prove transitory.

Is it vainglorious for us to infer that the old Continent, as we tend to think of Europe, has taken a leaf from our own historical experience, that it is translating into political reality our own motto, as it were, *E Pluribus Unum?* I think not. I believe we may take great encouragement and gratification from this manifest will of our European friends to apply principles tested in our own national experience to bring about a strong and united Europe.

The European Economic Community is far more than a mere customs union. But even in its purely commercial aspects it has a profound significance for us. The emergence of the Community means that we shall have on the two sides of the Atlantic Ocean two immense trading areas, two common markets, so to speak: the common market of the United States and the Common Market of Europe.

A NEW TRADING WORLD

These are the essential facts of the new trading world now being created. With the common market of the United States we are familiar—a trading area of fifty States among which trade flows freely and without tariffs or other obstructions but which is surrounded by a common external tariff. The Common Market of Europe comes to many of us as a new idea, but it should not; in its commercial aspects it is not far different from what we have known on our own continent—a common market presently of six states but on the verge of expansion, where internal trade can flow freely without tariff or other obstructions, the whole surrounded by a common external tariff.

I need hardly remind you that the existence of these two great trading areas—which between them will account for almost 90 per cent of the industrial production of the free world—will materially transform the trading world to which we have been accustomed. For American business, agriculture and labor it should mean great economic opportunity.

After all, the European Common Market is in many ways tailor-made for our type of industrial enterprise. We are the only industrial nation of the free world that has developed its industrial plant and its industrial techniques to serve a great mass market. Now for the first time we shall have the opportunity of utilizing our accumulated technical know-how, our experience with mass production and mass distribution, to establish our products in a market growing twice as fast as our own. It is a market which offers almost untold possibilities for expansion, for the European consumers are only just beginning to enjoy many of the modern consumer goods which Americans take for granted.

I recognize that American businessmen will not be able to enjoy the opportunities offered by this market without effort. Our industrialists will have to show ingenuity and resourcefulness. It will not be enough merely to attempt to sell our surplus products in Europe. We shall have to design products for use under very different social and physical conditions.

We shall have to apply our genius for distribution, for merchandising, to an entirely new market and shall have to learn to deal with habits and tastes different from those of America. The creation of this great market, the existence of these two great markets on opposite shores of the Atlantic, offer the possibility of a great expansion of transatlantic trade—provided that both we and our European friends are prepared to lower the level of the trade barriers that now divide us.

A great deal has been said in the last few months to the effect that American industry and agriculture will be under a disadvantage in dealing with the Common Market. In a sense this is true.

A manufacturer in Detroit selling to a customer in Hamburg will, of course, be under some disadvantage as against a manufacturer in Rome; he will have to sell his goods over a common external tariff while the manufacturer in Rome will not. But of course such advantages and disadvantages are reciprocal, since the manufacturer in Hamburg selling to a customer in Detroit will be at a similar disadvantage as against a manufacturer in North Carolina.

We start from a position in which the average levels of the external tariff walls of these two great markets—the United States and Europe—are not too far different. The expansion of transatlantic trade will depend to a considerable extent upon our ability and will, by agreement between ourselves and the Common Market, to reduce both of these walls. If we can bring this about we will have given further recognition to the fact of economic interdependence among the great industrial areas of the world—a fact which we have already recognized with the creation of the OECD, the Organization for Economic Cooperation and Development. We would at the same time have taken a long further step toward the development of an effective Atlantic partnership.

### NEED FOR TRADE EXPANSION ACT

The Trade Expansion Act of 1962 is the instrument which the President will need in order to achieve this result. It would authorize the gradual elimination of tariffs by the United States in return for concessions by the EEC on those products in which the United States and the EEC together supply 80 per cent of world trade—products in which we have shown we can compete. On others, tariff reductions of 50 per cent would be authorized, and these reductions would also be made reciprocally with nations outside the EEC. Tariff reductions negotiated with our principal trading partners will be extended to other nations on a most-favored-nation basis. There are provisions for preserving domestic industries essential to defense and for helping others meet import competition through adjustment assistance and other devices that would help keep American business and workers competitive and self-sustaining.

This broad new authority will enable us to bargain with the EEC and, by removing impediments to trade, expand export opportunities for all free-world nations. Our own industries—which now employ some three million workers directly producing for export—will have access to growing markets. Increased exports will enable our competitive industries to increase their employment, investment and profits, thereby stimulating the entire economy. . . .

To those who argue that our wages are too high for us to compete in world markets, let me point out that our exports exceed our imports by over $5 billion. In the machinery and vehicles industries, in which our workers are among the highest paid, we exported in 1960 four times as much as we imported. We exported more machinery and vehicles to the EEC countries than we imported from them. Our coal miners receive one of the highest hourly wages in American industry, yet we are the world's lowest cost producer of coal. American agriculture is especially competitive on world markets, and export markets are particularly important to American farmers. The produce of one-sixth of our harvested cropland is sold abroad; in tobacco the figure is one-third.

It is true that some of our producers, particularly those in handicraft or labor-intensive industries, are not competitive on world markets. On the one hand, we cannot allow the future of the free world—and this is what is at stake—to be forfeited for a small minority. On the other, we cannot callously stand by while this minority is injured. It need not be. In the case of an industry very important to you in North Carolina, cotton textiles, we were able to negotiate an agreement with major importing and exporting countries to ease the problem. Another way to ease the adjustment, a way entirely in keeping with the dynamism of the American economy, is to provide tax relief, loans and technical assistance to enable threatened producers to broaden or shift their production, introduce new processes, or modernize their plants, as well as through readjustment and relocation allowances to permit workers to learn new skills, which may be required as their employers shift to new products or processes, or find new jobs. Such trade adjustment assistance is provided for under the new Trade Expansion Act.

Actually, experience with such assistance in other countries indicates that when businesses and workers fully understand the necessity to meet competition they are usually able to do so without help. This has been the case under the European Common Market; producers deprived of protection have forgotten their first misgivings and have become competitive and are making higher profits. Far from suffering from unemployment, Western Europe today faces a shortage of labor.

Competition from abroad can lend a healthy incentive to domestic manufacturers and open their eyes to new opportunities. The postwar trend among American motorcar manufacturers was toward an all-purpose, eight-cylinder family car, with ever diminishing choice offered the purchaser. European imports did much to show that a two-car-per-family market existed, together with a demand for much greater diversification. Detroit is now offering far more variety in its products and—quite apart from the great advantages reaped by the consumer—is doing very well for itself.

### BENEFITS TO U.S. FROM NEW TRADE PROGRAM

I started out by indicating that I was going to speak of sacrifices our country should be prepared to make. But the Trade Expansion Act does not fall in that category. Its passage by Congress will mean a great deal to other peoples; but it will also mean a great deal to us. I am referring not to our stake in the health and cohesion of the free world—though that is beyond price—but to cash in our pockets. It will enable us to expand our markets in Europe. It will open important new markets for our products abroad, and increased trade will give our economy added vigor. We can expect significant new investment and the development of new products, which in turn will further expand our markets, domestic as well as foreign. Moreover, though we sometimes forget it, we are all consumers as well as producers. And certainly there can be no question but that the lowering of trade barriers will go far to insure that 180 million American consumers will obtain the best quality and widest varieties of goods at prices derived from vigorous competition.

I shall say one thing more on this subject. Either we believe in capitalism, in the freedom of individual enterprise, or we do not. And we do not if we hold with massive government intervention to distort and freeze the operation of the market. If we look to government to rig the game, we may as well look to it to play the hands. If we mean to discourage the forces of free enterprise all around the world, I can think of no better way of doing it—without even stirring from our chairs—than to shrink from competition behind unrealistic tariff walls.

Where there must be sacrifice is in respect of that large part of the human race which, while it will benefit from wider trade, cannot look to that alone for rescue.

OBJECTIVES OF FOREIGN AID

Can I, in a few minutes, say anything you do not know about the necessity for our foreign aid programs? I am not going to talk about the ability of the Communists to exploit human misery, or about the readiness of the U.S.S.R. and Communist China to move into the "have not" countries with their own aid programs as levers of ideological and political influence. I feel it is really not worthy of us to employ such a justification of our foreign aid. If we act in accord with what is worthy of us, we can leave it to the Communists to do the worrying.

We have been coming to the aid of our hard-pressed fellows on a scale unprecedented in human history. It began with a massive contribution to the victims of World War II—through UNRRA, the United Nations Relief and Rehabilitation Administration. I would not wish to think about what might have happened to such countries as Austria, Italy and France without this immediate assistance. Our next objective was the revival of Europe's economy—which the Marshall plan dramatically achieved. With that, and with our very large programs of aid to other war-wrecked countries—the Philippines, Korea, Japan—we discovered that what we were actually embarked upon was nothing less than an attack upon mankind's ancient enemies—want, sickness, ignorance, hopelessness. We were inspired, if by nothing else, by a realization that the exigencies of the mid-twentieth century left us no choice but to do what we could to bring a decent world order into being. To that end we have been carrying on various programs—Point Four, economic support for the common military burdens of our alliances, the Development Loan Fund, Food for Peace. We have come a fair distance. No one, however, can travel far abroad without being struck, to say the least, by the significance of the task remaining.

To bring about the Decade of Development the President has called for during the sixties, we have felt the need to concert the forces of the industrialized West. On our own side we have created a new agency in which for the first time the administration of all our programs of foreign assistance is combined. The Agency for International Development, a part of the Department of State, will, we believe, enable us to carry out more quickly, more effectively, and less expensively the work we have undertaken. It is our determination to manage it, not in a hardhearted but in a hardheaded way.

### MAIN FEATURES OF U.S. AID PROGRAM

First, we know that our loans or grants to another country can be no more than the extra, if critical, push. Economic and social development cannot be exported from one country to another. The main drive and the basic resources must come from within the country itself. None knows that better than we who have seen the transformation of the life of our own Southland within our own personal experiences. We have witnessed the magical partnership of education, improved health, and rising productivity; the partnership of education, research and extension; the partnership between opportunity and a personal and family yearning for a more decent existence. Development means advance on a broad front, an advance which can be achieved only by an entire people moving together. Education means, among other things, a more productive individual. Rising productivity means a more adequate tax base for schools and roads and the other necessities of public investment. Health is basic to work, and work is the indispensable ingredient in progress.

If we press others beyond our borders to conduct their public affairs with honesty and efficiency, it is because we know from our own experience that inefficiency and corruption are social wastes which no one can afford. If we press for the mobilization of local capital resources and adequate taxes, it is because we know that, otherwise, the great task of development will fail. If we urge the political and psychological mobilization of entire peoples in the effort, it is because we know that only an interested and dedicated people will succeed in rapid development under free institutions.

If we are resistant to those who would rely solely upon the threat of communism as a basis for our assistance, it is because we know that outside funds alone cannot meet that threat—and there are not enough funds to waste in such futility.

Second, we are moving rapidly toward aid which is related to longer range plans for economic and social progress. I have already spoken of the need to move on a broad front. Hit-or-miss projects, including projects designed to meet crises, are unlikely to make an enduring contribution. A solid structure of growth must have solid foundations—and this means doing first things first. This is why education and technical training have been emphasized more strongly, why potable water seems more urgent than a sports stadium, why housing is more attractive than monuments.

A third feature of our present program, thanks to Congress, is that we are able to make long-range financial commitments—subject to annual appropriations—in support of long-range planning by other governments. It is a powerful means for encouraging long-range commitments by those being assisted and yields larger harvests in self-help and realistic priorities.

I do not, by any tone of voice, mean to imply that an indifferent, halfhearted performance is the rule among governments with which we are cooperating. Far from it. Most of them are doing an admirable job under trying and difficult circumstances —far more trying and recalcitrant than we at a distance might suppose. It takes time to train teachers and extension workers. It takes unusual dedication for the educated to turn aside from lucrative urban opportunities to go into the villages and the countryside to serve as development missionaries. Old habits change slowly, and grudgingly. We in North Carolina have forgotten the violent agitation which resisted the first hookworm campaigns in this and neighboring states. But it is deeply encouraging to see governments and peoples gearing themselves for the great task of moving toward the unlimited promise of the modern age.

Finally, our aid programs are related to the combined effort of our vigorous partners of the industrialized West and of other nations in position to help. The burden of development is more than we can bear alone, and there is no reason why we should try. Indeed, there are important political reasons why aid across national frontiers should be as broadly based and as widely shared as possible. We attach the greatest importance to the movement of the OECD countries toward appropriating approximately 1 per cent of gross national product committed to aid for underdeveloped countries. We are deeply gratified to see regional and other arrangements through which underdeveloped countries are helping each other. And we have profound respect for the mobilization of broad support for such purposes by the specialized agencies of the United Nations. We are glad that Congress has given us the means, through our present aid program, for encouraging others to take an increasing share in this great adventure.

#### LOOKING TO THE WORLD OF THE FUTURE

I am fully aware of the fact that we have invested heavily in all types of foreign aid since 1945 and that we have done so despite the fact that we have much unfinished business in our own society. We have done so because these programs are an essential part of the main business of the nation—our commitment to freedom and to a decent world community of independent states, freely cooperating with each other in matters of common interest.

It is a matter of some importance that no one of the countries which have become independent since World War II has fallen behind the Iron or Bamboo Curtain, that no nation has willingly embraced communism as the result of a free election. It is of some consequence that the large majority of smaller countries members of the United Nations stoutly resisted the effort to destroy that organization through the troika proposals. It is reassuring to observe that Soviet blandishments and aid have not destroyed the stubborn insistence upon national independence by those who have been assiduously courted. It is of interest to see the Communist bloc less monolithic than Soviet leaders wish, with differences appearing which are deeply rooted in such old-fashioned notions as national feeling, national interest and national independence.

We can move through this period of tension and turmoil with safety and with confidence if we keep our eyes steadily upon the kind of world which is coming into being, and must come into being, in response to the aspirations of ordinary people in all parts of the world. It is necessary to be critical of our efforts; it is sometimes fashionable to be cynical about them. But we are a nation of builders and are at our best in building, even though we know that building is more difficult than tearing down.

. . . While most of his contemporaries were guided by their local provincialism, Washington had his mind not merely on the Thirteen Colonies alone but on the almost trackless continent beyond them. It was he who in 1790 caused to be designed for the infant Republic of a few million souls a Capital City so grand in its conception, so ample in its scope, that for generations its unfilled spaces provided amusement for the scoffers. Even Jefferson, no mean visionary himself, would have settled for a district a tenth the size. But not Washington. The years rolled by, the nation spread to the Pacific, spanned the continent with iron rails, commenced to climb skyward, became a world power. And at last, a century after the death of its first President, it had grown up to the Capital he had prepared for it.

With the pace of change what it is today we cannot expect

to look one hundred years ahead. We shall do very well to perceive dim shapes twenty years hence. But I believe we must try to do that, to foresee what the city of man may look like then, not making too much of the difficulties that lie in the way but conscious, as Washington would have been, of the possibilities. In that way we shall realize them and in the process find allies in all corners of the earth—the men and women of many lands who want the kind of world sketched out in the U.N. Charter, a world of peace and human dignity, of creative endeavor, of expanding frontiers for the human spirit.

## The Trade Expansion Act of 1962

*This sets forth succinctly the purposes of the new trade expansion legislation requested by President Kennedy.*

. . . . The Trade Expansion Act of 1962 is a new initiative, a new program to replace measures that have become outpaced by the march of world events. Its provisions take cognizance of the special problems and needs of this nation as it advances to meet the promises and the complex problems of the sixties.

### GROWING RECOGNITION OF INTERDEPENDENCE

Implicit in the provisions of this act is the recognition by the United States of the growing interdependence of the nations of the free world. United by the sovereignty of freedom, this family of nations is not only menaced by Communist ambition;

Portions of address before the Conference on Trade Policy, Washington, D. C., May 17, 1962.

it is challenged to prove its basic thesis that government by free choice can best answer man's demand for social and economic progress.

National security alone compels interdependence. Domestic goals—among them economic growth and higher living standards—increasingly call for cooperative measures among countries of the free world. Fiscal and monetary problems in today's world defy unilateral solution.

Nowhere is the recognition of interdependence more evident than in Europe today. The Common Market, the Coal and Steel Community, and EURATOM [European Atomic Energy Community] are the first institutions of the rapidly developing economic integration of Western Europe. Powerful forces are moving the European Community toward political integration as well.

Survival and growth have forced the nations of Europe to forget their historic antagonisms and unite. Through the pooling of resources and efforts, a mighty new entity is growing out of the chaos left by national rivalries and world war.

We became heavily engaged in the rebuilding of Europe the moment the American people fully recognized our common destiny with Europe in the postwar world, and we have strongly supported the move toward unity. NATO has emerged as the military arm of our partnership with Europe. We and the Canadians have joined with eighteen European nations in the Organization for Economic Cooperation and Development, an organization created to bring into closer agreement the economic and financial policies of the Atlantic community and, with Japan, to mobilize the energies and resources of the industrial free world in assisting the developing countries.

The Atlantic community is a going concern; Western Europe is prospering with a growth rate greater than ours; economic and social development in the underdeveloped countries is moving forward through concerted American and European efforts; the internal Communist threat in Europe has been largely dissipated. Strong NATO forces deter military adventurers. Partnership is working.

Last year the United States launched another great project

in partnership in another area—the Alliance for Progress. A mutual concern for the security of the Western Hemisphere coupled with the urgent need for economic and social advancement among our Latin neighbors prompted the creation of a development program of great dimension. Again the recognition of interdependence has resulted in a joint commitment to mutual assistance.

On a global scale the United Nations is working to control centrifugal world forces through programs attacking the scourges of poverty, illiteracy and disease, as well as through providing machinery for the settlement of at least some of the corrosive problems among its members.

It is in this context of the growing recognition of interdependence and the emergence of international institutions for cooperation that we must consider the question of expanded free-world trade.

I must stress that we are in a period of transition, of fluidity. But we can move in some confidence that the new patterns of integration in Europe, of development in Latin America, of independent nation-states in Africa and Asia, will progress along lines that will be congenial to our foreign policy objectives. We seek a close partnership with the industrial democracies, an alliance sharing the burdens and responsibilities of building and defending the free world. We seek to forge strong bonds with the developed nations and the developing nations, bonds that depend on assistance, cooperation and free choice.

Support for the less developed nations in their efforts to move toward self-sustaining growth and independence must include not only direct economic assistance but also a determination to provide markets for their products, so that they may earn the foreign exchange necessary to generate their own dynamism for development.

### CHALLENGES TO FREE-WORLD TRADE

Against our design for a world of free choice, the Sino-Soviet bloc has mounted an offensive—using trade and aid as a weapon—to bring these less developed nations into the Communist orbit. "We threaten capitalism," Premier Khrushchev has said, "by peaceful economic competition." In fact, in this period of revolutionary change and attendant instability, Communist coercion threatens to subvert the fundamental concept of a world community of free and independent peoples.

There are other dangers. Patterns of international trade will either bring the free world into closer harmony, or they will produce increasing discord. The formation of a protectionist European trade bloc, giving preferential treatment to associated states but discriminating against the United States, Japan and Latin America, would be disastrously divisive of the free world. European leadership, sharing our awareness of this fact, has pointed the market movement in the direction of liberal trade. The present Common Market countries showed themselves, in the round of GATT negotiations concluded last winter, prepared to bargain down their exterior trade barriers and to eliminate other barriers to trade with the outside world. The Common Market has set its external tariff rates at a level that is comparable to our own.

The time has come for the United States to indicate the nature of its response. We are challenged to lead in the negotiation of relationships with the Common Market area that will expand trade throughout all of the free world on a nondiscriminatory basis.

The President, in the Trade Expansion Act of 1962, has asked for the tools needed to negotiate. We must make concessions to get concessions. That the President get the powers he has requested is essential to free-world strength and unity, and thus the national security of the United States.

Needless to say, the trade bill alone will not expand trade. Much depends on our ability to use the authority effectively. As much depends on the initiative of American producers.

On the first requirement, that we negotiate effectively, I have no fears. Trade concessions will be made on a truly reciprocal basis, leading to expansion of trade to the mutual benefit of the parties concerned. Our trade negotiators act under a mandate to serve the national interest and protect the economic strength of the nation as a whole.

American negotiators have shown themselves time and time again to be good Yankee traders. The continued—in fact, tenfold —expansion of United States trade since 1934 proves their effectiveness. The lowering of tariffs is not their only objective; given effective bargaining power, they will continue to attack the many other types of restrictions that restrain trade. However, the effectiveness of our negotiators is dependent on their having the requisite bargaining power.

I might add, parenthetically, that a vigorous export promotion program, here and abroad, is being carried out by the State and Commerce Departments. The commercial officers of our Foreign Service will play a major role in increasing American business activity abroad through providing foreign market information and developing new trade opportunities.

Given the authority contained in this bill, the United States Government can and will secure agreements opening the possibility of substantially increased American exports. It will then be largely up to our producers and salesmen to capitalize on the opportunities. This new trading world will be intensely competitive. But competing is what we do best in this country.

The countries with which we strike trade bargains can be expected to exploit every new possibility to expand their exports to this country. Exploitation of the advantages offered us will challenge the aggressive spirit, initiative, and imagination that are the foundation of this nation's progress and power. We will be committed to a massive demonstration of the workability and applicability of free enterprise. What is needed is the effort. We have the capability; indeed, I am convinced that we have the competitive advantage.

The Trade Expansion Act of 1962 will give the President the authority to assure the United States continued leadership in the formative years of a great alliance of free nations. We are not given the choice of sustaining the *status quo*. Either we accept leadership or lay down our mantle and retreat to a perilous isolation. To meet the challenge demands total commitment on the part of the American people and total engagement of America's resources.

## Trade, the Commonwealth and the United States

*Great Britain's decision to seek membership in the European Common Market alarmed several countries of the Commonwealth, which had long enjoyed a protected position in the British market under the Commonwealth system of preferential tariffs. Individuals in some of these countries were mistakenly accusing the United States of having pushed the British into that decision. In May 1962, while in Australia for the ANZUS Council Meeting and in New Zealand for a one-day visit, Secretary Rusk explained the attitude of the United States toward European integration, tried to reassure Australia and New Zealand, and sought their cooperation in working toward a more open trading world. This excerpt from his speech at a dinner given by the New Zealand Parliament contains his main argument.*

Portion of address at Official State Reception, Parliament Buildings, Wellington, New Zealand, May 10, 1962.

In the 1950s, Western Europe achieved a rate of progress unprecedented in its long history. Japan also has attained an unparalleled rate of economic growth—a rate higher than the Soviet Union's or Western Europe's. And in the United States the increase—just the increase—in gross national product since World War I exceeds the total gross national product of the Soviet Union today.

## MOVEMENT TOWARD EUROPEAN INTEGRATION

One of our great tasks in building the free world, as we see it, is to strengthen the bonds among the more advanced free nations. These lie chiefly in the Northern Hemisphere but certainly include Australia and New Zealand.

For at least fourteen years the United States has favored cooperation and movements toward integration among the nations of Western Europe. Our attitude was stated in the legislation authorizing the Marshall plan and has been reaffirmed on many subsequent occasions by our Congress and by all our postwar Presidents. It has been supported consistently by the leadership of both of our major political parties.

We hoped, first of all, for a Europe which would submerge for all time the old feuds which cost the world so much in treasure and blood. We can almost say with certainty that after six hundred years we shall not have wars which originate within Western Europe. And beyond that, we have wanted to see a free Europe that is strong and vigorous. And we have believed that in union there is strength.

We on our side have never offered any blueprints for an integrated Europe. We have never tried to tell our Western European friends how, or to what degree, they should integrate. But when proposals which seemed to us constructive have originated in Europe, we have supported them. We looked with favor on the creation of the European Coal and Steel Community and, later, on the formation of EURATOM and the European Economic Community.

Generally the process of European integration seems to

us to have produced splendid results. Enlightened leadership has established a new relationship between Germany and her Western European neighbors. And economically Western Europe has forged ahead with unprecedented dynamism.

Now Great Britain seeks membership in the Common Market. It was her decision, not ours. We did not urge it. But when the British asked us, as old friends, for our views, we responded favorably. We hope that the current negotiations will soon be successfully concluded. We share with Britain the judgment that she can better maintain and enhance her strength inside the Common Market than outside it. And we think that the addition of British resources, skills and proven political capacities will greatly strengthen the Common Market.

ADJUSTMENT TO COMMON MARKET

Full participation by the United Kingdom in the great process of European unity—an objective so eloquently outlined in the Lord Privy Seal's opening statement last October—will be beneficial to the Community, to the British, to other European states and in fact to all of us. We firmly subscribe to this view, even though we realize that Britain's entry into the Common Market will create problems of adjustment for many countries, including New Zealand, Australia and the United States.

We are sympathetic with the problems faced by you and Australia because we face problems not greatly different in kind, even though different in degree. We share with you a considerable area of common interest. None of us belongs to the European Common Market. All of us are substantial exporters of temperate-zone agricultural products and interested in maintaining and expanding our markets for these products. We can, therefore, benefit by working together toward the creation of a trading world as open and liberal as possible.

Let me say quite frankly, as we face these momentous changes in the trading world, that we recognize the problems posed to you here in New Zealand by the Common Market. If you have a problem, then we have a problem. And this is because the United States has a great stake in your prosperity. It is neither necessary nor profitable for us to engage in theoretical debate or to lose ourselves in slogans. But what we must do is to sit down and find the practical answers to these practical problems.

As a step toward the changed trading world of the future, President Kennedy has requested the United States Congress to grant him broad powers to negotiate for a substantial reduction in trade barriers. At the same time the United States has welcomed the initiative in GATT of exploring the possibility of global arrangements for cereals, since it seems to us that, in a world of vaulting agricultural technology, arrangements on a global scale may offer the only effective solutions to our mutual problems, not only for cereals but for other key commodities.

## CREATING A MORE OPEN TRADING WORLD

The open trading arrangements we envisage are, it seems to us, a far better approach than the permanent maintenance of preferential systems. In fact the permanent extension of existing Commonwealth preferences, within the framework of an expanded Common Market, would seriously prejudice our vital interest in a world of expanding and liberal trade. At the same time we recognize that, in order to ease the problem of adjustment, transitional arrangements for many of these commodities may be necessary.

I should like to enlist the active support of New Zealand and Australia in working with us toward the creation of a more open trading world, including our own common market among the fifty States of the United States. And I am persuaded that a mutual appreciation of the problems which each of us faces, as well as a sympathetic understanding of the problems posed for the United Kingdom in taking the great step that is proposed, should go far toward creating a climate in which solutions can more easily be found.

We have not the slightest doubt that the Commonwealth can meet this challenge. We have seen it accommodate itself to new conditions in the past—in the last few years to the addition of many new members. We believe that this great stabilizing family of nations will be able to accommodate itself constructively to the problems of the future.

We in the United States feel that we have a great interest in the ties which make for solidarity within the Commonwealth. If we would have any hesitancy or criticism, it would be that perhaps the Commonwealth has not moved forward with the self-confidence which it deserved.

Let me reiterate that the enlarged Common Market will require adjustments by the United States too. But we do not believe that the prospect of temporary difficulties should cause us to oppose a move which promises so much for the free world as a whole and for the cause of liberty to which you and we are dedicated.

# VI.   FOREIGN AID

*Charting  a  New  Course  in  Foreign  Aid*

*This speech sets forth the philosophy and cardinal features of President Kennedy's foreign aid program.*

I am grateful for this chance to talk to the leaders of American business about some of the decisions facing us as we move into the decade of the sixties. Some of these we can make ourselves; some will be made by others. Together they will have far-reaching effect upon our future; they may determine issues of war and peace, freedom and tyranny, and the prospects for a decent world order.

My remarks will center around foreign aid—at a time when the London *Economist* says that there is desperate need for "the idealism of the old world to redress the aid-weariness of the new." I do not propose just now to talk about particular amounts of money for specific purposes; that will come later when the Con-

Address at United States Chamber of Commerce, Washington, D. C., May 3, 1961.

gress and the public take up the President's proposals for discussion.

What concerns me is not a certain number of dollars but whether we make history or submit to it, whether we retreat into our dreams or stir to realize them. For the decade of the sixties will see decisions made which will have a great deal to do with the shape of our world for the rest of this century.

I would suppose that some of these are:

Whether the established and productive societies of the West can combine their efforts to create a world environment of expanding freedoms and productivity essential to their own security and well-being.

Whether the Western world can build effective ties of genuine partnership with peoples of other areas, races, cultures, and circumstances.

Whether the large number of newly independent nations can find solutions for their urgent problems through free institutions or will succumb to the trap of totalitarian methods baited by the promise of rapid development.

Whether governments of those living in misery and want can evoke their primary asset, i.e., the energies of the peoples themselves dedicated to the task of making the sixties a decade of progress.

Whether we ourselves can find the talent, the persistence, the sophistication and the tact to labor with others, in the words of the United Nations Charter, "to promote social progress and better standards of life in larger freedom."

Whether troubled mankind can spin more effectively "the infinity of threads which bind peace together" in common tasks which make natural allies of us all.

### BASIC OBJECTIVES OF EXTENDING AID

My questions have had little to do with military matters. We face formidable military threats and shall need the combined arms of the free world to meet them. Surely we must not learn all over again that weakness can tempt aggression. Our foreign aid program includes military aid to help in building the common defense. But a primary task of policy is to support our purposes and build a decent world order by peaceful means if possible. Power is not a matter of arms alone. Strength comes from education, fertile acres, humming workshops and the satisfaction and pride of peoples. A vibrant society is not subject to subversion; determined defense is the easier when there is something to defend.

Nor have I emphasized the threat of communism. The threat is there, but foreign aid has more solemn purposes. In presenting the plan which bore his name Secretary George Marshall put it: "Our policy is directed not against any country or doctrine but against hunger, poverty, desperation, and chaos."

It seems to me that, as we look back over the past two decades, we have lost sight of the words of George Marshall. The aid programs of these two decades have been the creature of crisis and rapidly changing events, and the original Marshall concept has become blurred.

Foreign aid started with China in 1938 as military aid and became the great wartime weapon of lend-lease. But even before the war was over, we began a program of relief to war-ravaged regions—a noble international effort known as UNRRA [United Nations Relief and Rehabilitation Administration].

From relief we moved on to the historic Truman doctrine aid, which saved Greece and Turkey from military subversion, and from there to economic assistance, with a program that reached its pinnacle in the Marshall plan—not only one of the most dramatic strokes in history but also one of the most successful.

With the dawning of the 1950s came a new awareness of the needs of the underdeveloped nations and the inauguration of the Point Four technical assistance program. At the same time, however, we became increasingly preoccupied with building the military strength of the free world. The NATO treaty among the North Atlantic nations was followed in later years by the SEATO and the CENTO treaties. We formed a network of military bases throughout the world, and a massive military aid program that began in Europe soon became global in scope. In the later fifties the technique of bringing about economic development through long-term loans to underdeveloped areas was introduced into our aid program with the establishment of the Development Loan Fund.

The challenge now before us is different in character from that of the past. We must provide military assistance, but the larger task is only indirectly related to immediate security problems. It is concerned with preventing them. Unlike disaster relief, it is long-range in nature. Unlike the Marshall plan, it deals with nations which lack the governmental traditions, the industrial base, and the trained manpower of a modern economy.

As we enter the decade of the sixties we have an opportunity to stand back a bit, to learn from our experience of the past two decades, and to chart a more effective and intelligent course for the future.

LESSONS OF THE PAST

What are the principal lessons to be learned?

The first is that, if our aid is to be effective, we must have clear targets and objectives and a careful plan for achieving them. Too often in the past our aid has been governed less by the priorities of a well-planned program than by the needs and pressures of the moment: the need to preserve an alliance or friendship or protect an American military base; or the desire to counter a Communist aid offer or save an economy from imminent collapse. These needs were urgent; to some extent they will persist. But aid granted in this fashion is not necessarily best suited to the fostering of long-term development and the attainment of self-sustaining growth which will free nations of the need for outside assistance. This must be the paramount goal in the granting of aid in the sixties.

The attainment of that goal will require a carefully thought-out, long-range development effort in each country assisted. This bears directly on the second lesson of the past: that economic development is not an overnight matter. It is a time-consuming process that requires the steady application of resources and energy. It will not be achieved by hesitating, and sometimes spasmodic, annual steps. The yearly authorization and appropriations processes which govern the present aid program are simply not suited to the long-term economic development task of the sixties.

Third, we must recognize that the capital and financial assistance that brought such brilliant success to the Marshall plan is not, by itself, adequate to the requirements of the sixties. The Marshall plan countries were highly developed, with mature governments and institutions, skilled and literate people. Today, however, we are primarily concerned with assisting nations which lack the governmental experience, the industrial base or the trained manpower of a modern economy. Hence we are talking about total development—the building of a nation from its very foundations. Especially is this true of the newly emerging nations.

A fourth lesson is that various types of assistance—loans, grants, technical assistance, food and so forth—must be coordinated and administered by a single agency of the government. The aid programs of the past decade have been the creatures of unfolding and rapidly changing events, and today foreign assistance is administered by a variety of agencies. Clearly this is not the way to make the most effective use of each aid dollar.

Finally, we have learned that assistance is not likely to achieve its purposes if it is unconcerned with social objectives, if it merely serves to enrich the rich and perpetuate the gap between rich and poor that breeds discontent and revolt. The impoverished of centuries are awakening to the knowledge that a better life *can* be theirs. Social justice is an imperative of the 1960s. The fostering of social justice must, therefore, be a major objective of our aid programs—not because we wish to interfere, not because we wish to dictate, but simply because we wish our aid to be effective.

In charting our course for the sixties we must, I believe, return to the words of Marshall and follow the goal he enunciated fourteen years ago. The purpose of our aid program, he said, "should be the revival of a working economy in the world so as to permit the emergence of political and social conditions in which free institutions can exist."

This is precisely the goal of the new aid effort which President Kennedy has proposed to the Congress. It seeks to take advantage of the lessons of the past two decades and to chart a new course for the future.

### CARDINAL POINTS OF NEW AID PROGRAM

The cardinal points of this new program are:

First, improved and efficient administration. Under the President's proposal the existing aid programs now being administered by separate agencies will be brought under one roof, under a single director.

Second, long-term financing. The heart of President Kennedy's new program is his request for authority to make commitments for development loans over a five-year period rather than on the year-by-year basis under which the aid program has been operating. This is essential to making the most effective use of each aid dollar. It is a necessity if the new aid administrator is to:

Relate our assistance to long-range country plans for the attainment of self-sustaining economic growth;

Elicit maximum self-help efforts from those assisted;

Stimulate long-term help from other industrialized nations in a partnership effort to assist the underdeveloped areas of the world.

To achieve these ends the President has asked Congress for authority to borrow funds from the Treasury over a five-year period. He has chosen this method of long-term financing for the aid program principally because it has proved effective in some twenty-two existing lending programs of the Federal Government, including many you know well and support, such as the

Reconstruction Finance Corporation and the Federal Deposit Insurance Corporation and, in the international field, the Export-Import Bank.

This is not a new proposal in the aid field. President Eisenhower recommended borrowing authority for the Development Loan Fund in 1957. Nor will this deprive Congress of control over the aid program. All of the nonlending aspects of the program will continue to be subject to the usual appropriation procedures, which will afford Congress a full opportunity to review the entire aid program.

The third cardinal point of the new aid program is a strong effort by those assisted. This involves not only the use of their own resources but programs of social reform and the fostering of social justice. The granting of long-term commitment authority bears directly on this point, for these self-help efforts will call for sacrifice on the part of recipient nations—sacrifices they may be reluctant to make in the absence of assurances by us and others of long-term assistance. Conversely, if we are unwilling to make a moderate adjustment in our method of financing the aid program, many countries may wonder why they should take much more radical and difficult steps.

Fourth, the new aid effort will not be solely an American effort. It will be a partnership effort in which all of the industrial nations of the world will join.

The Senate has recently approved United States participation in an Atlantic grouping of nations known as the Organization for Economic Cooperation and Development—or OECD. One of the principal functions of this Organization is to coordinate the aid programs of the various member nations and to work toward formulas of equitable sharing of the task of helping the underdeveloped nations of the world. We have already had one meeting on this subject with our industrialized friends in which an excellent start was made. Procedures for aid coordination were established, a start was made on the question of burden sharing, and our allies agreed to the naming of an American chairman to head the OECD organization. Another such meeting is scheduled to take place in July.

THE "RIGHTNESS" OF FOREIGN AID

In his inaugural address President Kennedy said:

> To those people in the huts and villages of half the globe struggling to break the bonds of mass misery, we pledge our best efforts to help them help themselves, for whatever period is required—not because the Communists may be doing it, not because we seek their votes, but because it is right.

It is right because the per capita output in the under-developed countries is about one-twentieth of what it is in America; because 65 per cent of the peoples of these areas are illiterate, compared to our 2 per cent; because infant mortality is six times greater, life expectancy a little more than half. It is right because misery is a challenge to the best there is in us, because the responsibilities we accept are privileges, because we are the kind of people we are.

Foreign aid would be impelling were there no Sino-Soviet bloc, backing with energy and power their doctrine of world revolution. But the bloc is there, and what would be impelling becomes a matter of life and death for freedom itself. Beginning in the mid-fifties the bloc has moved into economic and technical assistance, with increasingly large resources and with considerable effect. They have found a device by which they hope to leap over or outflank the bastions of the free world and a means for pressing their campaign into every continent.

I recall, some years ago, a consultation with a distinguished Senator about an early aid program. Having heard the proposal he said, "We must do this, but if you want this kind of money you'll have to come in here roaring." Roar we did, but the roaring was discordant; it confused our purposes, misrepresented our motives and impaired our execution.

Vigorous public debate is vital to our democracy, but we could add great strength to our position if we could decide as a nation that foreign aid is a national necessity of the greatest moment in this period of dramatic historical change, that we accept it as a long-term commitment and give our President our steady and quiet support for this instrument of action in a troubled and dangerous world.

## The Foreign Aid Program
## for Fiscal Year 1963

*This statement summarizes the changes in the administration of foreign aid made during the preceding year, the guiding principles of the program, and the requirements for the ensuing year.*

. . . . Our present problem is not to justify the fundamental need for our foreign aid program but to determine and act upon the principles which will contribute most effectively to its success.

There are undoubtedly many significant factors which must be considered from time to time, but I believe we may underscore six basic propositions as our major guides:

1. *The fundamental and indispensable requirement for the development of a nation is the determination of its own government and people to move forward.* Our aid, no matter what its amount, cannot materially help those who will not help themselves. No country can make solid progress except by its own efforts, inspired by its own leadership and supported by the dedication of its own people.

The aid we can supply will be only a small portion of the total national effort needed. Our aid, for example, to the nations

Major portions of Statement to the Senate Foreign Relations Committee, April 5, 1962.

joining in the Alliance for Progress is less than 2 per cent of the total of their gross national products. Obviously, therefore, what is done by these nations with their own resources is crucial. These efforts must in all cases include mobilization of national resources, economic, financial and human. With national variations, they must include the willingness to undertake reforms important to progress—reforms in taxation, in land holdings, in housing and the broadening and improvement of educational opportunities. We must constantly bear in mind that our goal is not just economic development. It is equally and concurrently to increase social justice which will secure the benefits of progress to those masses who have so long suffered from poverty, ignorance and disease—and from the most cruel condition of all, hopelessness.

2. *Our resources should be devoted to fostering long-range economic and social growth.* We cannot prudently invest major resources on a crisis-to-crisis basis. Political stability cannot be assured unless there is steady progress toward long-term goals. We are inevitably and properly limited in the money and the skilled manpower we can invest in the progress of the less developed countries. We have no funds to spend on those projects which, however useful in themselves, do not significantly help advance the cause of national growth. We must continually press countries receiving our assistance to improve their planning and to use their resources in the most effective way. Our aid must be tailored country by country to concentrate on those programs and projects which will have the maximum effect on development.

3. *The education and training of the people of the nations we are aiding is vital to their economic and social growth.* Progress will not come from our aid dollars or materials but from the use which people can make of them. People are the dynamos which generate the power of development. They provide the minds, the will and the skills by which progress is made. It is essential that they have not only the will but the competence for the task.

Education in all its branches is fundamental. We have seen in our own country that our economic progress has paralleled our educational development. We could not wait to become rich before we built our educational system. We created it, and our skilled people created our wealth. This year we are particularly aware of this relationship because we are celebrating the hundredth anniversary of our unique system of land-grant colleges. Education of leaders, training of administrators and of technicians of all kinds must be central to the development programs of many of the new nations. The emphasis of our grant assistance in Africa and Latin America, especially, is and properly should be in this most basic field of human and social development.

4. *The progress of the newly developing nations should have the aid of all the industrialized nations of the free world.* Those which we aided in the past are now thriving. It is appropriate and practical that they should increase their contributions.

5. *Developing nations themselves have an opportunity to help each other.* They may do so by opening their educational institutions to others less well situated. They may share the lessons learned in the process of development. They may extend direct assistance within their capabilities. This is already occurring, and we can be encouraged by the response to this opportunity.

6. *Our aid program should be administered as efficiently as possible.* The administering agency should be organized to fulfill the requirements of the program and should be staffed by the most able personnel who can be persuaded to undertake this complex and important public duty.

PROGRESS IN THIS YEAR OF TRANSITION

If these should be our guiding principles, how have we applied them?

It is too early to make a full report. The new authorizing legislation became effective about 7 months ago, and the Agency for International Development came into being only 5 months ago. Yet I can report that significant progress has been made.

*Administration.* The needed administrative reorganization is under way. Mr. Fowler Hamilton, the new Administrator of the Agency for International Development, has reshaped the Agency on a regional basis capable of carrying out the new emphasis on well-planned country programs. He has enlisted the services of an able group to direct these regional programs and to administer the supporting functional staffs which will provide expert advice with respect to material resources, educational and social development, and development financing and private enterprise. Qualified employees of the old ICA [International Cooperation Administration] and the Development Loan Fund are now being integrated into the new AID organization, and a major search is under way in and out of Government for additional talented people to carry out the demanding and complex tasks of the program in Washington and the field.

*Self-Help.* I am encouraged by the growing evidence of the determination of the less developed nations to act vigorously for their own progress and by the multiplying examples of basic reforms and other measures of self-help. Many of these have, of course, been in preparation for several years. Others are of more recent origin. The Charter of Punta del Este contains a forward-looking agreement on goals to be achieved by the Latin American nations in a framework of cooperation. The goals they agreed on include a minimum rate of economic growth of 2.5 per cent per capita, a more equitable distribution of national income, economic diversification, the elimination of adult illiteracy by 1970 and the provision of at least 6 years of schooling for each child, the substantial improvement of health conditions, the increase of low-cost housing and progress toward economic integration.

It is true these are goals and not yet facts, but the agreement is in itself a substantial accomplishment and the determination back of it justifies the hope of substantial progress toward fulfillment. This hope is sustained by the series of reform measures which have been undertaken by Latin American nations since the Act of Bogotá less than two years ago.

*Planning.* We can be encouraged also by the progress which has been made in long-term planning in this year of transition. In Latin America many countries have made conscientious efforts to improve their planning processes. Several African countries—Tunisia and Nigeria are good examples—are developing realistic plans. India and Pakistan, of course, have well-developed plans, and others show promise. We must recognize, however, that many others face serious obstacles to adequate planning. For many the needed administrative experience is lacking. For some even the basic statistical information is not yet available. Where decisions must be made by democratic processes —processes which are among our basic objectives—these decisions may involve the same kind of debate, timing and resolution of difficulties with which we ourselves are familiar.

Long-range commitments are a spur to long-range planning, and such commitments have now been made with India, Pakistan, Nigeria and Tanganyika. The authority granted by the Congress has already provided encouragement to other countries to take the difficult steps necessary for development. We anticipate making commitments under the long-range authority in the near future with a few other nations where meaningful plans are now being formulated.

*Human Resources.* Our increased emphasis on the development of human resources is finding ready response in Africa and Latin America. Several nations have strongly recognized its basic importance to progress and have urged our assistance to educational and health programs they have worked out.

*Aid From Other Nations.* During the past year we have increased our efforts to coordinate and increase the flow of assistance from our allies to the less developed countries. Our NATO allies, together with Japan, are now providing in the neighborhood of $2.3 billion per year to less developed countries. A number of these other free-world countries are contributing to foreign assistance a portion of their gross national product comparable to that contributed by the United States. Unfortunately, however, much of the assistance from these countries is in the form of short-term loans with relatively high interest rates. Several nations have substantially liberalized their loan terms in the past year, but further improvement is needed. Significantly, the United Kingdom, Germany, France, Belgium, Canada and Japan have established new aid and lending agencies, evidencing their sense of responsibility in this area.

Several types of multilateral organizations and groups have been formed to encourage closer cooperation and coordination of effort among the nations supplying capital and technical assistance to the developing areas. Consortia organized by the World Bank are supporting the development plans of countries such as India and Pakistan. The Development Assistance Committee of OECD [Organization for Economic Cooperation and Development] is undertaking a coordinating role with regard to technical and capital assistance to countries where its members have substantial interests.

### THE USE OF FISCAL YEAR 1962 FUNDS

Mr. Hamilton and his colleagues will discuss in detail the uses to which the funds available for the first year under the new legislation are being put. I should like to stress, however, their indispensable value in supporting foreign policy positions the United States has taken in recent months. In the Far East, for example, these funds have made possible the buildup of military and economic strength with which the free people of Viet-Nam are combating the forces intent on destroying their nation. In South Asia these funds are contributing to the continued remarkable progress India and Pakistan are making with their well-developed programs. These funds are making possible the peacekeeping activities of the United Nations in the Middle East and in the Congo—activities which have turned aside what might otherwise have been the grave danger of involvement of major powers.

In Africa also these funds through loans and grants are providing for fundamental development of human and economic resources quite literally crucial to the building of whole nations. And in Latin America the availability of aid funds made it possible for us to support a free government in the Dominican Republic. In Latin America also I have already referred to the Charter of Punta del Este based in substantial measure on the assurance of aid from the United States and designed to bring about the peaceful evolution of a continent under conditions of free institutions.

In short, around the world, on five continents, our aid is fulfilling a major and indispensable role in support of the interests of our country and the preservation and strengthening of freedom.

The request before you is essentially for the authorization of funds for fiscal year 1963. It rests on the premise that the authorizing legislation enacted last year is sound. It asks for only one major change and a few minor ones. It does not provide at all for authorization for military assistance or development lending funds, since authorizations enacted for those categories last year extend through fiscal year 1963.

*Military Assistance.* I know, however, that you have a deep interest in military assistance, and I should like to report to you on the program for which $1.5 billion of funds are being asked in appropriations.

Military assistance remains an important part of the total U.S. defense effort. It is also the principal means by which there is sustained the worldwide collective security systems of which we are a part. You may recall that the Chairman of the Joint Chiefs of Staff said to you last year that no amount of money spent on our own forces could give the United States a comparable asset of trained, well-equipped forces, familiar with the terrain and in suitable position for immediate resistance to local aggression. . . .

Our military strategy today calls for a necessary flexibility. We do not wish to allow ourselves to become frozen in our choices so that we are limited either to submission to aggression against a free-world neighbor or compelled to resort to forces of unlimited and uncontrollable destruction. The availability of trained and equipped forces of Allied nations at the points where aggression may come and prepared to defend their own homelands is increasingly important to this vital flexibility of response.

The appropriation requested for fiscal year 1963 is $1.5 billion. It is $385 million less than was asked for last year and $200 million less than was authorized for fiscal year 1963. It is intended to continue the program of providing only that equipment and training which is needed to fill the gap between what the aided country can do for itself and what must be done to enable it to protect itself from internal subversion and external aggression. It is important also to the maintenance of a climate of stability and confidence favorable to economic and social progress.

One other positive benefit will come from our expenditures for military aid. We are placing emphasis on civic action projects in underdeveloped countries. Wherever possible, country forces receiving military assistance are encouraged to participate in developing public works programs such as roadbuilding, sanitation and communications. American aid in this area is particularly productive because it not only advances the progress of the nation as a whole but also brings home to its people the fruits of United States friendship and concern for their general welfare.

*Development Lending.* Funds needed for development lending in the coming year were also authorized last year. Dollar repayable development loans now constitute the major instrument of our foreign economic assistance program. In the current year they will make possible commitments of approximately $1,100 million for fundamental development purposes. Already loans have been approved for major transportation facilities, local credit institutions, public utilities, a cement plant and capital goods for development in eighteen countries.

For fiscal year 1963 over half of the funds requested will be for development lending. The present authorization for fiscal year 1963 is $1,500 million. The President has requested an appropriation of $1,250 million. (Additional funds are asked for the Alliance for Progress, which I shall discuss in a moment.) These new loan funds will be concentrated in countries which have sound and well-administered long-term development programs or the capability to carry forward individual projects which will contribute to national growth.

Funds at least in the magnitude requested are needed and can be effectively used during the coming year.

*Alliance for Progress.* The only significant legislative change sought this year is the enactment of a new title VI providing for the Alliance for Progress and authorizing its long-term support by the United States. The Alliance is unique among our regional programs in that it is based upon a mutual declaration of principles and goals and a procedure for review of country programs by a regional panel. These concepts were agreed upon by the United States and the Latin American Republics at Bogotá and Punta del Este. In addition, the authority and funds for our aid in support of the Alliance derive in part from legislation separate from the basic Foreign Assistance Act. The Alliance criteria and authorization should now be consolidated within the AID program both to simplify administration and to reiterate our adherence to these exacting standards and high goals.

The Alliance also differs from our other programs because we are dealing not with new countries but with Republics almost as old as our own. The struggle for orderly change of the entire social and economic structures of Latin America faces stubborn resistance from entrenched privilege and vitriolic opposition from a radical left for whom change means only violent revolution. We cannot expect the necessary changes to occur under conditions of orderly growth and long-term reform unless there is reasonable assurance that the critical increment of United States financial support necessary to success will be forthcoming over the long pull. We therefore strongly urge that Congress record its long-term support by authorizing $3 billion for the next four years of the Alliance. Such authorization will bolster progressive forces and provide a sounder basis for the kind of long-range planning required if the objectives of the Alliance are to be realized. It will provide for the alliance the same period of assurance of United States support as is provided for aid to other areas.

*Authorization of Funds for FY 1963.* The total *appropriation* which the President is requesting for fiscal year 1963 is $4,878 million—slightly more than Congress appropriated last year for AID and the Alliance. The new *authority* which is requested from this committee for appropriations this year totals $2,125 million.

Within this total we are requesting an initial appropriation for the Alliance for Progress of $600 million in loan and grant funds for next year as part of the $3 billion long-term authorization extending through fiscal year 1966.

*Development Grants.* The legislation before you asks $335 million authorization for development grant activities in fiscal year 1963 in areas other than Latin America. These funds are among the most crucially needed in the entire bill. Advances in education and technical training, improvements in health conditions, the development of able public administrators, and the creation of effective governmental institutions are essential to progress in most of the developing nations.

*Supporting Assistance.* In our effort to concentrate economic aid on development we cannot overlook the fact that supporting assistance will still be needed for a number of countries—primarily those on the periphery of the Sino-Soviet bloc which are subjected to direct and massive Communist pressures and must of necessity maintain armed forces greater than their economies can support unaided. We are asking for the authorization of $481.5 million for this purpose—20 per cent less than was requested last year. Most of this will go to three Far Eastern countries which are particularly threatened.

As we reported to you last year, it is our purpose to supplant supporting aid with·development loans as soon as it becomes feasible for any particular country. It is important to recognize that we are proposing supporting assistance for next year for eighteen countries fewer than those receiving such assistance this year. Although this judgment may require modification in light of events, we hope that this trend will be continued. In some cases the need for supporting assistance may persist for a considerable period.

*International Organizations.* As in past years we are requesting funds for voluntary contributions to multilateral programs conducted under the United Nations: These include the Expanded Technical Assistance Program and the Special Fund,

UNICEF [United Nations Children's Fund], the Palestine Refugee Program, the U.N. Congo Economic Program and others. This category also includes our contribution to the Indus Basin Trust Fund administered by the World Bank and to other international programs. The sum requested for these purposes is $148.9 million.

*Investment Guaranties and Savings.* We are well aware that private investment can make a most valuable contribution to progress in the less developed countries. But the investor in such a country may face special risks which he will not undertake without some form of protection. The investment guaranty program authorized by the AID legislation has been an effective incentive to such investment. We anticipate that in the next year requests by American businessmen for guaranties will exceed the funds available. We therefore are asking for additional investment guaranty authorizations.

*Contingency Fund.* Each of these requests for funds represents our best estimate of the minimum necessary to maintain the momentum of our economic and military programs. But I would like particularly to emphasize the importance of the President's contingency fund. Recent events have given us no basis for supposing that our responsibilities can be significantly reduced. The only assured prediction we can make is that the unpredictable will occur. We must be ready to move quickly to anticipate or meet new situations. The unprogramed reserve against the unexpected is, therefore, one of the most important elements in the foreign assistance program. The $400 million requested is not too great a sum to have available for emergency needs.

CONCLUSION

Our five months' experience under the Foreign Assistance Act of 1961 has demonstrated that the legislative framework of our foreign aid program is sound. The task of transforming the social and economic structures of less developed countries around the world will involve their energies for years to come; our own effort, relatively modest though it be, will require persistence and an assurance of continuing interest. The stakes are the security of the free world today and the shape of the world of tomorrow.

# VII.   CUBA, THE WESTERN HEMISPHERE AND THE ALLIANCE FOR PROGRESS

*The Communist Offensive
in the Western Hemisphere*

*This conference was convoked by a resolution
of the Council of the Organization of American
States to "consider the threats to the peace and
to the political independence of the American
states that might arise from the intervention
of extra-continental powers directed toward
breaking American solidarity." This meant, in
Secretary Rusk's words on leaving Washington
for the conference, the fact that "Cuba, a mem-*

Address at the Eighth Meeting of Consultation of Ministers of
Foreign Affairs of the American Republics, Punta del Este, Uruguay,
January 25, 1962.

*ber government of the Organization of American States, has made itself an accomplice to the Communist conspiracy dedicated to the overthrow of the representative governments of the hemisphere."*

. . . . For the second time in six months the nations of the Americas meet here in pursuit of their common goal—social progress and economic growth within a community of free and independent nations. But this time we come to take measures to safeguard that freedom and independence so that in the future we may devote all our efforts to social progress and economic growth.

We are assembled again on the eastern shore of a vast continent. Across this continent millions of our people are struggling to throw off the bonds of hunger, poverty and ignorance—to affirm the hope of a better life for themselves and their children. Last August we joined in a historic document, the Charter of Punta del Este, setting forth the goals, the machinery and the commitments necessary to transform that hope into reality. Last August we joined hands in a great alliance—the *Alianza para el Progreso.*

Since that time in every part of the hemisphere we have moved forward with fresh energy in fulfillment of the pledges we solemnly undertook to the people of the Americas. The task ahead is vast. Everyone in this hall knows the mighty effort which will be required to break the ancient cycle of stagnation and despair. But the need for action is urgent. Across the world the winds of change are blowing; awakening peoples are demanding to be admitted to the promise of the twentieth century. For Americans, north and south, this is a historical challenge. As the nineteenth century saw the Western Hemisphere enter the epoch of political independence, so the twentieth century— if those of us in this room, and the governments we represent, have boldness and faith—will see this hemisphere enter the epoch of economic abundance.

TASK OF DEVELOPMENT MEASURED IN YEARS

The means by which we seek our ends are the intelligence, decision and will of the governments and people of the hemisphere. We cannot hope to make progress unless the governments of our nations faithfully meet the needs of their peoples for education and opportunity, unless we press steadily forward with the measures of self-help and social reform which make development possible and spread its benefits among all the people. This work has already begun. Let me say that it is unfinished business in the United States itself. Many Latin American nations are engaged in national plans and programs, internal reforms and action to build houses, schools and factories, roads and dams. My own country has already made large commitments for this fiscal year and will have no difficulty in meeting the more than $1 billion pledged to the first year of the Alliance for Progress. We have together established international machinery to stimulate and review national plans.

This is a notable beginning. There is, of course, much more to be done. Our task is to be measured, not in the months of this year, but in the years of this decade. I wish there were some way in which we could transmit to you the depth of our affectionate interest in the economic and social prospects of this hemisphere. Perhaps you would forgive me for a personal recollection. Like millions of present-day North Americans, I spent my earliest years in what people would now call underdeveloped circumstances. We were prescientific and pretechnical; we were without public health or medical care; typhoid, pellagra, hookworm and malaria were a part of the environment in which providence had placed us. Our schools were primitive. Our fathers and mothers earned a meager living with backbreaking toil.

But the great adventure through which many of us have lived has seen the transformation of our lives in a short period— a transformation brought about by the magical combination of education, health and increasing productivity. On our farms we felt the impact of the indispensable partnership among education, scientific research and the extension of knowledge to those who could put it to practical use. Neighbor helped neighbor to build a house, a barn or to pass along news about new prospects and new methods. They joined together to build roads until public funds could take over the burden. They pooled their limited resources to hire a schoolteacher or a doctor. Bits of capital began to accumulate, and this was reinvested in growth and development. More and more young people managed to get to the university, and more and more of these brought their learning back to the benefit of their own people.

These changes did not take place without struggle. Years of thought and work and debate were required to prepare America for the necessary steps of self-help and social reform. I remember well the bitter resistance before Franklin Roosevelt was able to win support for the Tennessee Valley Authority, that immense network of dams and power stations and fertilizer factories and agricultural extension offices which has wrought such miraculous changes in our South. But a succession of progressive leaders, determined to bring about social change within a framework of political consent, carried through an "alliance for progress" within the United States.

Other parts of the hemisphere have experienced similar improvements. What has been done for some must now be done for all. It shall be our common purpose to labor without cease to advance the cause of economic progress and social justice within the hemisphere—to advance the autonomous and peaceful revolution of the Americas.

CHOOSING THE ROAD INTO THE FUTURE

There are those in every land who resist change—who see the society they know as the climax of history, who identify their own status and privilege with the welfare of their people, and who oppose the vital land and tax reforms necessary for the completion of our work. But their resistance is doomed to failure. The nineteenth century is over; and, in the twentieth, people across the earth are awakening from centuries of poverty and oppression to claim the right to live in the modern world. "The veil has been torn asunder," wrote Bolívar. "We have seen the light; and we will not be thrust back into the darkness." No one can hope to prolong the past in a revolutionary age. The only question is which road we mean to take into the future.

This is not a question alone for this hemisphere. It is a question faced everywhere in the world. On the one hand are those who believe in change through persuasion and consent— through means which respect the individual. On the other are those who advocate change through the subjugation of the individual and who see in the turbulence of change the opportunity for power.

I do not believe that I have to argue the moral superiority of free society anywhere in the Americas. I do not think, other things being equal, that any rational person would prefer tyranny to tolerance or dictatorship to democracy. But there are some who doubt the capacity of freedom to do the job, and turn in resentment and desperation to totalitarian solutions. They are wrong. History shows that freedom is the most reliable means to economic development and social justice and that communism betrays in performance the ends which it proclaims in propaganda. The humane and pragmatic methods of free men are not merely the right way, morally, to develop an underdeveloped country; they are technically the efficient way.

### FAILURE OF COMMUNISM TO MEET NEEDS OF PEOPLE

We meet here at Punta del Este to consider the tragedy of Cuba. There have been many elements in that tragedy. One was the failure of the dictatorship which preceded Castro to concern itself with the elementary needs of a people who had a right to be free. Another was the disillusionment of the hopes which rode with Castro at the beginning of his resistance movement. And now we see the Cuban people subjected to a regime which has committed itself to Marxist-Leninist doctrines at the very time when this answer to economic and social problems has proved itself to be brutal, reactionary and sterile.

If there is one lesson which we in the Americas can learn from observing what is happening from East Germany to North

Viet-Nam, it is that Castroism is not the answer to economic and social development. If there is tension in Berlin today, it is because of the failure of the regime in East Germany and the flight of tens of thousands of its people toward freedom and expanding opportunity. It is worth noting that vast areas of the world with remarkable natural resources have failed to provide even the elementary needs of food, contrasted with the surpluses which abound throughout much of the free world. The needs of the individual have been ruthlessly subjected to the requirements of the power-hungry apparatus of the state. What we know in the free world as the consumer is brushed aside, and men are called upon to submit themselves to the requirements of ambition and appetite.

Wherever communism goes, hunger follows. Communist China today is in the grip of a vast and terrible famine, which, in turn, has led to stagnation and decline of industry. There is hunger in North Viet-Nam. Whatever contribution communism has appeared to make to industrial development comes only because it does what Marx charged nineteenth-century capitalism with doing, that is, it grinds down the faces of the poor and forces from their postponed consumption the capital necessary for arms and industry. Communism—once in power—has turned out to be the most effective and brutal means known to history for exploiting the working class.

Recognizing its failure in the underdeveloped world, recognizing that its greatest enemy is the process of peaceful and democratic development, communism in recent years has concentrated—in Asia, in Africa, in the Middle East, now in our own hemisphere—on using the troubles of transition to install Communist minorities in permanent power. The techniques by which communism seeks to subvert the development process are neither mysterious nor magical. Khrushchev, Mao Tse-tung and "Che" Guevara have outlined them in frankness and detail. They seek first to lay the political basis for the seizure of power by winning converts in sections of the populations whose hopes and ambitions are thwarted by the existing order. They then try to capture control of broadly based popular movements aimed ostensibly at redressing social and economic injustice. In some cases they resort to guerrilla warfare as a means of intimidating opposition and disrupting orderly social progress. At every point the Communists are prepared to invoke all the resources of propaganda and subversion, of manipulation and violence, to maximize confusion, destroy faith in the democratic instrumentalities of change, and open up the way for a Communist takeover.

As for its claim to social justice, Chairman Khrushchev himself has given the most eloquent testimony of the inevitability of monstrous injustice in a system of totalitarian dictatorship. The crimes of Stalin—crimes fully acknowledged by his successor—are the inescapable result of a political order founded on the supposed infallibility of a single creed, a single party and a single leader. Under the banner of the classless society, communism has become the means of establishing what the Yugoslav Communist Milovan Djilas has termed the "new class"—an elite as ruthless in its determination to maintain its prerogatives as any oligarchy known to history.

Nothing shows more clearly the failure of communism to bring about economic development and social justice than the present condition of Europe. The bankruptcy of communism is etched in the contrast between the thriving economies of Western Europe and the drab stagnation of Eastern Europe—and it is symbolized in the wall of Berlin, erected to stop the mass flight of ordinary people from communism to freedom.

The proponents of free society need have no apologies. We have moved far beyond the rigid laissez-faire capitalism of the nineteenth century. The open society of the mid-twentieth century can offer the reality of what the Communists promise but do not and cannot produce, because the means they are using, the techniques of hatred and violence, can never produce anything but more violence and more hatred. Communism is not the wave of the future. Communists are only the exploiters of people's aspirations—and their despair. They are the scavengers of the transition from stagnation into the modern world. The wave of the future is the peaceful, democratic revolution symbolized for the Americas in the Alliance for Progress—the revolution which will bring change without chaos, development without dictatorship, and hope without hatred.

This is our faith. Because we have pledged ourselves to this road into the future, we have no more urgent obligation than to guarantee and protect the independence of the democratic revolution. Because communism has its own ambitions, communism everywhere directs its most intense effort to making democratic change impossible. It is in this setting that I ask you to consider the question of the purposes and methods of communism in our hemisphere.

CUBA'S DEFECTION FROM INTER-AMERICAN SYSTEM

If the one striking development of the last years in our hemisphere has been the rise of the Alliance for Progress, the other striking development has been the defection of Cuba from the inter-American system.

Let us be clear about the character of the problem presented by Castro and his government. We have no quarrel with the people of Cuba. As this week we have welcomed a free Dominican Republic back into the inter-American community, so we look forward to the day when a free and progressive government will flourish in Habana and the Cuban people can join with us in the common undertakings of the hemisphere.

Many of us in this hemisphere had no quarrel with the avowed purposes of the revolution of 1959. Many rejoiced in the aspirations of the Cuban people for political liberty and social progress. Nor would we have any quarrel with changes in the economic organization of Cuba instituted with the consent of the Cuban people. Our hemisphere has room for a diversity of economic systems. But we do condemn the internal excesses of the Castro regime—the violations of civil justice, the drumhead executions, the suppression of political, intellectual and religious freedom. But even these things, repellent as they are, have been known to our continent. If kept within the confines of one unhappy country, they would not constitute a direct threat to the peace and the independence of other American states. What we cannot accept—and will never accept—is the use of Cuba as the means through which extracontinental powers seek to break up the inter-American system, to overthrow the governments of other countries, and to destroy the autonomous democratic evolution of the hemisphere.

The Castro regime has extended the global battle to Latin America. It has supplied communism with a bridgehead in the Americas, and it has thereby brought the entire hemisphere into the frontline of the struggle between communism and democracy. It has turned itself into an arsenal for arms and ammunition from the Communist world. With Communist help Dr. Castro has built up the largest military establishment in Latin America.

Within the United Nations the Cuban delegation has abandoned its brethren of the hemisphere to play the smirking sycophant for the Communist bloc. Out of the thirty-seven rollcall votes taken on the most important issues in the last session of the General Assembly, a majority of the members of the Organization of American States voted together thirty-five times. But, of these thirty-seven votes, Cuba voted thirty-three times with the Soviet bloc and only five times with the OAS majority. Cuba opposed the resolution appealing to the Soviet Union not to explode the 50-megaton bomb; it was the only delegation in the United Nations, besides the ten avowed members of the Soviet bloc, to do so. In the same manner Cuba alone joined the Communist bloc to oppose the resolution calling for a nuclear test ban treaty with international controls. On several occasions Cuban representatives followed other members of the Communist bloc in walking out of the General Assembly when delegates of states not approved by the Soviet Union dared take the floor.

PREVIOUS OAS ACTIONS AGAINST COMMUNISM

At the seventh meeting of foreign ministers at San José in August 1960, our governments together rejected any attempt on the part of the Communist powers to exploit the political, economic or social troubles of any American state. Since San José the Cuban government has aligned itself more flagrantly than ever with those dedicated to the overthrow of the inter-American system and the destruction of inter-American freedom. The Soviet-Cuban communique of September 20, 1961, and the Chinese-Cuban communique of October 2, 1961, both signed by President [Osvaldo] Dorticós, proclaim an identity of views on foreign policy between the Cuban and the Soviet and Chinese Communist regimes. Only a few weeks ago Dr. [Raúl] Roa, the Cuban Minister of Foreign Affairs, made clear once again that the primary allegiance of the Castro government is not to its brethren in the Americas but to its comrades beyond the Iron Curtain. "The socialist camp, led by the invincible Soviet Union, is with the Cuban revolution," Dr. Roa said. "We are neither alone nor helpless. The world is with the Cuban revolution, and the future belongs entirely to the universal socialist society that is coming, and of which, forever, Cuba already forms part."

When Dr. Castro himself said on December 2, "I am a Marxist-Leninist and I shall be a Marxist-Leninist until the last day of my life," he could have surprised only those who have paid no attention to the evolution of the Castro regime. This public oath of fealty to Marxism-Leninism underlines Dr. Castro's commitment to the Leninist use of deception and violence, to the Leninist contempt for free institutions, and to the Leninist injunction that obedience to the international Communist movement is the highest duty.

Driven by this Marxist-Leninist faith, the Castro regime has dedicated itself, not to the struggle for democracy within the hemisphere or even within Cuba, but to the perversion and corruption of this struggle in the interests of world communism. Part III of the report of the Inter-American Peace Committee sets forth the ties of the government of Cuba with the Sino-Soviet bloc, its subversive activities within the hemisphere, its violations of human rights, and the incompatibility of its behavior with the Charter of the Organization of American States.

Fourteen years ago at Bogotá the Ninth International Conference of American States in its Resolution XXXII on "The Preservation and Defense of Democracy in America" declared that "by its anti-democratic nature and its interventionist tendency, the political activity of international communism or any other totalitarian doctrine is incompatible with the concept of American freedom." This resolution condemned "interference by any foreign power, or by any political organization serving the interests of a foreign power, in the public life of the nations of the American continent." The American Republics solemnly resolved "to adopt, within their respective territories and in accordance with their respective constitutional provisions, the measures necessary to eradicate and prevent activities directed, assisted or instigated by foreign governments, organizations or individuals tending to overthrow their institutions by violence, to foment disorder in their domestic political life, or to disturb, by means of pressure, subversive propaganda, threats or by any other means, the free and sovereign right of their peoples to govern themselves in accordance with their democratic aspirations."

Three years ago at Santiago the foreign ministers of the American Republics reaffirmed the Bogotá resolution in the Declaration of Santiago, condemning "the methods of every system tending to suppress political and civil rights and liberties, and in particular the action of international communism or any other totalitarian doctrine."

No one can doubt, on the basis of hard evidence compiled by committees of the OAS and known to every observer in our hemisphere, that the Castro regime has placed itself in a position of systematic and contemptuous hostility to these principles of our inter-American system. Beyond the evidence every delegate in this hall knows in his mind and heart that those behind Castro hope to overthrow his government and every other government in Latin America. The Castro regime, by repudiating the principles and philosophy of the inter-American system and making itself the American agent of world communism, has created a clear and present danger to the prospects of free and democratic change in every country in Latin America. The time has come for the American Republics to unite against Communist intervention in this hemisphere. We believe in the inter-American system. We stand on the principles of the Charter of the Organization of American States. We are faithful to the ancient hope of a hemisphere of free democracies, bound together in independence and common purpose. Else we would reject that hope, forsake our faith itself, exposed in its isolation to every gust of political or ideological fanaticism.

The Alliance for Progress is the best way of attacking the longrun sources of the Communist appeal—poverty, hunger and ignorance. But the Alliance cannot by itself provide a means of warding off the shortrun Communist tactics of disruption and subversion. Vitamin tablets will not save a man set upon by hoodlums in an alley. If the Alliance is to succeed, we need to protect the democratic processes of change; we need a shield behind which constructive measures can take effect in steady and secure progression. We have seen the effect of Communist disruptive tactics in other lands and other continents. Let us take action now to guard our own continent and our programs of democratic reform against those who seek to replace democracy by dictatorship, those who would transform our fellowship of free states into a bondage of satellites.

I am confident that this meeting of foreign ministers will hearten the democratic forces of this continent by making it clear that we will not stand still while the enemies of democracy conspire to make democratic change impossible. Against Dr. Castro's Communist allies let us reaffirm our faith in our own good neighbors; let us commit our minds and our hearts to the success of our free Alliance for Progress.

FOUR MAJOR ACTIONS TO TAKE AGAINST CASTRO

What is our working task here at this meeting? I suggest we must move in four major directions:

First, we must recognize that the alignment of the government of Cuba with the countries of the Sino-Soviet bloc, and its commitment to extend Communist power in this hemisphere, are incompatible with the purposes and principles of the inter-American system and that its current activities are an ever present and common danger to the peace and security of the continent.

Second, we must now make the policy decision to exclude the Castro regime from participation in the organs and bodies of the inter-American system and to direct the Council of the Organization to determine how best to give rapid implementation to this decision. Within our own competence, since the Inter-American Defense Board was created by a meeting of consultation, we can and should now exclude the government of Cuba from membership in the Inter-American Defense Board. This step would correct at once the most obvious incongruity arising from the participation of a regime aligned with the Sino-Soviet bloc in a body planning the defense of the hemisphere against the aggressive designs of international communism.

Third, we must interrupt the limited but significant flow of trade between Cuba and the rest of the hemisphere, especially the traffic in arms.

Fourth, we must set in motion a series of individual and communal acts of defense against the various forms of political and indirect aggression mounted against the hemisphere. The acts of political aggression which the Castro regime is committing have an immediate and direct impact in the general Caribbean area near the focus of infection. Yet with one exception there is not a foreign minister present whose country has not felt the impact of the interventionist activities which constitute essential elements of the international Communist design. We must find adequate means to strengthen our capacity to anticipate and overcome this constant gnawing at the security of our peoples. In particular we should direct the Inter-American Defense Board to establish a special security committee to recommend individual and collective measures to the governments of the American states for their greater protection against any acts or threats of aggression, direct or indirect, resulting from the continued intervention of Sino-Soviet powers or others associated with them.

## A FEW BASIC FACTS TO CONSIDER

As we confront these decisions let us face, as old friends and neighbors, a few basic facts in our situation. The weight of Communist aggressive techniques is felt unequally among us; the nature of the Communist threat is understood in different ways among our peoples; and the OAS itself is confronted, as a body, with a form of aggressive action relatively new in its history.

We have heard references to the intrusion of the cold war into this hemisphere. There may be some who wonder whether the Americas are being caught up, as innocent bystanders, in a struggle among the giants.

But let us think clearly about what the cold war is and what it is not. The Communist world has dedicated itself to the indefinite expansion of what it calls its historically inevitable world revolution. The cold war is simply the effort of communism to extend its power beyond the confines of the Communist bloc and the effort of free men to defend themselves against this systematic aggression. The cold war would have been unknown to us had the Soviet Union determined, at the end of World War II, to live in peace with other nations in accordance with its commitments under the Charter of the United Nations. The cold war would end tomorrow if those who control the Communist movement would cease their aggressive acts, in all the many forms. Nothing would be more gratifying to the citizens of my country than to have the Soviet Union bring about the revolution of peace by a simple decision to leave the rest of the world alone.

But the cold war is not a contest between the Soviet Union and the United States which the United States is pursuing for national ends. It is a struggle in the long story of freedom between those who would destroy it and those who are determined to preserve it. If every nation were genuinely independent, and left alone to work out its relations with its neighbors by common agreement, the tensions between Washington and Moscow would vanish overnight.

Speaking last October before the Twenty-second Communist Party Congress, Mr. Khrushchev said: "We firmly believe that the time will come when the children and grandchildren of those who do not understand and do not accept communism will live under communism."

This is his belief. Were it only his belief we need not care;

but it is also the program of action of the Communist powers—
and about that we care a very great deal.

We know that the Communist effort to impose their system
on other nations and peoples will fail and that the next generation will dwell in a community of independent nations, each
freely pursuing the welfare of its people. We know this is so because history confirms that freedom must win because it is rooted
in the nature of man and in his relations with God.

Our problem today is to combine a sense of the necessities
of the harsh realities with the dreams upon which civilized man
has steadily built. A shining future is waiting for us in this hemisphere—a future in which every child will have a decent chance
for life, for education, for medical care, for constructive labor
and creative contribution; in which every Republic on this continent will cooperate to improve lagging standards, to elevate
culture and to raise man to his full dignity in freedom.

We have the talents, the resources and the aspirations. We
need not retreat into the murky shadows of a conspiratorial society developed on the steppes of central Asia, because we can
move ahead in the great tradition of a civilization which was
born in the free discourse of the early Mediterranean world
more than 2000 years ago, was nourished in Western Europe,
and came to this hemisphere to be extended by Bolívar and San
Martín, by Martí, Jefferson, and Lincoln.

Our task today is not to let a petty tyrant who has appeared
among us divert us from these great tasks but to put him in his
place while we proceed with the great adventure upon which we
are embarked together.

*Closing Statement at Punta del Este
Conference, January 31, 1962*

*This followed the adoption of resolutions ex-
cluding the government of Cuba from participation in the inter-American system.*

. . . . We have been discussing the Communist offensive in
this hemisphere, an offensive which is a worldwide offensive, an
offensive which is engaging American forces in some fashion in
every continent, an offensive aimed at us all—at our traditions,
our institutions, our governments and our respective ways of
life.

We have agreed here on a very great deal; and there is no
doubt in my mind that this organization and the nations which
make it up have come a long way in defining both the creative
and the defensive tasks which we must undertake if our societies,
challenged by this offensive, are to continue to develop in harmony with their past.

We have had some difficulty on only one point: how to
give effect to the simple fact which we all recognize, namely that
the official character and policies of the present government of
Cuba are incompatible with the presence and participation of
that government in the principal business of the Organization
of American States.

When we return to our foreign offices, we shall return to a
troubled world, a turbulent world, to such matters as Berlin and
Laos, Viet-Nam, the Congo and the many other points where
the struggle to maintain the principles of independence and
human freedom goes forward. There is one lesson that derives
from our experience with these problems and in dealing with
the Communist offensive over the past seventeen years. Communism works unceasingly to exploit every difference of view, every
difference on national perspective within the free world. The

friends of freedom must stand together. For wherever freedom is threatened, every man is threatened. But this does not mean that we must be unanimous on all points. This is not a meeting of the Warsaw Pact. This is a meeting of the organization of free and independent American states.

I would wish to say just a word about Cuba. I had intended to say more, but the representative of that government has demonstrated today the principle of self-exclusion. We have listened here as I have listened in many forums over many years to the mixture of threats and half-truths and untruths, to corrupt statistics and corrupt definitions of democracy and legality, which are the hallmark of Communist public oratory. The representative of the Cuban government has told us that we shall see a system of police states spread throughout this continent. The figure on the knee of the ventriloquist, of course, says what the ventriloquist says. In party congresses, in public declarations, the leaders of this world conspiratorial movement have made it eminently clear that they do mean to do what they can to bring about their world revolution.

That effort must fail. It shall surely fail, because the strength to guard against it is in the hearts of men throughout the world, because we have a different vision of the future. We see a hemisphere which will remain true to its historical commitment, to human rights and to democracy, as we understand it and as men have been talking about these concepts for more than 2000 years—a hemisphere in which each nation develops its own version of a productive, modern society, consistent with its culture and its traditions and its aspirations, and cooperating freely with its friends across international borders. And we see, as others have seen at this meeting, a Cuba released from its nightmare and returned to the family of American states.

I can assure my colleagues that, in the policies of President Kennedy and of the American people, behind this vision of the future lies the strength, the resources, and the faith of the people of my country.

## Report to the Nation on the Punta del Este Conference

I have reported to President Kennedy on the recent meeting of inter-American foreign ministers in Punta del Este, and he has asked me to share this report with you.

We met there with the other American Republics to decide what we should do together to meet the mounting Communist offensive in our hemisphere. This offensive is worldwide, but there is no part of it which concerns us more intimately or more seriously than the systematic subversive attack under way in the Americas, spearheaded by the present regime in Cuba.

It is for that reason that I should like to talk to you this evening about this conference and its results. First, a word of background. In August 1960, seventeen months ago, there was a meeting of foreign ministers which discussed the Cuban problem in San José, Costa Rica. At that time the foreign ministers agreed to condemn outside intervention in the affairs of this hemisphere, and they reaffirmed in broad terms their faith in democracy and their rejection of totalitarianism. But they were not then prepared to take concrete steps aimed at the Communist offensive in general and Cuba in particular. In fact Cuba was not even named in the declaration, and some delegations said that it should not be interpreted as applying specifically to Cuba.

### COMMUNIST NATURE OF CASTRO REGIME

But during these past seventeen months there has been a far-reaching change in the attitudes of both governments and peoples.

The Communist nature of the Castro regime has become more apparent to all—and so have its aggressive designs.

The Castro regime voted consistently with the Communist bloc at the United Nations. It built up its military strength with

Delivered over radio and television, February 2, 1962.

the help of Communist arms. It used its embassies in Latin America as centers of espionage and subversion. Thirteen American governments broke off all diplomatic relations with Cuba. It sought to intimidate, subvert and harass free governments and nations, as reported to our meeting by the Inter-American Peace Committee of the OAS [Organization of American States]. And Castro himself, in early December, publicly confessed what everyone had come to know: that he is a Marxist-Leninist and would be until he dies.

At the same time it became apparent throughout the Americas that Castroism was *not* the answer to their hopes for economic and social progress. They saw many Cubans who had originally joined with Castro in the honest belief that they were striking a blow for democracy and for economic and social reform become disillusioned with his dictatorship and his subservience to a foreign power. And, perhaps most important of all, they saw new hope and real action in President Kennedy's Alliance for Progress, a peaceful, constructive, and cooperative effort by free men to achieve rapid economic and social progress through free institutions.

## ACCOMPLISHMENTS OF MEETING

We met at Punta del Este against the background of these changes. What was accomplished?

First, in a strong resolution that named names and minced no words, we declared unanimously—except for Cuba, of course —that the Castro-Communist offensive in this hemisphere is a clear and present danger to the unity and freedom of the American Republics. Even as we met, reports came in from several countries of efforts by small Communist-led minorities to disrupt constitutional government and the will of the majority.

Second, the ministers agreed, again unanimously, that the hemisphere is bound together by two powerful ties: by its commitment to human rights, social justice and political democracy and by its commitment to exclude from this hemisphere the intervention of outside powers. On these grounds we concluded, again unanimously, "That the present Government of Cuba, which has officially identified itself as a Marxist-Leninist government, is incompatible with the principles and objectives of the inter-American system."

Third, on the basis of this unanimous conclusion, a two-thirds majority decided "That this incompatibility excludes the present Government of Cuba from participation in the inter-American system." Seventeen had declared that "the present government of Cuba has voluntarily placed itself outside the inter-American system." Included in this majority were those who felt themselves to be, and are, under special attack by Castro communism.

Fourth, recognizing that the threat of Cuba is an active threat to the security of the hemisphere and not merely a matter of ideological incompatibility, the foreign ministers, once again unanimously, officially ejected the Cuban regime from the Inter-American Defense Board, where their representatives had already been excluded from confidential discussions. In addition we established special machinery within the OAS to recommend joint action that can block Communist subversive activities before they reach the level of insurrection or guerrilla war.

Fifth, this meeting decided, again unanimously, to prohibit trade and traffic in arms between Cuba and the other American countries. No American government is now selling arms to Cuba, but we are determined to do everything necessary to stop illicit trade or traffic to or from Cuba within this hemisphere.

Sixth, the Council of the Organization of American States was asked to explore further trade restrictions, applying to Cuba the same kind of machinery that was applied last year to the Dominican Republic, and giving special attention to items of strategic importance.

Seventh, and finally, the foreign ministers unanimously recognized that the struggle against communism in this hemisphere is not merely a question of a defense against subversion but of positive measures as well—economic, social and political reforms and development, to meet the legitimate aspirations of our peoples. In this spirit the governments committed themselves anew to the great constructive tasks of the Alliance for Progress.

SIGNS OF STRENGTH OF OAS

The rollcall of votes on these resolutions provided a dramatic demonstration of two important points.

First, that Cuba stands alone in the Americas. No other nation voted with its delegates in opposition to any of these resolutions. We listened to their longplaying records of invective and abuse and then got on with our business. They made no progress with their threats and pleas, they could find no comfort in any differences among the rest of us, and finally they withdrew altogether.

The other point is that honest debate was a sign of strength in the Organization. Unless we know that the votes which are cast represent the convictions of the governments, the votes themselves would fail to carry conviction. The fact that differences were registered is an insurance that the unanimity, when expressed, was genuine.

There was no disagreement over the incompatibility of the Cuban regime and the inter-American system. But some governments sincerely felt that additional legal and technical steps were necessary before the exclusion of Cuba from participation in the official agencies of the system could be finally settled. While they abstained on that vote, however, all joined in the condemnation of communism and the present Cuban regime.

Those who spoke for our own Government were united in their efforts and their satisfaction at the result. President Kennedy's leadership and the respect in which our neighbors hold him were evident throughout the conference.

We were fortunate in having as advisers to our delegation the chairmen and ranking minority members of the Senate and House subcommittees on inter-American affairs: Senator Morse, Senator Hickenlooper, Congressman Selden and Congressman Merrow. They were of great help. We worked on a nonpartisan basis, with full cooperation between the executive and legislative branches. And every American can draw satisfaction from the results of the conference.

But there was an even larger result. An international organization such as the Organization of American States, the OAS, can maintain its vitality only if it faces up to the issues—no matter how difficult—which the moving course of history places on its agenda. Because the problems posed by Cuba and the Communist offensive in this hemisphere affected each government somewhat differently, there has been some uncertainty about whether the OAS was capable of taking hold of this crucial issue on a collective basis. I believe that uncertainty has now ended.

The OAS demonstrated that it is a living political body capable of reconciling different points of view in order to move ahead together. It has proved itself capable of boldly facing a problem of utmost gravity and taking constructive steps toward a solution. It has proved itself capable of sustaining a lively debate on a matter of law and procedure without losing its poise or its underlying unity. Above all, it has demonstrated how democratic nations, bound together by commitments of principle and geographic association, can conduct serious business as friendly and dignified partners.

No conference could, by itself, eliminate the problem of communism in this hemisphere. But the results of this conference were deeply reassuring. The hemisphere has taken a long stride forward.

### NO QUARREL WITH CUBAN PEOPLE

I might conclude with a point on which there was, again, unanimity. An empty seat at the OAS table is no cause for joy. The rest of us have no quarrel with the Cuban people—only with the regime which has fastened itself upon that country. Our Latin American friends are bound to the Cuban people by powerful ties of culture and tradition. We ourselves expelled colonialism from Cuba and provided for its independence. And that is why all delegations joined in a common hope that we shall be able to welcome a free government of Cuba back into the family of the hemisphere.

We talked at Punta del Este about defending the hemisphere against the Communist threat, because that was the subject of our meeting. But defense is only a part of the job. Our main business is the great creative task of building in these continents vibrant societies, firmly rooted in the loyalty and pride of their peoples, societies which are secure from attack primarily because their own people would not have it otherwise.

## The Alliance for Progress in the Context of World Affairs

The Alliance for Progress represents the most important common venture in the long history of our hemisphere. On its success depends the individual welfare of hundreds of millions of our people, the independence and freedom of many of our nations and the continued flourishing of that civilization which our ancestors built in the wilderness and which their successors have struggled to bring to full flower. . . .

For us, the Alliance is a special part of an indivisible whole. For it rests on those indissoluble ties of geography and history, of common culture and common interest, which have always bound our nations together. It rests on the realization that this hemisphere is part of that Western civilization which we are struggling to protect and that many of the highest values of that civilization have found their richest expression in the life of the nations to our south. It rests on the special responsibilities of the United States in this hemisphere—responsibilities which exist independently of the cold war, or a Soviet military threat or the demands of nations newly freed from colonial rule. It is an alliance which my country has joined because of our realization that the destiny of the United States is irrevocably joined to the destiny of our sister Republics of the New World. . . .

Portions of address at the School of Advanced International Studies of Johns Hopkins University, Washington, D. C., April 25, 1962.

SHATTERING THE "WALL OF GLASS"

The drive toward economic development is essentially a product of the Western technological revolution. It was this revolution that has provided man with the capacity to emerge from centuries of poverty and hunger and ignorance. And it was also this revolution that awakened man's realization that such capacity was within his grasp.

Suddenly, in the years following World War II, it became apparent that the vast unbridgeable gulf between the rich and poor nations had become a wall of glass. On one side of that wall were the capital, the scientific advances, the technological skills of the industrialized nations, and on the other the poverty and hunger and the fierce desire for a better life of the great masses of the underdeveloped continents. The shattering of that wall, the application of the tools and wealth of the industrialized nations to the needs of the poorer nations, became, and still remains, the central issue of our time. We have confronted this problem with the new tools of economic aid, national planning and social reform. Yet it is clear that the successful completion of this task will require new breakthroughs of thought and action —the devising of new tools and techniques for the creation of capital and credit, for trade and the spread of technology. We will have to look afresh at all the institutions and procedures we have developed to speed up growth within each country of wealth and productive capacity. For only new efforts of imagination and intellect will enable us to shatter the glass wall and liberate the undoubted capacity of our society to bring, and bring rapidly, a better life to man.

. . . Although the Alliance springs from the special relationships between the American nations, it embodies basic principles of development which are of broader application. It is a product of the experience both of Latin America and of the United States since World War II—a period during which the United States has devoted greater resources to the assistance of others than any other nation in the history of the world. These resources have helped to sustain economies in many parts of the world, have met emergency human needs and assisted nations to launch

programs of development. Yet we must also admit that some of
this money has been ineffective. Some of it has disappeared, van-
ished without a trace of permanent effect on the lives of the people it was meant to help. It was this experience that has taught
us that solid development is not possible without at least three
basic conditions.

### MOBILIZING NATIONAL RESOURCES AND ENERGIES

First, no nation can develop unless it possesses its own inner
determination to progress. This means the mobilization of national resources and energies, the use of national institutions
and, above all, an intangible dedication of national spirit and
will—a singlemindedness of purpose and an unrelenting determination which is essential to all great human achievements and
without which development is not possible. If this condition is
present, then external resources can give a vital if marginal boost.
If it is not present, then no amount of external help will leave a
permanent trace on the life of the nation.

No free nation will demand of its people the sacrifices which
the Communist nations demand—the loss of liberty and the
rigorous regimentation of daily life. Such sacrifices destroy the
goal of freedom for man; they are unnecessary even in economic
terms and do not yield progress. But neither can we make the assumption that economic development is painless, that it can be
achieved without arduous labors and sacrifice; it may require increased taxes or the yielding up of large estates, curbs on consumption or the barring of luxury imports. But such sacrifices
are mild indeed compared to the Communist alternatives, and
they will ultimately yield greater abundance for all.

This first condition, under the name of self-help, is an essential component of the Alliance for Progress and of economic development everywhere.

### EXAMPLES OF SELF-HELP

With this in mind it is heartening to see the many examples
of effort and will which the nations of this hemisphere have

made in an effort to improve the welfare of their people. These examples are not only significant in themselves, but they indicate the strength of spirit which characterizes this hemisphere and which holds such high promise for the far greater effort ahead. Let me cite a few of these examples of self-help and cooperation among our American Republics—examples which antedate the Alliance for Progress.

Local Colombian initiative led to the formation of the Colombian Technical Institute aimed at developing badly needed technical and scientific skills for all Latin America.

The Mexican Ministry of Agriculture has developed one of the finest institutes of agricultural research in the world. Agronomists from all over Latin America and twelve from the Near and Middle East are there learning skills to improve the agricultural production of their countries.

The University of Chile has one of the finest programs of advanced economic training in this hemisphere. Of the fifty-seven students enrolled in the graduate school of economics, forty-five are from outside Chile, and the faculty is rapidly becoming a leading source for highly trained economists throughout Latin America.

Peruvian private initiative has built up the fishmeal industry from its inception in 1950 to the point where Peru is now the world's largest exporter of fishmeal and stands third only to Communist China and Japan in terms of total production of fish products.

Bolivia has doubled its number of school buildings in the past decade, largely through the efforts of local communities.

Under the Venezuelan land-reform program, which began in March 1960, four million acres have already been distributed to 44,000 families.

In Argentina the Nobel Prize winner, Dr. Bernardo Houssay, after resigning from the University of Buenos Aires in a protest against Peronism, built one of the hemisphere's finest institutes of biology and experimental medicine, relying principally on local subscriptions.

Costa Rica, a country with a population of only 1.2 million, has implemented one of the hemisphere's most successful programs of education; as of now 240,000 students are enrolled in schools of all types.

Mexico has achieved an increase of 223 per cent in its agricultural production in the last twenty years. Once a large importer of corn and wheat, Mexico has in the last six years become self-sufficient in both crops. And the nation as a whole has become virtually self-sustaining in the agricultural field.

The Mexican record in the field of public health has been impressive. The antimalarial campaign which began in 1957, when 25,000 Mexicans were dying each year from malaria, was so effective that in 1960 not a single Mexican died from malaria.

These and thousands of other examples serve to illustrate the range and effectiveness which is possible to private and public initiative within a free society. It is, in fact, one of the principal advantages of a free society that it liberates the energy and initiative of thousands of individuals and groups in the service of human welfare.

### MEETING DEMAND FOR SOCIAL JUSTICE

Second, no real economic development, consistent with the goals we have set ourselves, is possible without a social structure which permits the great mass of people to share in the benefits of progress and which affords each man the fair expectation of social justice. This often means basic, even revolutionary, changes in the structure of society. Outmoded systems of land tenure which allow a few to hold great estates while most agricultural workers are landless must be swept away. Tax systems which exempt the wealthy from their just share of the burden of development must be revised. And all the institutions of society must be carefully scanned to insure that they are not instruments for maintaining the privileges of a fortunate few.

Some of these changes are necessary for rational development. But many of them do not find their justification in the calculations of economists or the formulations of planners. They are vital because no government and no nation can carry forward the process of development without the support and help of its people. And people will only give their assistance when they are convinced that the government is serving their interest, that they are not being exploited on behalf of a minority, and that they and their children will have equal access to land, jobs, and education. People can be called upon for the sacrifices which development demands when they are convinced that everyone is sharing those sacrifices and that there will be a just distribution of the progress which sacrifice brings.

I am fully aware that these fundamental social reforms are not made without controversy. We are deeply committed to democratic processes, and we know from our own experience that economic and social reform involves vigorous debate, time and adjustment of contending views. The great human forces which have unleashed the drive for development in the last several years also demand social justice as a part of that development.

### DEVELOPING HUMAN AND MATERIAL RESOURCES

The third requisite for development is also the most obvious: the human and material resources necessary to permit a nation to build the basic economic structure which will produce long-term growth.

In our rush to create new capital we often neglect the importance of the human resources necessary for economic development. But factories and roads and bridges will not be built without men to plan them, to engineer them and to manage them. The programing of economic development itself requires the application of a hundred skills; and the implementation of these plans requires thousands of men to run the factories, teach new methods to the farmer and guide the public administration of the developing society. The history of economic progress in all countries is proof that general education and the development of skills are the most productive long-run investments which can be made in the future of any nation.

Let me say a word here about the element of time. It is a truism to say that each nation has consumed centuries in getting to where it is today. But in development, decades or even centuries can be jumped over because of the transferability of knowledge and technical skills. We are celebrating the one hundredth anniversary of our land-grant colleges, but that does not mean that it will take a hundred years to equal that experience elsewhere. The rapid growth of educational systems and institutions of higher education throughout Latin America in the postwar period has been deeply encouraging and lays a solid base for the training of the manpower needed for national development. It is no accident that sharply increased attention is being given within the alliance to the training of leaders, for people remain the bottlenecks for the accomplishment of great human tasks.

Of course large sums of capital will be needed. Much of it will be mobilized within the developing country. But the United States also accepts its obligation to supply a substantial share of the external assistance needed for the success of the Alliance for Progress. These funds can come from only one source—the ordinary taxpayers of the United States. We have no magic mountains of gold; the Alliance is for us a people's effort, just as it is in the rest of the hemisphere. President Kennedy has pledged us to a mammoth ten-year effort. And we intend to live up to that pledge in the years to come.

With the fulfillment of these three conditions, and with unremitting effort by all of us, we can insure the success of the Alliance for Progress. And with these same instruments we can also help bring a better life to men and women in other parts of the world.

The Alliance for Progress represents an acceptance by all nations of the hemisphere—North American as well as South—of our common responsibility to create an American civilization where no man is forced to live out his life in hunger or hopeless poverty, where every man has the right to hope for a better life for himself and his children.

We approach this task confident of the unparalleled creative power of free societies. We approach this task with the knowledge, evolved from experience, of what we must do to advance the development of the American nations. We approach this task with the same unyielding will which created a civilization in a wilderness and subdued a continent to the service of freedom.

And when we succeed in our Alliance—as we shall succeed—then we will have created a hemisphere where every man will be liberated from material bondage in order to pursue unhindered the ceaseless quest of the human mind and heart. In this way the basic goal of my country, and of yours, will have been fulfilled.

### ADDITIONAL REMARKS

I wonder if I might conclude with just a personal observation or two.

We in this country are aware of the fact that in this great effort which we have called the Alliance for Progress we are in a real sense the junior partners—junior because the effort which we can commit will be considerably less than the efforts which will be committed by all the others. Of the large sums of capital needed for new investment in the next decade perhaps some 20 per cent of it will come from external sources, and of that more than half will come from us. But there remains the 80 per cent which will be mobilized by the peoples of the countries of the hemisphere themselves. As far as we in the United States are concerned, the sums of which we are talking are on the order of 2 per cent of the gross national product of the other members of the alliance; 98 per cent is their responsibility and their contribution. I hope that we in this country can recognize that we are the junior partners and, in good manners and good spirit, that we are in relationships with mature societies with vast problems on their hands, with peoples to lead, peoples to educate, with efforts to mobilize, and that we can understand their problems even though many of them seem far away.

The second has to do with what may turn out to be the most difficult part of all our Alliance effort. We are dedicating ourselves to a decade of impatience. That is the meaning of the Alliance for Progress. Now it is customary for free men to take their deepest common commitments for granted and to exaggerate the importance of their marginal differences. One of our problems therefore within the family of the hemisphere is to discover how to combine urgency—desperate urgency—with a kind of common feeling which will preserve the unity and fellowship of this hemisphere.

In certain respects we must not expect too much. Will there be those who will be discontented with the pace of the effort? Of course. Some will think the movement is too slow. There will be a few who think, in their own situations, that the movement is too fast.

Will there be some of us here in North America who will be impatient with the rate of progress in one or another country or several below the border? Of course. Will there be countries in the hemisphere who will be somewhat disturbed because a neighboring country seems to be moving somewhat more rapidly than one's own country? Yes. Will there be hard negotiations in allocations of resources? Surely. Will there be problems to solve as one neighbor helps another in any one of the dozens of ways in which help is going forward? Yes.

All these things are true. All that means is that free peoples are doing business with each other in a common effort through free procedures. Therefore we shall be debating domestically as well as internationally. We shall be negotiating seriously and hard. We shall be dissatisfied—steadily and continually dissatisfied, I hope—because whatever we do will still leave us the great unfinished business of freedom ahead, but our job is to get on with this great alliance, with a solidarity which our commitment to the peoples of this hemisphere requires, and keep these marginal differences within bounds. Because we approach this task confident of the unparalleled creative power of free societies and we approach this task with the knowledge evolved from experience of what we must do to advance the development of the American nations. We approach this task with the same unyielding will which created a civilization out of a wilderness and subdued a continent to the service of freedom. . . .

# VIII. BERLIN, GERMANY AND NATO

*The most dangerous issues between the Soviet Union and the West have centered on Germany and its traditional capital, Berlin. Although Berlin lies more than 100 miles behind the Iron Curtain in the Soviet-occupied zone of Germany, it is not a part of that zone but a separate political entity for which the four major allies of the war against Hitler assumed joint responsibility. The Western Allies occupied the western sectors of the city, the Soviet Union its eastern sector.*

*Attempts by the Soviet Union to force the Western Allies out of West Berlin, thus opening the way for the absorption of West Berlin into Communist East Germany, have pro-*

duced a series of crises. The first of these began in 1948 when Stalin severed all land and water routes between Berlin and the Western zones of Germany. The Berlin blockade was overcome by allied countermeasures, including an airlift in which American, British and French airmen flew in 2,343,301 tons of supplies, and by the fortitude of the West Berliners. In May 1949, the Soviet Union abandoned the blockade.

The second major assault on the freedom of West Berlin was launched by Khrushchev in November 1958. In essence, it was a threat to annul Western rights in Berlin and to make West Berlin a demilitarized "free" city. This led to a series of talks and negotiations, culminating in a Big Four summit meeting in Paris in May 1960—a conference not formally convened because Khrushchev used the U-2 incident to break it up.

During the early months of 1961, Khrushchev indicated that he still regarded Berlin and Germany as urgent questions. President Kennedy decided, and Khrushchev concurred, that a direct exchange of views, without at-

*tempting negotiations, might be useful. These
talks were held June 3-4, 1961, in Vienna.
They were, in President Kennedy's word,
"somber."*

*An aide-memoire which Khrushchev handed
to President Kennedy on June 4 marked the
formal beginning of the third major assault on
West Berlin.*

*General readers not familiar with this subject
may find it useful to read for background
Berlin-1961 (Department of State Publication
7257).*


## The Soviets Cannot Extinguish
## Western Rights


*Khrushchev liked to call the situation in Berlin
"abnormal." He did so again in a harsh speech
on June 21, 1961.*

. . . Due to the *de facto* division of Germany, the entire
situation in that country is abnormal. The Soviet position in re-

Excerpts from Mr. Rusk's news conference of June 22, 1961.

gard to this matter is predicated on the belief that the division of Germany is normal, that the division of Berlin is normal and that the sole abnormality that persists is West Berlin. This is not a formulation of the problem which is acceptable to the United States.

The militant tone of the speeches made yesterday in Moscow by Chairman Khrushchev and other Soviet leaders must be a source of keen disappointment to those who seek to advance the cause of peace. The effect of these speeches, as the Soviet leaders must have known, can only be to heighten world tensions. The Soviet leaders are aware that they cannot, by any action on their part, extinguish the rights of the Western powers in Berlin. Although cloaked in the propaganda line that all that they propose to do is to sign a peace treaty with a portion of Germany which they control, their intention is to renounce unilaterally obligations assumed in solemn international agreements. In this connection I might recall that the State Department on March 24, 1960, released the text of the basic agreement concerning the areas which the respective forces of the four occupying powers would occupy in Germany and Greater Berlin.

The United States and its allies have assumed certain basic obligations to protect the freedom of the people of West Berlin. Western forces are in the city by right and remain there to protect those freedoms. The people of West Berlin welcome and support those forces, whose presence gives tangible expression to our obligation. It is obvious that the United States could not accept the validity of any claim to extinguish its position in Berlin by unilateral action.

Since the Soviets precipitated the present Berlin crisis in November 1958, the United States and its allies have repeatedly confirmed their position both on the substance of the problem and on their willingness to seek peaceful solutions. I need not review here the history of the long and frequent exchanges of diplomatic notes, of the Geneva Conference of Foreign Ministers of 1959, and of discussions which have taken place at the level of heads of government. In all of these the United States and its allies have been sincerely motivated by a desire to end the tensions over Germany and Berlin which the Soviet threats have created.

But such solutions cannot be at the expense of our obligations and of the basic principles of freedom and self-determination.

There are many contradictions and historical fallacies in the present position of the Soviet leaders. Chairman Khrushchev's description, in his speech of yesterday, of the alleged origins of World War II will scarcely impress any serious historian.

The Soviets talk constantly of peace but threaten the obvious peace which exists in West Berlin. Having purported to turn over East Berlin to the so-called German Democratic Republic, in violation of existing agreements, they now propose to move in upon the position of West Berlin. If the world is full of anxiety and uneasiness over Berlin, this arises directly from the threat of the Soviets to the rights of others and to the liberty of the West Berliners rather than to anything in the present situation in Berlin.

Demands and threats which create a crisis over a subject which involves the vital interests of other people do not promote that real peace which the world desires.

The United States and those associated with us are clear and firm about our obligations to ourselves and to the people of West Berlin. . . .

## We Stand Firm But Are Willing To Talk

*On July 17, 1961, after consultation with the United Kingdom, France and the Federal Republic of Germany, the U.S. replied to the Soviet aide memoire of June 4. We gave notice that we would defend the legal rights on which the freedom of the people of West Berlin depended.*

Excerpt from Mr. Rusk's news conference of July 27, 1961.

*On July 25, in a report to the nation on the
Berlin crisis, delivered by television and radio,
President Kennedy announced a series of measures to strengthen our military forces. West
Berlin, he said, "has now become, as never before, the great testing place of Western courage
and will, a focal point where our solemn commitments, stretching back over the years since
1945, and Soviet ambitions now meet in basic
confrontation."*

. . . . The President in his speech to the Nation indicated
our broad approach to the issues which have been created by the
Soviet moves with respect to Berlin. I think he made two things
very clear: one, that we and the free world must prepare ourselves to be firm and to defend our rights, if necessary, in that
city. This is not only because of West Berlin itself, but because
of its involvement with our stake in the world situation right
around the globe. He also made it clear that there is room for
discussion, that we expect that negotiations will in fact at
some stage take place, and that we and our allies will try on our
side to find opportunities for a peaceful adjustment of a situation
which could be very dangerous.

We are not going to be able to talk about the details of the
proposals which may be discussed with other governments or
with the Soviet Union in the weeks and months ahead. Assistant
Secretary [Foy D.] Kohler, Mr. [Henry H.] Fowler of the Treasury Department, and Mr. [Abram] Chayes of the State Department, and others are leaving today to go to Europe to continue
consultations with our allies.

I shall be going over the first week in August to meet with

the Foreign Ministers of the United Kingdom, France and Germany, also to meet with the North Atlantic Council, where we can continue our consultation with our NATO partners, and to meet with American ambassadors from European capitals. We shall be in the process of consultation steadily on a day-by-day basis.

I think that it would not be possible, and certainly would not be wise, to try to spell out in advance the details of any negotiating positions which we may be formulating or considering with our allies. The President's statement gave some broad indications of the possibilities that might open up, but the details of what might be possible must await the events and consultation. . . .

. . . . There have been proposals, as you know, in the past that dealt with the possibility of meeting the position to some degree that has been taken by the Soviet Union, such questions as the matter of armaments or activities in West Berlin. That is a matter of record.

But to go from those particular points of details to details in future proposals on negotiations I think would not be proper at this time. If there are concerns about security in central Europe, those are concerns which to a very considerable degree—I will put it stronger than that—those are concerns which in any event are unreal, at least as seen from the West, because we have been living with a certain *status quo* in Germany and central Europe for some sixteen years without ourselves taking the initiative to change that *status quo* by force. There have been many proposals for improving it or settling it or changing it by peaceful means.

There may be those who are concerned about—as the Soviets indicate they are—the rearmament of Western Germany. But Western Germany is a part of the great western European community, which acts as a community, and its attitude on these questions, as is the attitude of Germany, is not to provoke a war over matters which can be settled by peaceful means. There are assurances in the situation which have been there and which I think contribute to the peace in this situation. . . .

*Excerpt from remarks outside the White House after meeting with the President, August 3, 1961, just before Mr. Rusk left for Europe to confer with Foreign Ministers of the Western Allies and the North Atlantic Council.*

. . . President Kennedy has already told our own people—and indeed the people of the rest of the world—how we see this Berlin problem. It is essentially a very simple problem. There is peace in Berlin and there is no need to disturb it. There is freedom in West Berlin and we cannot allow that freedom to be undermined or destroyed.

Now there are some who think that it is negative or old-fashioned to be in favor of the status quo. We ourselves and the West would like to see an improvement in the status quo. And since 1946 the West has made many suggestions for changing the situation in Germany so that we can have permanent peace and a permanent settlement in that country. But we cannot admit to a change in the status quo at the cost of peace and freedom in central Europe.

I have no doubt whatever that our NATO Alliance, that the great Atlantic Community, will meet this problem with unity and firmness and determination, but also with reasonableness, and a readiness to discuss, which characterizes this great, experienced Western community of nations.

There is no reason why this problem cannot be solved by peaceful means if those others beyond the Iron Curtain are willing to approach it in the same spirit. President Kennedy has indicated to the entire world this combination of firmness and readiness to discuss, which must be characteristic of a responsible, great nation.

This is no time for recklessness—recklessness in word or in deeds. But may I point out that one can be reckless in two directions, in giving away essential positions, which only postpone the day of tragedy to some future date, or a recklessness of rash action not thoughtfully pursued; and I am quite sure that the

Western Alliance will be reckless in neither one of these directions.

## The Berlin Wall

*Statement for the Press, on August 13, 1961, when the Communists began erecting a barrier between East and West Berlin.*

The authorities in East Berlin and East Germany have taken severe measures to deny to their own people access to West Berlin. These measures have doubtless been prompted by the increased flow of refugees in recent weeks. The refugees are not responding to persuasion or propaganda from the West but to the failures of communism in East Germany. These failures have created great pressures upon Communist leaders who, in turn, are trying to solve their own problems by the dangerous course of threats against the freedom and safety of West Berlin. The resulting tension has itself stimulated flights from the East.

Having denied the collective right of self-determination to the peoples of East Germany, Communist authorities are now denying the right of individuals to elect a world of free choice rather than a world of coercion. The pretense that communism desires only peaceful competition is exposed; the refugees, more than half of whom are less than twenty-five years of age, have "voted with their feet" on whether communism is the wave of the future.

Available information indicates that measures taken thus far are aimed at residents of East Berlin and East Germany and not at the allied position in West Berlin or access thereto. However, limitation on travel within Berlin is a violation of the four-power status of Berlin and a flagrant violation of the right of free circulation throughout the city. Restrictions on travel between East Germany and Berlin are in direct contravention of the Four Power agreement reached at Paris on June 20, 1949. These violations of existing agreements will be the subject of vigorous protest through appropriate channels.

## Exploratory Talks

*After two series of meetings with the British, French and German Foreign Ministers (the first in Paris early in August 1961, and the second in Washington early in September), Secretary Rusk began a series of bilateral U.S.- U.S.S.R. exchanges on Berlin and related subjects. He met three times with Foreign Minister Andrei A. Gromyko in New York in late September on the margin of the U.N. General Assembly. This particular exchange included a meeting between the President and Foreign Minister Gromyko in Washington on October 6, 1961. It was followed by a series of five meetings in Moscow between U.S. Ambassador Llewellyn E. Thompson and Foreign Minister Gromyko stretching from early January through early March. Secretary Rusk then met*

Excerpt from news conference, October 18, 1961.

*six times in Geneva with Foreign Minister
Gromyko from March 12 to March 26 on the
margin of the meeting of the eighteen-power
Disarmament Commission. This was followed
by six conversations in Washington between
Secretary Rusk and Soviet Ambassador Anatoliy
F. Dobrynin, three meetings between Secretary
Rusk and Foreign Minister Gromyko in July
in Geneva on the margin of the Laos Confer-
ence, and further August meetings in Washing-
ton between Secretary Rusk and Ambassador
Dobrynin.*

*Secretary Rusk also participated in inter-Allied
talks on Berlin at the time of the NATO Conference in Paris in December 1961, in Athens
in early May 1962 and during the course of his
trip to Europe in June 1962.*

. . . . I know that you will wish to know whether I have
any comments on Chairman Khrushchev's speech of yesterday.
Let me say that I have not yet received the full text in transla-
tion and would not wish to characterize it in general terms. In a
speech of this character the excerpts which are received early
might be affected by additional material which would be in the
complete text, and these matters in fine print sometimes are important. From the portions which I have seen it is clear that
Chairman Khrushchev ranged widely over the field of foreign
affairs and said a good many things which could not be supported
by the record.

Today, however, I would comment on one statement he made. He said:

> If the Western powers show readiness to settle the German problem, then the question of the time of signing a German peace treaty will not be of such importance. We shall then not insist that the peace treaty be signed without fail by 31 December, 1961.

This confirms publicly what has been said in private talks, including our talks with Mr. Gromyko. His public statement, indicating that he does not assert an ultimatum with respect to time, may serve to reduce tension somewhat. But his general observations about the German and Berlin problems show little, if any, change from what has been said before. He did not go into details, but one would not expect him to in a general review of this character.

Our discussions in recent weeks with the Soviet Union are properly called exploratory talks. They have not been negotiations but an attempt to discover whether a basis for negotiation exists. In this process we have kept our allies fully informed, both through the ambassadorial group in Washington and in NATO.

When a serious and dangerous difference arises, there are various ways of dealing with it. One would be for the two sides to growl publicly at each other until something happens. Another is to establish contact in order to clarify the situation and to guard against a catastrophe which might be brought on by ignorance, miscalculation or mistake. In the modern world I believe that it is important that great powers not lose contact with each other in the presence of a severe disagreement. Exploratory talks can clarify an understanding of vital issues and our determination to defend them. They can also discover whether there is any basis for negotiations which might lead to a peaceful conclusion. We believe that responsible statesmen must keep in touch with each other—not despite the difficulties and dangers but because of them.

If systematic negotiation can occur at some point, that does not insure that an agreement can be reached. The object would be to reach an agreement which fully protects the legitimate vital interests of both sides. But since governments have, not unexpectedly, different views as to what these interests are, negotiation does not always succeed.

There has been considerable speculation about differences among the Western Allies with respect to the handling of the problem of Germany and Berlin. I do not wish to pretend that there have not been differences, but it is important for us to know, and for Mr. Khrushchev to know, what these do and do not mean. There is complete agreement in the West on the nature of our vital interests in Germany and Berlin and on the necessity for defending those vital interests. There is general agreement on the need for preparations to meet a severe crisis if one develops. There has been some disagreement on the timing and nature of contacts with the Soviet Union; these have more to do with procedure than with substance. It would not be correct to believe that there is any crisis within the West with respect to Germany and Berlin. Consultations among the Four Powers most directly involved in Germany and Berlin continue on a daily basis, and on a regular basis in NATO. Whether a particular group of experts meets in a particular place, or whether tentative arrangements for such a meeting do not materialize, is not as important as the basic unity on which we are proceeding and the regular consultations which are going forward. . . .

## The Future of Germany

. . . I don't believe that the permanent peace in Europe can be achieved until the German people have a right to determine their own future. I think we in the West, and certainly we in the United States, believe that we should not take any for-

Excerpts from transcript of interview over the first program of German television produced by Radio Free Berlin and North German Radio, February 28, 1962. Mr. Rusk was interviewed in Washington by five German correspondents.

mal steps or any juridical action which would bar the way for the German people to determine their own future. I do not foresee any *de jure* recognition of the East German regime, nor do I foresee any formal *de facto* type of recognition of the East German regime.

Now we know that East Germany is there as a matter of fact, and we act in accordance with that fact. But we do not wish to take any action which stands in the way of the eventual right of the German people to determine their own future. . . .

I have noticed an occasional press report out of the Federal Republic which expresses some sort of misgiving. I would like to speak to that very directly.

A great alliance does not draw its strength from weekly injections from a hypodermic needle. The basis of the strength of a great alliance is in deep commitments, deeply felt by the peoples and the governments of nations.

Now this NATO alliance is a fundamental arrangement among the Western nations. It is at the heart of the policy of the Western nations, including the policy of the United States. The defense of Western Europe and the defense of the United States are indivisible. They cannot be separated; and that every German would recognize if he would put himself in the position of an American, and try to decide what is essential for the defense of the free world.

Now we are in regular contact, daily contact between our two governments, talking about the great issues of the security of our great alliance, and our two countries. Any German can look around him and see, in many parts of Germany, American soldiers. Those soldiers are not tourists; they are there for a serious purpose. They are there for the mutual defense of Germany and the United States within the framework of the NATO alliance.

Now we do not wish to inflate words by making regular speeches at each other, because these speeches would soon be boring. What we have done, what President Kennedy has done, has been to reaffirm the most elementary and basic commitments of the United States toward our mutual safety and our mutual interests.

And I think there is no basis for any sense of uncertainty within the alliance about the strength of the alliance, and particularly about the attitude of the United States.

. . . Now it is quite true that in the present situation there seems little likelihood of an early movement toward a German reunification. It is also, I think, quite true that the West and the East have no intentions of using force and moving into a world war to change that situation. But the reunification of Germany continues to be a political objective which we take very seriously. . . .

The most immediate question in front of us has to do with the security, the safety, the viability, the freedom of the city of West Berlin.

It is against the position of the West that the Soviet Union has moved once again in recent months to bring pressure. We in the West, the three occupying powers, as well as the NATO alliance, have declared very specifically that the safety of that city, and our presence there, and its access with the rest of the world, are of vital interest to the West.

So far, there does not appear to be a common basis with Moscow on guaranteeing or securing those vital interests. I have no doubt that if those essential interests are adequately and thoroughly recognized that other subjects could come up, but I would not specify what you refer to as "European security."

I think perhaps the context in which these broad questions of security can best come up would be in the disarmament discussions in Geneva. But I do not see a direct linkage between the vital interests of West Berlin and specific questions involved in "European security" at this stage. . . .

## Strengthening the Western Alliance

*NATO, the North Atlantic Treaty Organization, began April 4, 1949, with the defensive alliance signed by Belgium, Canada, Denmark, France, Iceland, Italy, Luxembourg, the Netherlands, Norway, Portugal, the United Kingdom and the United States. Greece and Turkey joined in 1952, the Federal Republic of Germany in 1955. The NATO Council, composed of the foreign ministers of the member states, holds two regular meetings annually.*

*The cohesion and strengthening of NATO have been prime concerns of U.S. policy.*

. . . . I shall be leaving this weekend for meetings in Paris. First, with the foreign ministers of the United Kingdom, France and the Federal Republic of Germany, and then for the annual ministerial meeting of the NATO Council, where we shall be joined by not only the foreign ministers but ministers of defense and of finance.

We shall, of course, in the foreign ministers' meeting, be talking about the German problem. I want to underline the importance of keeping our eyes on the main ball as we think about the German problem. That there are margins of difference among the Western governments as to how, specifically, we might proceed to deal with this question is a matter of general knowledge. But the differences which really count are those

Excerpt from news conference, December 8, 1961, shortly before departure for Europe.

which exist between Moscow and the West. That is the heart of the matter. That is the cause of the crisis. That is the problem to be resolved.

The West is united on an understanding and appreciation of the vital interests that are involved, but the problem of peaceful settlement is whether the Soviet Union will recognize and respect these long-established rights and vital interests in that situation.

At the NATO meeting we anticipate that a number of things will be discussed which will maintain the increasing momentum of the Atlantic community, in its economic development, in its growing military strength, and in the strengthening ties between the Atlantic community and the rest of the free world. We feel that the NATO and the Atlantic community are on the move and that the momentum of this movement should be maintained. . . .

### Statement on arrival at Athens, May 2, 1962, for meeting of the North Atlantic Council.

I am very pleased to visit Greece, which has an especially warm place in the hearts of Americans because of the dedication of its people to liberty.

In Ottawa—just about one year ago—President Kennedy spoke of the "irresistible tide" *for* freedom and *against* tyranny that began here in Greece some two and a half thousand years ago. That tide of freedom, he said, is the wave of the future.

Our meeting here in the next few days is perhaps best characterized as part of the normal and established conduct of business of this alliance. But at the same time we are reminded simply by our presence here what it is we stand for, and why the tide of freedom—of which the President spoke—is in the long term indeed irresistible as long as there are those who will work and sacrifice for that cause.

For the immediate future, I wish I could hold out a prospect for relaxation, but I cannot. It is true that there may be the appearance of some slight improvement in the international scene —and even this much is welcome. But it is a long way from the appearance to the reality, and the reality is not even in sight.

And so we must get on with the important work of the alliance. That work does not consist only of the meetings of the Council of Ministers. It consists also of the year-round work of the Permanent Council, the secretariat and the military commands to build the strength and cohesion of our alliance. In a very real sense, this work is never finished. It will be the purpose of the ministerial meeting to carry forward this continuing task by appraising where we stand and by furnishing further guidance to the permanent authorities of the alliance.

Finally, I want to thank our loyal Greek allies, who have kindly offered to be our hosts and wish them health, continued progress and prosperity.

# IX. SOUTHEAST ASIA

*The Importance of SEATO*

*The Southeast Asia Treaty Organization (SEATO) was formed by a collective defense pact of Thailand, the Philippines, Pakistan, Australia, New Zealand, France, the United Kingdom and the United States, signed at Manila, September 8, 1954. By a protocol its protective arm was extended to cover Laos, Cambodia, and the Republic of Viet-Nam.*
*At the time of this seventh meeting both Laos and the Republic of Viet-Nam were under assault by Communist guerrillas. In Laos, troops of Prince Souvanna Phouma, neutralist former premier, also were in revolt, and the rebel forces, both Communist and neutralist, were*

Address at seventh meeting of Council of Ministers of Southeast Asia Treaty Organization, Bangkok, March 7, 1961.

*being assisted by a Soviet airlift. The Soviet government had declared, however, that it favored a neutral Laos and had taken up a proposal by Prince Sihanouk of Cambodia for an international conference to settle the Laotian question. On March 23, just four days before this meeting, the United Kingdom, after consultation with the U.S., had agreed to a Soviet proposal to convene a conference. However, this agreement was conditional upon a verified cease-fire in Laos. The Soviet reply, which was generally favorable, did not come until April 1, three days after this meeting adjourned. Thus, when Secretary Rusk spoke, it seemed highly uncertain whether a Communist takeover could be prevented unless members of SEATO put armed forces into Laos.*

This seventh meeting of the Council of Ministers of SEATO brings us back to the realities which gave birth to our alliance. We can regret that our meeting in this lovely capital of Thailand occurs in such troubled times, but it is perhaps symbolic that we return today to the city in which our first meeting was held in 1955.

The hard fact is that this particular meeting finds the treaty area in a situation full of danger for the future of its nations and peoples—a possibility clearly envisaged at the time of the founding of the treaty. The United States does not believe that such a situation can be ignored.

The principle of collective security for defense is as old as the history of nations. Even though we may be considered ourselves one of the principal world powers, we do not rely exclusively upon our own arms to defend ourselves but look to the collective strength of defense organizations in which we have joined around the world. The words and actions of aggressive powers have demonstrated clearly, both to us and to the allies with which we have associated ourselves, that collective effort is necessary if we are to insure our continued existence as free nations.

We are, as a people, naturally interested in our own freedom; yet we have on numerous occasions demonstrated our willingness to come to the aid of others who are themselves threatened—both where we have local treaty obligations and where, as in Greece or in Korea, we had no obligations except those imposed upon us by the U.N. Charter and by our sense of responsibility to other freedom-loving nations.

This sense of responsibility has no geographical barriers. Our attention here is focused on Southeast Asia. The people of this treaty area, no less than elsewhere, have an inherent right to create peaceful, independent states and to live out their lives in ways of their own choosing. Loss of freedom means tragedy whether that misfortune overtakes a people on any continent or any island in the seven seas.

Let no one suppose that the peoples of Southeast Asia, whether members of this Organization or not, are innocent victims caught up somehow accidentally in power struggles between powerful external contending forces. The objects of aggressors, in their efforts to expand their dominion, are the people and the territory that lie in their path. This is the issue here. Were this issue laid to rest by an abandonment of such ambition, the United States would welcome the resulting reduction of tensions and the ushering in of a world under law. But we cannot imagine the survival of our own free institutions if areas of the world distant from our own shores are to be subjugated by force or penetration. We cannot hope for peace for ourselves if insatiable appetite is unrestrained elsewhere. We confess a national interest in freedom, but it is a national interest which we share with other nations all over the globe—which becomes thereby a common interest of all who would be free. If we are determined, as we are, to support our commitments under SEATO, it is because peace is possible only through restraining those who break it in contempt of law.

We sincerely regret that this meeting must be preoccupied by security matters related to the threat which faces the Kingdom of Laos and the Republic of Viet-Nam, both states lying within the treaty area of this Organization. Our more basic purpose is to assist the peoples of this area in realizing those noble aspirations of life for which man was created.

We would be much happier if money spent here on arms, which we have furnished at the request of the legitimate governments of the states in the area for their own defense, could have been spent on the development of the human and material resources of the area—the harnessing of the great Mekong River for the enrichment of the lives of all the people of this area, the building of great highways to bind the peoples of this area together in friendly intercourse, the improvement of the lot of the people themselves, those living in the country, cities, towns and villages—their health, their welfare and their education.

These are the goals for which the money spent on arms could more happily be devoted. Only through the attainment of these goals can there emerge the feeling of unity and purpose among the people and states of the area which will give them a basis for collective action to improve their own wellbeing. We in the United States continue to help the nations of this area in their development and in the furtherance of their peaceful pursuits, as appropriate through SEATO, through the Colombo Plan, through the United Nations and through arrangements undertaken directly between us.

In the final analysis the protection of personal freedom and national independence must stem from the individual and collective efforts of peoples themselves, based on their own desires and motivations. Small states are not, however, able to defend themselves alone against aggression or interference in their internal affairs by outside powers. Until the nations of this area are able to live with reliable assurance against external threats, we will continue to assist them toward this end.

Three newly independent states, one of them divided, emerged from the deliberations which attended the breakup of Indochina. Even before they had had a chance to organize as states and to create viable economies and social structures, they were under attack by the same forces which had subjugated northern Viet-Nam. During their short national existence they have not been given the chance to develop to the point where they could protect themselves against further subversions or aggressions.

We believe, and we feel confident that our views are shared by the other members of this Organization, that it is our obligation to assist the peoples of Southeast Asia in their fight for their freedom, both because of our responsibilities in connection with the formation of these states and because of the duties undertaken in the formation of the SEATO organization.

Speaking for my country I wish to assure the members of this Organization and the people of Southeast Asia that the United States will live up to these responsibilities. It is our sincere belief that all of the states of mainland Southeast Asia can themselves resolve their purely internal problems. In these, of course, we have no desire to interfere. We will, however, continue to assist free nations of this area who are struggling for their survival against armed minorities directed, supplied and supported from without. We will assist those defending themselves against such forces just as we shall assist those under attack by naked aggression. We feel confident that our fellow SEATO members share our feeling and will likewise meet their commitments under this treaty. A primary purpose of this meeting of the Council of Ministers is to determine how this can best be done.

## Statement on return to United States, March 31, 1961.

The meeting of the Council of Ministers of SEATO in Bangkok was highly productive. We were much encouraged by the discussions there and by the unity achieved.

The most important fact about the SEATO meeting was the demonstration of its solidarity and the determination of its members. The meeting expressed its support of efforts for cessation of hostilities and for peaceful negotiations to achieve a neutral and independent Laos. Should these efforts fail, however, members are prepared to take appropriate action. The ministers also expressed their resolve not to acquiesce in the attempted takeover of south Viet-Nam.

All of us meeting in Bangkok were deeply concerned with the seriousness of the threat to Laos and south Viet-Nam. Some of our friends in SEATO are very close to these dangers. But even those of us far from that area recognize the threat to our own security and wellbeing. The resolve of the SEATO members is an important element in the maintenance of the peace in that part of the world and in the preservation of the independence of the peoples of that area.


# The Neutralization of Laos

*Under the co-chairmanship of the Soviet Union and the United Kingdom, this fourteen-nation conference convened on May 16, 1961.*

In late April we received an invitation to an international conference on the Laotian question. On Monday evening last, the co-chairmen announced the opening of the conference and stated that "this conference is solely concerned with the international aspects of the Laotian question." We are here to take part on that basis because the Laotian question is urgent, in relation both to the people of that troubled country and to the peace of

Statement at International Conference on Laos, Geneva, Switzerland, May 17, 1961.

Southeast Asia. We wish to say at the beginning how gratified we were that His Royal Highness Prince Sihanouk [of Cambodia] was able to open our sessions last evening with wise words aimed at moderation and a genuine attempt to reach a satisfactory solution.

At the outset . . . I believe it necessary to raise a matter which we believe to be the first order of business in this conference. A number of invited governments, including the United States, considered that this conference could not meet with any hope of success unless there had been achieved a prompt and effective cease-fire. We received on May 12, the date proposed for the opening of our sessions, a report from the ICC [International Control Commission], which said that the Commission are satisfied that a general *de facto* cease-fire exists and such breaches as have been informally complained of are either due to misunderstanding or to factors such as the terrain, the nature of disposition of forces, both regular and irregular, of all parties.

Information from Laos indicates that rebel forces continue to attack in a number of localities and that rebel troop movements are occurring which are prejudicial to an effective cease-fire. The most serious of these violations have taken place in the Ban Padong area near Xieng Khouang, where artillery and infantry attacks are continuing against Government forces. The Royal Lao Government has made formal complaint to the ICC chairman.

Surely . . . the cease-fire and proper instructions to the ICC are matters of first importance. This is something which cannot be postponed. An effective cease-fire is a prerequisite to any constructive result from our proceedings; a failure of a cease-fire would result in a highly dangerous situation which it is the purpose of the conference to prevent. I would urge that the co-chairmen take this up immediately in order that the situation be clarified and the ICC given the necessary authorizations and instructions.

There is another point which affects our ability to come to a satisfactory result. We do not believe that this conference is properly constituted without due provision for the delegates of the constitutional government of Laos. The Royal Laotian

Government, empowered by the King and Parliament to govern Laos, represents that country in the United Nations and in other international bodies. It is the only authority resting upon that nation's constitution and the means established by law for registering the wishes of its King and people. We do not see how we can make good progress without the presence here of the Government of Laos, and we regret, though understand, why it does not consider that it can be here under existing circumstances. We believe that this, too, is a matter which requires the immediate attention of the co-chairmen in order that this conference of governments may have the benefit of the participation of the Government of the very country which we are discussing.

Before I turn to what I had intended to say about the questions before the conference, I should like to thank the Secretary of State for Foreign Affairs of the United Kingdom [Lord Home] for his constructive and helpful contribution of last evening. We find ourselves in general agreement with his suggestions and hope that the conference can settle down quickly to the detailed provisions required to give them effect.

### THE REAL THREAT TO PEACE IN SOUTHEAST ASIA

I also listened with interest to the remarks of the representative from Peiping [Chen Yi]. He made certain statements about the United States which were not true and not new. We have heard them often before. Indeed, I rather thought that his statement of them on this occasion was less violent than language to which we have become accustomed. To leave open the possibility that those at this table are prepared to find some common basis for the settlement of the Laotian question, I shall comment upon his remarks with the restraint enjoined upon us by Prince Sihanouk.

There is only one problem of peace in Southeast Asia and, indeed, in many other parts of the world. It is whether those who have wrapped around themselves the doctrine of the historical inevitability of world domination by their own particular political system merely believe it or will attempt to impose it upon others by all the means at their disposal. The real issue is whether peaceful co-existence is what normal language would indicate it means, or whether it means an all-out and continuous struggle against all those not under Communist control. The real threat to peace in Southeast Asia is not from south to north, nor from across the Pacific Ocean. The threats are from north to south and take many forms. If these threats should disappear, SEATO would wither away, for it has no purpose but to maintain the peace in Southeast Asia.

We cannot settle this argument in this conference, for it involves commitments of the Communist world which they would undoubtedly not yield in this discussion, just as it involves the commitments of free peoples who are determined to perfect and cherish freedoms still evolving from more than 2,000 years of struggle against tyranny in all forms. What we *can* do here is to discover whether we can agree that the people of Laos should be permitted to live in their own country without interference and pressures from the outside.

We note the statement made by the representative from Peiping that he "is ready to work jointly with the delegations of all the other countries participating in this conference to make contributions to the peaceful settlement of the Laotian question." We ourselves are prepared to work diligently to discover whether there *is* agreement in the conference on the questions before us.

Promptly after assuming office President Kennedy said: "We strongly and unreservedly support the goal of a neutral and independent Laos, tied to no outside power or group of powers, threatening no one, and free from any domination." In early exchanges with Chairman Khrushchev, the latter affirmed his commitment to a neutral and independent Laos, and there was useful discussion of the example of Austria. Other spokesmen of other governments, including a number represented here, have declared their desire for a neutral Laos.

The King of that country, on February 19 of this year, declared: "We desire to proclaim once more the policy of true neutrality that Laos has always sought to follow. . . . Once again we appeal to all countries to respect the independence, sovereignty, territorial integrity and neutrality of Laos."

I have already indicated that we believe the most immediate problem is to insure an effective cease-fire, to give the ICC the necessary and relevant instructions and to give it the resources required to carry out its vital task.

TASK OF INSURING A NEUTRAL LAOS

Next we must turn to the problem of insuring a genuinely neutral Laos. In this task, of course, most of us in this conference act as outsiders. We cannot impose on Laos anything which that country and its people do not truly want for themselves. In this particular instance we are fortunate that the expressed desires of the international community seem to coincide with what the people of Laos themselves want. Almost every nation here has expressed itself in favor of a neutral Laos.

But what does this mean? Neutrality is not simply a negative concept. A neutral Laos should be a dynamic, viable Laos, making progress toward more stable political institutions, economic wellbeing and social justice. A truly neutral Laos must have the right to choose its own way of life in accordance with its own traditions, wishes, and aspirations for the future.

It is, of course, too early in the conference to present detailed proposals for achieving this end. But it is not too early to begin considering the broad outlines of a program directed to the goal.

As my Government sees it, such an outline would involve three separate points.

First; a definition of the concept of neutrality, as it applies to Laos, which all of us gathered here could pledge ourselves to respect. This definition must go beyond the classical concept of nonalignment and include positive assurance of the integrity of the elements of national life.

Second; the development of effective international machinery for maintaining and safeguarding that neutrality against threats to it from within as well as without.

Third; Laos will need, if it wishes to take its place in the modern world, a substantial economic and technical aid program. We believe that such aid could be most appropriately administered by neutral nations from the area and that it should be supported by contributions from many states and agencies. We do not believe that a neutral Laos should become a field of rivalries expressed through foreign aid programs on a national or bloc basis. But we do believe that the Laotians should benefit from the enlarged possibilities of better health, broader education, increased productivity which are opening up for mankind in all parts of the world.

A word more is perhaps in order about each of these points.

### RESPECTING THE NEUTRALITY OF LAOS

First, *neutrality*. To be neutral, in the classical sense, means not to be formally aligned with contending parties. Certainly we want this classical neutrality for Laos. But in today's world, with modern modes by which one government may subtly impose its will upon another, mere nonalignment is not enough.

Foreign military personnel, except for those specified in the Geneva Accords, should be withdrawn from Laos. But we mean *all*, not just those assisting the forces of the constituted Government of the country at its request. There is no problem about the withdrawal of the limited U.S. military personnel assisting with the training and supply of Government forces if the "Viet Minh brethren" and other elements who have entered Laos from the northeast return to their homes.

We have no desire to send military equipment into Laos; if international arrangements can be reached about forces and equipment, there would be no problem on our side.

We have no military bases in Laos and want none. We have no military alliances with Laos and want none. We have no interest in Laos as a staging area or as a thoroughfare for agents of subversion, saboteurs or guerrilla bands to operate against Laos' neighbors.

If all those at this table can make the same commitments and support international machinery to protect Laos and its neighbors against such activities, we shall have taken an important step toward peace in Southeast Asia.

Finally, neutrality must be consistent with sovereignty. It involves safeguards against subversion of the elements of the state which is organized, directed or assisted from beyond its borders. In the end we must find a way to let the people of Laos live their own lives under conditions of free choice—and under conditions which permit the continuing exercise of choice to adapt institutions, policies and objectives to the teachings of experience.

In the Final Declaration of the Geneva Conference of 1954, the parties pledged themselves to respect the sovereignty, the independence, the unity and the territorial integrity of Laos. The intervening years since 1954 have demonstrated as a practical reality that, for Laos, sovereignty, independence, unity and territorial integrity cannot long be maintained unless others also are willing to respect the neutrality of Laos.

We invite the nations of this conference to join in a solemn recognition and pledge of respect for Laotian neutrality. We invite all here to join in developing adequate machinery for protecting this status and with it the sovereignty, independence, unity and territorial integrity of Laos as well.

### MACHINERY FOR KEEPING THE PEACE

Second, *machinery for keeping the peace.* The Geneva Conference of 1954 spent most of its time in discussing international machinery to supervise and control the introduction of arms and military personnel into the Southeast Asian area. Despite those labors, that machinery has not proved effective in controlling military activity and in keeping the peace in the area. It has, however, given us a body of experience upon which we can draw in an effort to build better than our predecessors.

That experience suggests a set of principles or criteria by which we and the world will be able to judge whether the international controls developed here will effectively serve the ends for which they are designed.

The control machinery must have full access to all parts of the country without the need for the consent of any civil or military officials, national or local.

It must have its own transportation and communication equipment sufficient to the task. These must be constantly available to and under the sole orders of the control body.

It must be able to act on any complaints from responsible sources, including personnel of the control body itself, responsible military and civil officials in Laos, the governments of neighboring countries and of the members of this conference.

The control body should act by majority rule with the right to file majority and minority reports. It should not be paralyzed by a veto.

There should be some effective method of informing governments and the world at large about a finding by the control body that the conditions of peace and neutrality, as defined, have been violated.

If we are successful in giving practical meaning to the idea of a neutral Laos with international assurances against aggression and intervention, Lao armed forces could be reduced to the level necessary to maintain its own security.

This is the yardstick by which we can measure the prospective effectiveness of any control machinery for Laos. This is the yardstick which will influence the attitude of the United States toward the work of this conference. In short, pledges and promises must be backed by effective controls, effectively applied to maintain a genuinely neutral Laos.

### COLLECTIVE ASSISTANCE EFFORTS

Third, *economic and technical development for Laos.* The energies of the Lao people have too long been diverted from the constructive work of establishing for themselves and their children a better society and a better life. Schools, hospitals, agricultural improvement, industry, transport and communications, improved civil administration—all are needed, and urgently, if the promise which the twentieth century holds out to all men is to be realized for Laos. Such improvement in their way of life is not only the right of the Laotians. It is also, I am convinced, a necessary condition of an independent and neutral Laos.

Unfortunately the resources necessary to permit such improvement at the required speed are not available in Laos itself. It is necessary that as many countries as possible supply the resources needed.

The United States would be willing to contribute to such a program. The United States has already contributed sizable amounts in material support and effort to assist the people of Laos in this program of economic and social development. It is a matter of regret that any portion of this effort has had to be expanded to meet the threat to the security of Laos. Certainly one of the prime tasks for this conference is to devise means so that collective assistance efforts for Laos can be dedicated to the peaceful pursuits of people and to bringing the benefits of modern science and technology to the masses.

We believe that such assistance might usefully be administered by an organization of neutral nations of the area. We invite the U.S.S.R. to join with us in underwriting the cost of such assistance. Let us make Laos the scene of a cooperative effort for peaceful construction.

Mr. Chairman, I wish to inform the conference that I am one of several ministers who plan to return to our posts toward the end of this week. It was my announced intention when I first arrived. Our delegation will be led by Ambassador at Large [W. Averell] Harriman, one of our most distinguished public servants and most experienced diplomats. But official propaganda has begun to say that my departure means an attempt to sabotage this conference. It is not important that such propaganda is false; it is important that such propaganda bears upon the bona fides of those at the table.

In conclusion, Mr. Chairman, I do hope that all of us at the conference can keep our minds upon the Laotian people, who have suffered much and endured much during the past two decades. Let us find ways to let them lead their own lives in peace. They are few in number and need not be caught up in larger issues. Let us affirm that it is *their* country and not an appropriate target for ambitions with which they need not be involved. We shall contribute what we can to the success of this conference; if each can contribute, a good result can be accomplished.

*After protracted negotiations, complicated by difficulties in persuading the different factions in Laos to combine in a new government under Prince Souvanna Phouma, agreements on the neutrality of Laos were signed on July 23, 1962.*

*Remarks at the Plenary Session of the International Conference on Laos, at Geneva, Switzerland, July 21, 1962.*

When this Conference convened here in Geneva fourteen months ago, I suggested that the task before us was to "discover whether we can agree that the people of Laos should be permitted to live in their own country without interference and pressures from the outside." It is satisfying to come back today and to participate in this session during which it is being recorded that such an agreement has been reached. This is an event of considerable significance and the formal signature of this agreement next Monday should be an occasion which will be greeted with hope and satisfaction by all the peoples of the world as it has been greeted here with satisfaction by participants in this conference.

We have, unfortunately, heard certain distortions of fact from one or two discordant voices here this morning. I am ignoring these efforts to inject disruptive propaganda into the final sessions of this conference because the sources themselves know better than most the true facts of the situations to which they referred.

In a larger and more pragmatic sense these agreements are

a beginning. The documents which we approve today will have life and meaning not in their signature but in their implementation. The words which we record are an affirmation of the actions to which we commit ourselves. The United States will faithfully observe the letter and the spirit of these arrangements, and subscribes to them with every expectation that all other signatories will do the same. We believe that this is the only way in which an international climate can be established to permit the restoration of peace to Laos.

We believe, furthermore, that these agreements, scrupulously observed, will assure the future independence and neutrality of Laos. The International Control Commission, which has been authorized, with the concurrence of the Royal Government of Laos, to assist in the execution of these agreements, can contribute greatly to these ends and must have support from all of us. But it is also to the co-chairmen that we must look for a major responsibility of assuring the continuation of the international climate that has been established here with respect to Laos. I should like to take this occasion to express the genuine appreciation of my Government for the task the co-chairmen have already performed in bringing these agreements into being, and to assure them of our continuing support in connection with the new obligations and responsibilities which they are about to assume.

The peace, the independence and the neutrality of Laos are essential pre-conditions for the more tangible blessings of prosperity and unity to which, after so many years of turmoil, the people of Laos are entitled. It is our hope that, in turning from the waste of war to the pursuits of peace, the agriculture and industry of Laos will flourish and that the rewards of this economic revival will benefit all the people of the country. To assist in bringing this about, my Government is prepared, if the Royal Lao Government so requests, to provide certain economic and technical assistance. It is hoped that other Governments which feel themselves able to do so will be similarly prepared to help.

All these hopes for the future of Laos rest, of course, on the assumption that there will be unity of purpose and peace within Laos. My Government has carefully studied the governmental program announced by the Provisional Government of National Union and notes the particular significance which that program attaches to its immediate tasks. Among the most important of these, in the interest of peace in Laos, is the integration of all Lao armed forces into a single army loyal to the Government of National Union.

We feel it appropriate therefore to express the earnest hope that all parties in Laos will work together to assist the Government in the swift and smooth achievement of its program.

There is a procedural point which I wish to note for the record. It was mentioned by Lord Home: namely, that the participation of our Delegation in this Conference, and the signature of the documents which emerged from it, do not imply recognition in any case where it has not previously been accorded.

Finally, I wish, on behalf of President Kennedy, my Delegation and the American people, to express to His Highness, Prince Souvanna Phouma, and to the Prince's colleagues in the Government of National Union, our best wishes for their fullest success in the carrying out of their new and arduous tasks, which all the world will be watching and which will be of intimate interest to us all.

*Excerpts from interview on "Washington Conversation," CBS television network, September 2, 1962.*

. . . . We were under no illusions that, when these declarations were signed, this ended the Laotian problem. This is the beginning. Compliance with those declarations on the part of everyone concerned is essential if that question is to come out right.

. . . . There was the alternative, which we could not accept, of Laos being taken over by the Communists.

There was the alternative of our throwing into that land-locked country a large number of American forces. . . .

Now, I think this attempt to let the Laotians determine their future has been worth the effort; and . . . we will know in the next several weeks or months whether that attempt can succeed.

## *The Aggression Against Viet-Nam*

*Early in 1962, in response to an appeal from the Republic of Viet-Nam for aid to meet the growing Communist guerrilla attack, the United States increased substantially its assistance to the Republic.*

. . . I would like to open today with a statement on Viet-Nam. We have noted recent comments from Peiping, Moscow and Hanoi about the nature and purposes of American aid to Viet-Nam. I should like, therefore, to make a brief comment on that situation.

### COMMUNIST AGGRESSION AGAINST VIET-NAM

These comments from Communist capitals wholly neglect the fact that the Republic of Viet-Nam is under attack of Communist guerrillas who are directed, trained, supplied and reinforced by North Viet-Nam—all in gross violation of the 1954 Geneva Accords. Irrefutable evidence of this illegal and aggressive activity has been made public; I can add that what is known publicly is strongly and conclusively reinforced by intelligence information.

Excerpt from news conference, March 1, 1962.

United States military and economic assistance and technical advice are being extended to the Republic of Viet-Nam at its request to assist the Vietnamese people to maintain their independence against this aggression. There have been other examples, in almost every continent, of this type of aggression.

The United States is assisting with training, logistics, transportation and advisory personnel to enable the Government of Viet-Nam to deal with this conspiratorial effort to take over that country by violent means. We have no combat units in that country, and we have no desire for bases or other United States military advantages. All we want is that the Vietnamese be free to determine their own future.

In reference to the demand by the Communists that the cochairmen of the 1954 Geneva conference and other countries concerned consult regarding Viet-Nam, the United States is always prepared to talk about situations which represent a threat to the peace, but what must be talked about is the root of the trouble; in this case it is the Communist aggression against Viet-Nam in disregard of the Geneva Accords.

The President made it clear last December in responding to the Vietnamese request for assistance that

. . . our primary purpose is to help your people maintain their independence. If the Communist authorities in North Viet-Nam will stop their campaign to destroy the Republic of Viet-Nam, the measures we are taking to assist your defense efforts will no longer be necessary.

There is no threat to the peace of Southeast Asia from the south or from across the Pacific Ocean; the threat comes only from the north, from those who have declared their intention to force the rest of the world into their pattern—despite the fact that no people has yet chosen that pattern in a genuinely free election. There can be peace overnight in Viet-Nam if those responsible for the aggression wish peace. The situation is just as simple as that. . . .

# X. THE FAR EAST
# AND THE PACIFIC

*The Importance of ANZUS*

*This address followed a two-day meeting of the
ANZUS Council. ANZUS is the mutual secu-
rity treaty of Australia, New Zealand and the
United States, signed September 1, 1951*

Prime Minister Menzies—whom all the world knows as
"Bob"—Prime Minister Holyoake, Mr. Calwell, [Robert G.
Menzies, Prime Minister of Australia; Keith Jacka Holyoake,
Prime Minister of New Zealand; Arthur A. Calwell, Leader of
the Opposition, Australian House of Representatives] Your Ex-
cellencies Ministers of State and distinguished members of the
Parliament:

I am deeply grateful for this warm and friendly reception
you have given me this evening. Those of you who know intimately the political system of the United States will know how
sincerely a Secretary of State says that.

Portions of Address at Parliamentary Dinner, Canberra, Australia,
May 9, 1962.

. . . . It is a great personal pleasure to visit Australia for this first time. My longing to do so has been nourished quite literally throughout my life, from the stories of exploration and adventure I read as a boy—my State of Georgia, too, was founded by refugees from the debtor prisons of England—all the way from those early stories to the kind invitation which your Prime Minister extended to our meeting of ANZUS here in Canberra.

Australian friends at Oxford, law school studies of appeals to the Judicial Committee of the Privy Council, associations in World War II and Korea, team play with your delegations to the United Nations, cooperation with your scientists and your scholars while I was at the Rockefeller Foundation—these are among some of the ties which make this visit deeply satisfying, quite apart from the official business we meet here to transact.

### COMMON HERITAGE OF UNITED STATES AND AUSTRALIA

Like all other Americans, I feel at home here, not only because of your warm hospitality but because of our common heritage, our common institutions, our common values, our common purposes. Our legal systems have the same roots. We are as one in our respect for individual human rights and the practice of political and social democracy.

You know, it just occurred to me that those sentences sound trite. But let's be careful. These simple, elementary things turn out to be the most important, and one of the problems about letting them become trite is that we may let them lose strength by inattention—by taking them for granted.

We share the pioneering spirit which goes with the settling and development of continents. We have a common, or at least a vaguely similar, language, and a common tendency to enlarge—or shall I say enrich—it by coining new words.

We are both among the inventors of a federal system—arrangements, Mr. Prime Minister, which continue to make a rich contribution to political wisdom where unity and diversity must find reconciliation. We haven't begun to see the end of the story of this federal idea in the world in which we live.

You have a special capital district, as do we. And, like ours, we think yours is beautiful.

If we Americans have any complaints about you Australians they are that some of your runners and swimmers are rather too fast and that your policy in regard to the Davis Cup is unconscionably monopolistic. Years ago, in writing your Ambassador in Washington to congratulate him on Australia's victory in the Davis Cup matches, in typical Yankee style I decided to do a bit of timesaving forward planning. I made myself a stack of mimeographed letters, and now all I need to do is to fill in the date.

I am not prepared to concede that a similar letter will be necessary for the America's Cup, but I must of course at this stage recognize the possibilities. I have a feeling that perhaps it will be the turn of Sir Howard Beale to send a letter to me.

But let me congratulate you on a victory in another field—the first place won by your shortwave broadcasts in a recent worldwide poll.

The excellence which sometimes dismays us as competitors makes us treasure you all the more as allies and comrades.

AN ENDURING PARTNERSHIP

Many tens of thousands of Americans know from direct personal experience how good it is to have Australians and New Zealanders at their side in times of peril. One of these Americans arrived at Guadalcanal nineteen years ago last month to take command of a PT-boat. He became well acquainted with the neighboring waters of the South Pacific, first by cruising on them and then by swimming in them for some forty hours after his PT-boat was rammed by a Japanese destroyer and he and his crew were presumed lost. And lost or captured they all would have been, almost certainly, but for some friendly islanders and an Australian—one of that intrepid band of Australians and New Zealanders who risked their lives in lonely vigil behind enemy lines, as watchers over half a million square miles of Melanesia. President Kennedy has asked me to convey his warmest regards and best wishes to the people of Australia this evening, and a special personal greeting to Reg Evans [one of the Australian watchers referred to previously].

It is altogether fitting that this meeting of ANZUS should coincide with the celebration of the twentieth anniversary of the Battle of the Coral Sea. Coral Sea Week not only commemorates our joint struggle but signifies our enduring partnership.

When the ANZUS treaty was signed on September 1, 1951, Secretary of State Acheson said that it "only puts into words strong ties and purposes already in existence." And when I look back to that day of signing, at which I was present, I find in this present journey a journey of sentimental affection. I also recall —and this should be important to you—that the ANZUS treaty was a result of the most close cooperation between Secretary Acheson and Mr. John Foster Dulles, who were working at that time in complete harmony with respect to issues such as those we are talking about today.

Indeed I think it may be said that no defensive alliance was ever more firmly anchored in the solid realities of common interest, and common ideals and mutual confidence. As we have fought side by side to defend liberty in the past, so we stand today, resolved to preserve freedom against another grave threat. Our vital common interests are not confined to the Pacific; they are worldwide. We are locked in a global struggle, and in its outcome our fortunes—both yours and ours—are indissolubly welded.

### U.S. VIEW OF WORLD STRUGGLE

I should like to outline briefly how the Government of the United States looks upon this world struggle. . . .

*[The middle sections of this address dealt with main objectives of U.S. policy, the Communist program for world domination and the crisis*

*over Berlin. They are omitted here because their substance appears elsewhere in these selections.]*

. . . . In Southeast Asia, likewise, the free world has vital interests which you and New Zealand and we, with our other allies in SEATO, have special obligations to protect. At present, two adjoining nations, Laos and the Republic of Viet-Nam, are being subjected to aggression from the north.

We seek a united and an independent Laos. We believe that the interests of Laos, of Southeast Asia and of the free world as a whole would be served by a neutral Laos. The Soviets informed us that they too favored an independent and neutral Laos. International agreement on this stated objective was achieved at Geneva, and under this agreement all foreign troops would be required to leave Laos. As yet, however, the leaders of the principal political factions within Laos have not agreed on the composition of a coalition government. And I cannot honestly report that the end of this crisis is plainly in view.

In Laos there is a precarious cease-fire. But next door, in South Viet-Nam, is a country under active assault by thousands of men trained, infiltrated, in part supplied, and certainly directed, from north of the 17th parallel.

The Viet Minh have systematically violated the Geneva Accords of 1954 since the day of their signing. But they were unable to prevent South Viet-Nam from making remarkable economic and social progress, while hunger and misery made a mockery of the Communist claims to have created a paradise in North Viet-Nam. The success of the new nation to the south doubtless prompted the renewed and stronger Communist effort to destroy it. This assault is directed not just against soldiers but against the village school teacher, the village extension worker, the malaria eradication team, the local tax collector, the rural postal carrier.

This is a prime example of what the Communists call a "war

of national liberation." In reality it is a gangster war of horror and assassination. The stakes are greater than South Viet-Nam itself; the independence of all the peoples of Southeast Asia is involved.

In the last several months the United States has substantially increased its assistance to the people of South Viet-Nam. You are helping there in significant and growing ways, but there is more for all of us to do in that situation. We should like to see many other free nations also lend a helping hand, for aggression against Southeast Asia must not be allowed to succeed.

While we are determined to check aggression, we persistently seek areas of overlapping interest with the Communist nations. We were encouraged a few years ago when the Soviet Union joined Australia, the United States and other nations in the treaty on Antarctica. . . .

I have been speaking of our policies toward the Communist world. Let me turn for a moment to the great constructive task: the building of the strength of the free world.

One of the bastions of the free world is Western Europe, which has attained levels of wellbeing and rates of economic growth beyond the dreams of a decade ago. At the same time it has made dramatic progress toward integration—integration which is settling for all time the historic enmities which led to two world wars.

Is it really possible to comprehend what it means in our own minds that after 500 or 600 years we are just about at the point where we can say, "World wars will not start over intra-Western European conflicts"? How much that can mean to your country and mine, which have been in two world wars because of those conflicts.

And now the United Kingdom seeks admission to the Common Market. We hope these negotiations will succeed. In our view the more comprehensive integration of Western Europe would add immensely to the strength and the stability and the security of the entire free world. But we recognize that it would require adjustments by all of us, for we stand at the threshold of a new trading world. The challenge is whether it is to be an open system.

Our response to this challenge is the President's trade expansion program, now before our Congress. Our purpose is to negotiate major reductions in the Common Market's tariff in return for similar reductions in our own tariff. The heart of our policy is to open further the two great common markets—that of Europe and that of the fifty American States—to the goods of the free world. We remain opposed to any drift of Europe toward a closed economic society, or to new preferential arrangements related to the Common Market.

We hope that Australia, similar in so many ways to the United States, will wish to join us in freeing further the channels of trade and specifically in tariff negotiations to this end with the enlarged Common Market within the framework of GATT.

Tomorrow night in Wellington I shall say more about trade and some of these other questions, and I hope you may regard my talk there as coupled with my remarks tonight. If we can deal with these practical trade problems as practical problems, I am sure that we can find answers which deal with our vital interests and can satisfy the needs of both our countries, because we, too, have some economic problems with the prospective Common Market, just as we know you do.

### AID TO THE UNDERDEVELOPED NATIONS

I should like to emphasize here, however, the crucial importance of our assistance to the hungry half of the world where the concepts of human liberty and dignity are so often threatened by mass poverty. Here the Communists seek to play upon frustration, internal weaknesses and old resentments. But the advanced countries of the free world have more solid resources—not only superior material and technical resources but the spiritual and humanitarian resources of democratic societies. To apply these to the building of the underdeveloped nations is a task for the entire free-world community.

Australia is already making a very substantial contribution through the Colombo Plan and otherwise. We know also that you have opened the doors of your universities to thousands of students from Asian countries and that many of these students receive financial help from your Government. In helping to build a peaceful world community you also keep alive one of the commandments of the frontier society from which we both have sprung, that of helping your neighbor in his adversity.

I hope you will indulge me for a moment while I cite a few figures indicating what my countrymen are devoting to this dual task of protecting and building the free world. We maintain more than 2,800,000 men under arms. Of these—perhaps you hadn't realized—nearly 1,100,000 are deployed outside the continental United States, on land or afloat.

We have more than forty allies. We are extending technical and financial and, in some cases, military aid to many other nations. Altogether we are providing direct financial assistance to approximately seventy-five countries.

These outlays for defending and building the free world amount, this year, to nearly $54,000,000,000, or 24,000,000,000 Australian pounds.

I don't need to say this to you people, who are putters in this business, but we do have to say it to many of our friends in these other countries because they seem to think that we have some magic mountain out of which we can shovel gold that makes no difference to anyone. These are taxpayers' dollars. They total close to 10 per cent of our gross national product and average approximately $300 for every man, woman and child in the United States. Additional funds are sent abroad by our philanthropic foundations or privately invested by companies and individuals.

And I hope that you will sometimes agree—and I'm sure you do agree—that at least we are trying to do our share.

Our investment in the peaceful exploration of space also is substantial. Next year it will be about $3,800,000,000, or 1,700,-000,000 Australian pounds. And it will rise in ensuing years.

PROJECT MERCURY

We are grateful to you for your indispensable assistance in Project Mercury and in the whole field of space research and exploration. I think first of the cooperation of your Government and your scientists and technicians. And I would remind you that we are working together to build the most powerful radio telescope in the world, to be located near this city. I think also—and no American can avoid it these days—I think also of the citizens of Perth, who lighted the path of Colonel Glenn on his historic triple orbit of the globe. They touched the hearts of all his countrymen—indeed, I think I may say, of hundreds of millions of other citizens of the free world whose hearts were with him. (Incidentally, judging from my own experience, many of those hearts were beating much faster than Colonel Glenn's during those memorable hours.)

.     .     .

*Our Duties in the Pacific*

*After the ANZUS Council Meeting in Canberra, Secretary Rusk made a one-day visit to New Zealand.*

. . . . The long association between New Zealanders and Americans began during the Pacific whaling and sealing operations of the early nineteenth century. An American consulate was opened at the Bay of Islands in 1839.

But over and beyond these commercial associations, which continue at the present time, Mr. Prime Minister, Americans and New Zealanders committed their courage and their resources in voyages of discovery and exploration in Antarctica. In latter years, for example, Sir Hubert Wilkins was sponsored by the American Geographic Society when he made his epic flight over Graham Land.

Portion of address at Parliamentary Dinner, Wellington, New Zealand, May 10, 1962.

Our own Admiral Richard Byrd looked upon New Zealand sincerely as his second home. The monument recently erected on Mount Victoria is a testimonial not only to Byrd's work but to the good will and friendship of the people of New Zealand for Americans. And we are grateful for the warm hospitality so graciously extended by all New Zealanders, and especially by the people of Christchurch, to Byrd's successors, the personnel of Operation Deepfreeze.

These congenial special connections are but a few of the strands in the stout fabric of our friendship. We are woven together by common language, common insitutions, common purpose, common belief in the rights of man and in government by the people and for the people and of the people.

When I think of the democracy of New Zealand I think of an observation made in 1835 by the young Frenchman, Alexis de Tocqueville, in his book *Democracy in America*. In the introduction he wrote: ". . . amongst the novel objects that attracted my attention during my stay in the United States, nothing struck me more forcibly than the general equality of condition among the people. I readily discovered the prodigious influence which this primary fact exercised on the whole course of society."

The "general equality of condition among the people" is noteworthy in your society also. New Zealand stands as a leader among the nations in providing for the social welfare of its people. And you are justified in being proud—more proud than we can be—of the racial harmony you have achieved. You have come as close as any nation to realizing in practice some of the great truths of the American Declaration of Independence, that all men are born equal, that "they are endowed by their Creator with certain unalienable Rights, that among these are Life, Liberty and the pursuit of Happiness."

Together we have fought to defend our common way of life. As I said last night in Canberra, many tens of thousands of Americans know from direct personal experience how good it is to have Australians and New Zealanders at their side in times of peril. One of those Americans is our Ambassador to New Zealand [Anthony B. Akers]. Another, who also commanded a PT-boat, had a close call in the South Pacific but lived to fight another day and to occupy the highest office in my country. President Kennedy asked me to convey to the people of New Zealand his warmest regards and best wishes.

## COMMITMENTS IN ANZUS AND SEATO

We stand today shoulder to shoulder in the defense of liberty. We are allies through ANZUS and SEATO. In ANZUS we have just had a most useful meeting in Canberra. ANZUS is securely rooted in common purposes and, indeed, common necessities. I can do no better than to repeat the words spoken by my old and dear friend Sir Carl Berendsen, then your distinguished Ambassador to the United States, when the ANZUS treaty was signed on September 1, 1951:

> The treaty therefore rests upon the solid basis of common interests and ideals, upon the regard and affection of the respective peoples, upon their common desire for peace and upon their common determination to resist aggression. It reflects also the inescapable facts of geography on the one hand and, on the other, the especial perils to which the Pacific may be exposed in the course of this world-wide conflict between liberty and slavery with which the whole of mankind is today oppressed.

Beyond ANZUS, we have our common obligation through SEATO to defend Southeast Asia against aggression. This is a commitment of vital importance. In fulfilling it, we on our side shall do whatever may be necessary.

## THE ISLAND WORLD OF THE PACIFIC

Another deep and abiding interest which you and we share is in the stability and welfare of the great island world between North Cape and Hawaii. Although few New Zealanders or Americans gave the matter much thought, until January of this year our countries actually shared a common frontier in the Pacific: that between American Samoa and your former Trust Territory of Western Samoa. The fact that we were hardly conscious of facing each other across an international boundary is, I think, a confirmation of our close relations.

But when I think of stability in the island world I do not mean stagnation or lack of progress. The peoples of the Pacific Islands are expanding their horizons and developing their skills at an increasing rate. Their aspirations are keeping pace with their development. While the dependent territories of the Pacific vary in their level of development, all of them are being brought increasingly into the dynamic 1960s.

To the United States and New Zealand, to our ANZUS partner Australia, and to our European associates in the South Pacific Commission, this trend presents both a challenge and an opportunity. We must assist the people of the island territories in making economic, social and political progress. We must do this in a cooperative manner, without imposing arbitrary economic barriers or new spheres of economic influence.

To carry forward this task, while preserving peace and stability in the region, obviously will call for wisdom and experience on the part of the administering powers. And for much of that wisdom and experience I am sure we shall find ourselves turning to you, in face of the record which you have established in that regard. You have made a notable contribution through the skillful and understanding manner in which you have administered the Trust Territory of Western Samoa and prepared the way for its transition to independence.

## U.S. NUCLEAR TESTS

There is, of course, another aspect of the Pacific Islands scene that commands our attention at present. My country is carrying out a series of nuclear tests, based on Christmas and Johnston Islands. I know that you are aware that President Kennedy's decision to conduct these tests was made with great reluctance, only after examining carefully every possible alternative. The Soviet resumption of testing on a massive scale and the unyielding Soviet refusal to agree to a meaningful test ban treaty gave us no other rational choice. To have decided otherwise would have been a betrayal of our responsibility for the defense of the free world.

. . . . My country has expended very large sums in assisting the underdeveloped countries. And we have now a program of aid geared to the needs of systematic and long-term development. But we think the task is one for all the advanced countries of the free world—and even for those which may not have large economic resources but do have skills which others lack.

New Zealand is to be congratulated for its fine accomplishments under the Colombo Plan. And if there is a New Zealander who has a chance to be in New Delhi, for example, let me urge you to savor a thrill of quiet satisfaction by visiting the All-India Institute of Medical Sciences, which was launched by an initial £1,000,000 grant by New Zealand under the Colombo Plan. One of the great institutions of Asia has now appeared on the basis of that remarkable initiative and encouragement first given by this country to India.

We are struck also by the technical assistance that has been provided by countries of the Far East with limited resources—in some cases countries which themselves are receiving aid. I am thinking in this case, for example, of India itself. And this is all to the good. We must all extend ourselves to do what we can, regardless of our size, our population, our wealth. Every bit helps, both materially and in promoting good feeling among men. . . .

In this common effort, agricultural surpluses are more of an asset than we have perhaps realized. This ability to produce more food and fiber than we can consume or readily market—which you and our Australian friends and a few other countries share with us—has caused problems for us and among us. But let us remind ourselves that these are the kinds of problems with which most of the people of the world would be delighted to be afflicted. For in some cases they are problems of abundance—although we recognize that in your case they are the problems of furnishing the sinews of your national existence.

Nowhere is the contrast in efficiency, however, between communism and the free way of life more evident than in food production. Wherever the Communists take control, food production seems to falter and tends to decline. East Germany used to produce a food surplus; now it has a food deficit. The Soviet Union is continuously beset with difficulties in food production. The record of Communist China is even more disastrous; hundreds of millions of Chinese live on the edge of subsistence.

We have been using portions of our surplus of food and fiber to assist the less developed countries. In carrying out these programs we have taken care to assure that they do not interfere with the normal marketings of other nations which export agricultural products.

As you know from our recent initiative in the Food and Agriculture Organization, we think there is an opportunity for collective international action among all agricultural producing nations to explore new techniques of making this rich bounty available for the welfare of the less developed countries. But at the same time we must press ahead with the search for collective means of bringing supply into reasonable balance with effective demand. We know from experience that a decline in agricultural prices does not automatically result in less production but, on the contrary, may stimulate the producer to try to increase his income by producing still more. In the United States one of our most stubborn problems has been to maintain and improve farm income while reducing agricultural surpluses and costs to the taxpayer.

I am aware that the economy of New Zealand is basically oriented to animal agriculture. The United States now takes more than two-thirds of your beef and veal. And you are our principal supplier of carpet wool—at the rate, I am told, of more than fifty-two million pounds a year.

The prosperity of our agriculture also depends to a large extent on exports. About one-quarter of our overseas earnings come from agricultural exports. American farmers, especially the producers of wheat, cotton and rice among other important items, have a tremendous stake in expanding trade.

Sound international arrangements for bringing supply and effective demand into better balance will require a high level of responsibility on the part of both major producers and major consumers. Such arrangements should, we think, work toward the goal of regard to the most efficient producer—and under any such system New Zealand would be in first-class condition.

Here again is an area in which New Zealand and the United States are confronted with similar problems. While we think we can see the right objective, we do not pretend to be certain of the best road to it. We expect that the experience and judgment of your people will be helpful in this challenging task.

### TRADE IN BASIC RAW MATERIALS

We must also be prepared to concert with the producers of basic raw materials—by and large the less developed countries—to prevent collapses of prices which would wipe out their hard-won gains and perhaps plunge them into economic crises.

Here, too, producer and consumers should be prepared to seek international arrangements stabilizing prices of key commodities, thus providing an indispensable breathing spell during which longer term solutions may be found. Some countries may find their solutions through diversification and industrialization, others through the discovery of new markets for old materials. The process of economic development generally will create new demands for many raw materials and encourage the transfer of capital and manpower from the production of commodities which are chronically in surplus.

Perhaps the most difficult problem for the advanced nations is to accept low-cost industrial products manufactured in the developing countries. But if these countries are to develop they must be able to sell their fabricated goods on our markets. The underdeveloped and the advanced countries must work together in finding a solution to this problem. The former must be conscious of the impact of their goods on established markets, and the latter must be prepared to open wider their own doors.

In the great overall task of assisting the underdeveloped nations to modernize their economies and societies, we expect to see an integrated Western Europe play an increasing role. As Western European production continues to rise, more of it becomes available for this purpose. Likewise Japan is able to play an increasing role in assisting the development of other countries. It falls to all the affluent countries of the Pacific to assume special responsibility for the economic development and stability of this region.

### THE COMMON PURPOSE OF ALL MANKIND

The new era now unfolding, of partnership between the advanced nations and the underdeveloped, is far better than the old order. It rests on the truth that mankind is one and on a common purpose to make life better for the human race. There could be no more challenging task, no greater mission. For in helping to build the free world, as in defending and extending freedom, we cherish you as among our closest friends and stoutest comrades.

In some of the last words of Franklin D. Roosevelt: "The only limit to our realization of tomorrow will be our doubts of today. Let us move forward with strong and active faith."

## *The Importance of Japan*

*In June, 1961, during the visit of Prime Minister Hayata Ikeda to Washington, Japan and the United States agreed to establish a joint Cabinet committee to meet annually. The first meeting was held in Hakone, Japan, November 2-4, 1961. Secretary Rusk led a delegation of seven, including five members of the U.S. Cabinet.*

Portion of opening statement at meeting of Joint U.S.-Japan Committee on Trade and Economic Affairs, Hakone, Japan, November 2, 1961.

We shall talk frankly and intimately here together. I hope—indeed I am sure—that we shall each be wiser when we have concluded this interchange.

We are meeting together as partners. We have, in broad measure, common beliefs and a common dedication. Our peoples are committed to the principles of a free and open society. They hope and work for a world order of peace with justice. These shared convictions and aspirations are the firm foundation of our partnership.

We have other things in common. Japan and the United States are two of the world's leading industrial powers. The peoples of both our countries possess the magic key to industrial achievement; they have the genius to create and adapt technology and to organize their resources for extraordinarily productive ends.

As advanced industrial powers our countries have mutual interests of a special kind—and mutual responsibilities. Not the least of our responsibilities is to assist the less-developed nations. President Kennedy has said, with great wisdom, that this decade of the sixties is the decade of development. There can be no decision more challenging or worthy than for the peoples of great powers, such as Japan and the United States, to devote a growing part of their resources to help the underdeveloped nations advance toward that level of economic competence where they can play useful and constructive roles in today's turbulent world.

We shall talk together during the next two days not only as friends but as customers of each other. In the area of commerce, as in other areas, we are mutually dependent. We are your best customer; after Canada, you are our best customer. Last year our total merchandise trade with each other amounted to more than $2.5 billion. This year it will be larger still.

As our two countries continue to become more prosperous, the volume of our trade should continue to grow. I see no necessary limit to the expansion of this mutually profitable exchange of goods, and we shall certainly seek to encourage it. My government, under President Kennedy, is committed to a liberal commercial policy, and I know that this also is the case with your government under Prime Minister Ikeda.

And now, if my colleagues will indulge me, I should like to close on a personal note. My association with Japan, as some of you know, goes back a number of years. I have played a small role in the recent history of the relations between our two countries. I have been honored with the friendship of many of your people. I am deeply gratified that our meeting has given me the opportunity to return to Japan at this time. It is good to see old friends and to visit again this beautiful land. For me, our session is already a success because it has brought me back among you.

*Remarks at dinner given by the Japanese Cabinet Ministers attending the Hakone Conference, Fujiya Hotel, Miyanoshita, November 2, 1961.*

. . . . The atmosphere here at Hakone, where we have had a beautiful sunny day, reminds me of two wholly different kinds of international discussions—as different as the night and day. I have been involved in both types during recent weeks. The one is a discussion between those who are deeply committed to common purposes, who understand what each other is trying to do, who can trust each other's purposes and share mutual aspirations. In such talks, the object is to find the most appropriate means for accomplishing what we are agreed we should try to achieve. That is the kind of talk we are having here at Hakone.

The other type of negotiation is between those who cannot agree on the kind of world in which we want to live, where trust and confidence are not present. Negotiation becomes exceedingly difficult simply because communication itself is almost impossible.

This contrast emphasizes our appreciation for the warmth of the welcome with which you have received us, a welcome equalled only by the beauty in which we find ourselves in this lovely place. Of course, we face problems; they are complex and difficult rather than simple. For many of them I am confident that we can find answers; there may be some with which we must wrestle a while longer. But a problem unsolved must be remembered against the background of all that is right between us, the things which go well, the agreements achieved, the infinity of threads which bind our two peoples together in peace.

On behalf of President Kennedy and the American people, we thank you, Mr. Minister, and the people of Japan for their traditional hospitality on this heartwarming occasion.

## Our Continuing Interest in Korea

*Following the Hakone Conference in Japan, Secretary Rusk paid a brief visit to the Republic of Korea, a nation with whose affairs he had been intimately involved as Assistant Secretary of State for Far Eastern Affairs during the first two years of the Korean war. As his remarks indicate, he had visited Korea in 1951 at a low ebb in the war.*

Mr. Prime Minister, on behalf of President Kennedy and the American people, I thank you most sincerely for this warm welcome which you and your colleagues have given us; and I salute the officers and men of this distinguished honor guard which has made our reception so impressive. It is a source of real satisfaction to me to be able to gratify a long-felt desire to visit Korea again. I was last in your country in 1951. At that time, circumstances, of which you and we have a painful memory, prevented

Reply to welcoming address of Prime Minister of Republic of Korea, General Yo Chan Song, Kimpo Airport, Seoul, November 4, 1961.

my leaving Pusan, and I was unable to come to your brave capital city.

. . . . We have noted with gratification the zeal and energy with which Chairman Pak [of the Supreme Council for National Reconstruction] and his colleagues have tackled the problems which historically have confronted South Korea and which have been most acute since the end of the conflict so treacherously begun by the Communists in 1950. Progress has been made, and I am confident that with persistent cooperative effort by all sectors of the Korean people, guided by wise leadership, much more will be accomplished in the months ahead.

The United States has assisted in no small way in the rehabilitation and regeneration of your country which was devastated so clearly by the fighting of ten years ago. Let me reassure you firmly and solemnly that my government will continue to assist you as necessary and in conformity with the progress and development you yourselves can achieve. We know you are striving for accelerated economic and social development while ever menaced by Communist forces massed north of the demilitarized zone. We stand alongside of you with many thousand American troops in the United Nations command, which provides the shield behind which you can pursue your goal for your families. In a word, Mr. Prime Minister, we are allies, and we are friends. It is as a friend of Korea and its delightful people, a friend deeply interested in your safety, welfare and increasing prosperity that I visit you today. It is also as a representative of my government which is a friend and ally of Korea. This makes me doubly glad to be here.

## China and the United Nations

*Since 1950 the Soviet bloc, with the support of some other countries, has attempted to expel the representatives of the Government of the*

*Republic of China from the United Nations and all its organs and to replace them with representatives of the Chinese Communist regime. The U.S. has consistently opposed the entry of the Peiping regime to the U.N. and its component bodies.*

. . . . The problem on the Chinese seat in the United Nations is essentially this. Since about 1950 we have been trying to deal with that question through what is called a moratorium, that is, a vote at the beginning of each session of the General Assembly which would simply say: We will not consider this question until next year.

Now, this moratorium has been successful in postponing this issue for about ten years. I helped to invent the moratorium when I was in the Department before, under Mr. Truman.

In the last three or four years our delegations to the United Nations have been reporting that there is an increasing feeling in the United Nations, particularly with the large number of new members coming in, that this moratorium formula will no longer suffice to deal with the question, that there will be more and more delegations who will think that at least the question ought to be debated on its merits and not be simply postponed, regardless of their attitude on the merits of the question.

Now, this is the essence of the parliamentary problem of the General Assembly of the United Nations, where there is no veto, where a bare majority can, in the normal course of events, deal with procedural questions.

The principal problem from the point of view of those of us who recognize and support the Government of the Republic of China on Formosa is that this question might come to a vote as a credentials question, that is, as a procedural question aimed at the rather simple issue as to which delegation shall be accredited by the General Assembly to occupy the seat called China.

Excerpt from news conference at Chicago, June 27, 1961.

We ourselves believe that this would be a very serious step for the General Assembly to take, because this is not just a technical procedural question of credentials; it is a problem of the most far-reaching political importance. It is of great importance, of course, to the Republic of China on Formosa. It is of very great importance to the United States. And we believe it is important to the U.N.

So, in the face of this parliamentary problem, it is going to be necessary for all of the members, including ourselves and the Government of the Republic of China, to consider how this issue can be handled from a parliamentary point of view in the General Assembly of the United Nations. . . .

*At the Sixteenth General Assembly, the U.S. abandoned the moratorium formula and, in conjunction with Australia, Colombia, Italy and Japan, introduced a resolution declaring that any proposal to change the representation of China is an "important question" requiring a two-thirds majority under article 18 of the U.N. Charter. The General Assembly adopted this resolution by a vote of 61 to 34, with 7 abstentions. It rejected the Soviet proposal to seat the Communist Chinese by a vote of 48 to 37, with 19 abstentions.*

## No Settlement in Sight

*Since August 1, 1955, the U.S. and the Chinese Communist regime have engaged in talks at the ambassadorial level. These were begun in Geneva and transferred to Warsaw, Poland. Up to September 1, 1962, there had been 112 of these ambassadorial talks.*

REP. HARRIS B. MCDOWELL, JR. of Delaware: Those meetings are still continuing in Warsaw?

SECRETARY RUSK: Yes, sir. But no progress has been reflected there, because Peiping insists that the *sine qua non* for any normal relationship is the abandonment of Formosa.

Excerpt from testimony before House Foreign Affairs Committee, April 9, 1962.

# XI. AFRICA, THE MIDDLE EAST AND SOUTH ASIA

## Our Policy in Regard to the Congo

United States policy with regard to the Congo is consistent with our general foreign policy and our attitude toward Africa as a whole. Briefly stated, that attitude is (a) to help the African peoples form societies and governments that will be truly independent and consonant with their own consciences and cultures; (b) to maintain and promote the strong ties of culture, friendship and economic life that already exist between the new nations of Africa and the nations of Europe and America; and (c) to cooperate in every way acceptable to both the Africans and ourselves as these new countries strive to produce the political stability, economic progress and level of education that are essential to a free society.

In pursuit of these broad objectives, the United States has strongly supported efforts to preserve the territorial integrity of the Congo. Like almost every country in the world, the United States has firmly opposed efforts by Kasai, Katanga, Orientale or any other province to secede. This is our policy because there is no legal, moral or practical basis for the secession of any of these

Statement before the Subcommittee on African Affairs of the Senate Foreign Relations Committee, Jaunary 18, 1962.

provinces; nor is there reasonable evidence that secession is the will of the majority of the population of any province involved.

Just how did the United Nations became involved in the Congo? Memories tend to fade, even after only eighteen months.

You will recall that tribal fighting and mutiny in the Congolese Army occurred in the first week of July 1960, immediately after the Congo became independent. During the night of July 8 many Europeans fled from Léopoldville, and Belgium announced the return of Belgian troops to protect life and property.

The new Congolese Government reacted violently to the return of Belgian forces. On July 12 that Government requested urgent dispatch of United Nations forces to the Congo to protect the national territory of the country and avoid a threat to international peace.

On the same day on which the Congo Government requested United Nations aid, it also requested direct United States military aid. Three days later the Congolese President [Joseph Kasavubu] and Prime Minister [Patrice Lumumba] cabled Chairman Khrushchev, "We have to ask the Soviet Union's intervention, should the western camp not stop its aggression."

The urgent problem was to restore public order and to permit the withdrawal of the Belgian troops without leading to internal collapse in the Congo.

President Eisenhower rejected from the start any direct intervention by the major powers. In reply to the Congo Government's request for United States forces, the United States stated that any assistance to the Government of the Congo should be through the United Nations and not by any unilateral action by any one country, the United States included.

Why was this decision taken? The alternative to United Nations intervention would have been violence and chaos and a ready-made opportunity for Soviet exploitation, which the United States would have been compelled to counter. There was no alternative to limited intervention on the part of the United Nations if a direct confrontation of the great powers in the heart of Africa was to be avoided. Thus the United States strongly supported United Nations action in the Congo. Looking back it seems obvious now that this was the right choice.

SOVIET EFFORTS TO GAIN FOOTHOLD

It seemed clear by August 1960 that, if the Congo was to remain free and independent, United States support of the United Nations would have to be sufficient to permit United Nations operation in the face of a Soviet onslaught. Despite United Nations resolutions to the contrary, the Soviet Union was pouring personnel, materials and political agents into the Congo to establish what the Communists hoped would be a foothold in the heart of Africa. Secretary-General Dag Hammarskjold challenged the Russians because of evidence which accumulated in August and September that each Soviet Ilyushin aircraft was bringing in political agents. When the Soviets refused to halt these activities, the United Nations Command closed major airfields in the Congo to all but United Nations traffic. Shortly thereafter President Kasavubu ordered the Soviet and Czechoslovak Embassies to close, and several hundred Russians and Czechoslovaks were forced to leave the Congo.

It was this blocking by the United Nations of the Soviet takeover scheme that provoked the Soviet Union to declare political war on Secretary-General Hammarskjold and to begin the campaign for a troika directorate that would handcuff the world organization. The Communist bloc has refused to finance any part of the U.N.'s operations to restore political stability and bring economic progress to the Congo.

The United States supported the first government of the Congo—a government that was a compromise under which Joseph Kasavubu, a moderate trained in a Catholic seminary, became President and Patrice Lumumba became Premier.

Lumumba's ouster from office by President Kasavubu in September 1960 was followed by a period of political turmoil. Not until July 1961 did the parliamentarians again meet to give approval to a government. Despite appeals by U.N. officials and American and European diplomats, Katangan Provincial President Moise Tshombe, after hesitations, decided not to let his party's parliamentarians participate in the formation of a new government. Thus he chose to miss an opportunity to play an important role on the national stage. Even without the hoped-for support of Katanga, moderate forces prevailed in the new government.

Kasavubu, of course, remained Head of State and Commander in Chief of the Armed Forces. The new Prime Minister and Defense Minister was Cyrille Adoula, an able and dynamic leader of a trade union organization that is affiliated with the free trade union movement, the ICFTU. [Antoine] Gizenga was given the post of First Vice Premier in the new government.

Most of the forty-two-man Cabinet were true Congolese nationalists who were moderate in their views. The United States view was that the Adoula government was not only the legal product of parliamentary process but that it represented the only hope of achieving a stable, secure Congo.

It was obvious, however, that there were two main dangers to the Adoula government: the political insurrection of Gizenga, who in effect withdrew from the government and attempted to create a new redoubt in Stanleyville, and the continued armed secession of the Katanga. The first was a political problem that had to be dealt with by the Congolese themselves. This effort came to fruition on January 15, when the Congolese Parliament voted overwhelmingly to censure Gizenga, thus removing him from office. The U.N. responded rapidly and effectively to Prime Minister Adoula's appeal for aid in restoring law and order in Stanleyville in the face of armed insurrection

PROBLEMS OF KATANGA SECESSION

The problem of the Katanga secession was more difficult to deal with because it involved the active participation of foreign mercenaries who had taken up arms against both the U.N. and the Congo Government. So strong were the sentiments of nationalism of the Congolese people regarding the secession of southern Katanga that it became clear that no government would survive in the Congo unless it demonstrated progress in reintegrating the Katanga. It was obvious that failure to bring the Katanga back into the Congo would mean civil war and the ensuing chaos on which the Communists have capitalized in other parts of the world.

It was also clear that the moderate strength of Mr. Tshombe and his party leaders and the economic wealth of their area were needed in the central government. U.N. officials and U.S. and European diplomats therefore made repeated efforts to achieve the reintegration of the Katanga through conciliation and peaceful means. One of the difficulties was that foreign elements, not responsive to their own governments, sought to convince Mr. Tshombe that through military force he could maintain his secession.

The U.N. sought to remove the mercenaries, in accordance with the February 21, 1961, resolution, so as to clear the air for a peaceful settlement. The mercenaries refused to leave, cut off the U.N.'s lines of communication, and resorted to violence. The U.N. fought to protect itself and to establish conditions under which it could pursue its objectives with reasonable security.

While it deplored the loss of life and the isolated acts of barbarism that grew out of warfare, the U.S. supported the U.N. in its limited military action because the alternative was to acquiesce in Katanga's secession and permit the civil strife that inevitably would result in a big-power clash.

When Tshombe indicated a desire to negotiate, President Kennedy set in motion efforts which resulted in Mr. Tshombe's meeting with Prime Minister Adoula at Kitona. We are pleased by the statesmanship shown by Prime Minister Adoula and Mr. Tshombe in reaching an agreement at this meeting. Mr. Tshombe has indicated that he will abide by the agreement he signed at Kitona. If so, the Congo's political crisis may be moving toward an end and both the Congolese and the U.N. can turn their attention from military effort to the peaceful task of restoring the economy of one of the wealthiest countries in Africa.

The U.N. role in military matters can be brought to an end with a political settlement on constitutional and other questions among the Congolese themselves and through U.N. assistance with the training and organizing of the Congo's own security forces. Technical assistance in administrative, economic and social fields will undoubtedly be required for a considerable time. It is simple but correct to say that the U.N.'s purpose is to help achieve as rapidly as possible the conditions which will permit the U.N. to withdraw, leaving full responsibility to the Congolese themselves. We support them in that objective.

## Our Purposes in Africa

Q. Mr. Secretary, as far as Africa is concerned, I wonder if you'd explain our policy there. Some of our allies, like Britain, France, Portugal, feel that we are fanning the flames of national-ism a little too quickly for them. Would you comment on that?

A. I think the deep commitments of the American people on such matters are pretty widely known. We are a people who take pretty seriously the notion that governments derive their just powers from the consent of the governed. We have felt that satisfactory relationships between a Western people and a non-Western people can be established, provided they rest on con-sent.

There are many independent countries, members of the United Nations, who at one time were part of the British Empire. In general, the conditions under which they became independent, given the enlightenment of British policy, has left the way open for a close, friendly and cordial relationship between these inde-pendent countries and the mother country.

The relations between many of the French-speaking Afri-can states and France have been very good, because of the con-ditions under which they separated, or because each side decided that it wanted to sustain good relationships.

Now, we don't see how the relations between the West and the non-West can be built up over any period of time on any satis-factory basis unless this vital element of consent is present. We

Excerpts from interview in *U.S. News and World Report,* issue of January 29, 1962, published at Washington. Copyright 1962, United States News Publishing Corporation.

don't go out and conduct crusades on this matter. The demand for independence is present within these countries, the nationalist movements are there, and we think that accommodation has to be made with them.

Q. How does our policy on self-determination fit into our program for a central Government in the Congo?

A. Well, if you applied self-determination to every tribe or group in the Congo that might assert it, you might have twenty-five or thirty or even more units.

Mr. Tshombe's immediate supporters make up about a third of the population of Katanga. [Tshombe is President of Katanga.] If one were to insist that South Katangans should have self-determination, then the Balubas in the north of Katanga would want some self-determination. We see no outcome down that trail except a breaking up into many factions of a country which could, under some sort of a federal system, deal with its problems.

A principle like self-determination is extremely difficult to apply in detail. In the broadest sweep of national movements it has considerable validity, but it does not lend itself to an exact basis for constitutional construction in country after country. After all, I came from the part of the country where we tried to exercise a certain self-determination once upon a time.

. . . . Q. Isn't much of this unrest stimulated by the Communists? Any country could produce this nationalistic trend that you speak of—

A. I think that you'll find—at least I have found in talking with many leaders of these newly independent countries—that they recognize that there is a great problem, and there is a moderation among many of them with respect to remaining problems of colonialism in terms of timing, in terms of circumstance.

But what they are very much afraid of is that the notion that a country is not ready for self-government would be used to prolong colonial regimes far beyond their time. . . .

Q. Do you consider South Africa to be a remaining problem of colonialism? Or just what do you consider South Africa to be?

A. I think the basic problem there is a multiracial society which has not been able to work out satisfactory relations among

the races. It is not, strictly speaking, I think, a colonial problem
—any more than I would suppose that some of our problems here
are colonial.

Q. Just what are U.S. objectives vis-à-vis South Africa?

A. We do not agree with them on the racial policies which
they apply within their own country. We have made our disagreement known. But, on a great many other international problems, we work closely with them and would like to cooperate
with them. . . .


## Our Interest in CENTO

*The Central Treaty Organization, or CENTO,
is a defensive alliance of Turkey, Iran, Pakistan
and the United Kingdom, formed in 1955. Before the withdrawal of Iraq, one of the original
signatories, in 1959, it was known as the Baghdad Pact. Although not a member of CENTO,
the United States is pledged to assist all three of
the Middle Eastern members in repelling aggression, through bilateral agreements signed
March 5, 1959, as well as through NATO in the
case of Turkey, and through SEATO in the
case of Pakistan. The United States is represented on the CENTO committees and sends*

Address at opening public meeting of the ninth session of the
CENTO Ministerial Council, Ankara, April 27, 1961.

*observer delegations to the sessions of the CENTO Ministerial Council.*

. . . . Anyone who surveys the present world scene must conclude that there are certain points of real danger, but it would be a blind or foolish man who did not also see the great promise of the future. The problem of our times is to meet, to deal with and to remove the points of danger, but even more vigorously to build on the promise.

The free world is growing steadily in vitality and in the development of its potentials to improve the economic and social standards of its people. There is abroad in the world a new vigor and liveliness in the hopes of free men and in the measures being undertaken to bring about their realization.

It is all the more remarkable that such gains are being made at a time when free nations must devote a considerable portion of their resources to defense purposes, to provide for the common defense while promoting the general welfare.

Self-defense is a prime responsibility of all nations. If it is to be effective and adequate, cooperation is essential. This is the underlying truth of CENTO. The zeal and dedication which CENTO members have shown in their efforts to find solutions to common problems is most impressive. I also find impressive what has been accomplished by the Organization through its several committees. The going has not always been easy, but hurdles are to be surmounted, not accepted. Though still young in years, CENTO has weathered its early trials; it has remained undeterred by verbal attack, it has shown dedication to tasks at hand, and it has achieved results in a number of fields of endeavor which inspire respect for the past and confidence in the future.

These efforts have never been, nor will they be, aggressive, for CENTO challenges no one. It directs its efforts toward a common defense against those who might seek to challenge its partners.

But CENTO's energies are wisely not limited to military defense alone. Its members have understood the need to direct their individual and collective efforts to protecting the institutions of a free society and obtaining freedom from want and fear. They are knitting the bonds of friendship and respect and also the bonds of common aspirations as they work together to deal effectively with the economic and social problems that beset their citizens, as do men everywhere.

In these high tasks of defense and development, the United States is glad to associate itself with the members of CENTO. The United States has sought in the past to play a helpful part in supporting the member states' cooperative defense efforts and remains today as convinced as ever that collaboration continues to be the surest means for achieving this objective. We pledge our continued cooperation for our mutual security, in the knowledge that security for all means security for each.

As President Kennedy recently stated, we live at a very special moment in history, when many parts of the world, including the area in which the CENTO regional members are situated, are determined to maintain their independence and to modernize their ways of life. The needs are enormous, not merely to resist the pressures of those who would extend their influence through direct and subversive means, but even more importantly to enable economic growth and political democracy to develop hand in hand. It is our continued purpose, together with others who have also been heavily blessed with the bounties of the industrial age, to work with those not yet so well favored who seek through mobilization of their own energies, resources and plans to meet the requirements of today and the needs of tomorrow. . . .

*Portion of address at opening of tenth session of the CENTO Ministerial Council, London, April 30, 1962.*

. . . . We are once again in the midst of various international gatherings. Last month there convened the disarmament conference in Geneva. Following this tenth session of the

CENTO Council there will be, as you know, a meeting of the NATO Council in Athens. Thereafter I plan to travel to Australia to confer with our allies of the ANZUS treaty.

In all these meetings there is one general theme, a common denominator which links the peoples of the free world—to reaffirm their determination to stand together for peace and security. Through joint efforts we seek to preserve the integrity of our homelands, to maintain and enhance our cherished traditions and institutions, and to reassert the right of free men to their own independence and freedom of choice. These are the high purposes we promote and defend, and these meetings are a useful means of concerting our actions toward the attainment of our objectives.

I should also like to note the fact that the present series of nuclear tests in which the United States and the United Kingdom are engaged is fully consonant with the collective security objectives of the free world. President Kennedy indicated, in his address on March 2, that military security requirements would compel the United States to undertake certain atmospheric tests if the Soviet Union failed to agree to an effective test ban treaty. Since that time every avenue of obtaining Soviet agreement has been explored. The Soviet Union has thus far been unwilling to agree to an effective treaty banning all nuclear testing, despite many efforts by the United States and the United Kingdom to meet its view on particulars. In the circumstances the United States has had no choice but to assume its responsibility to look to the common defense and conduct a limited series of atmospheric nuclear tests.

We know, perhaps better than many others, what it means to struggle with the dilemma for which a solution has thus far eluded us. The United States must treat the testing of nuclear weapons in the same way it approaches any other aspect of defense preparations. The arms race cannot be ended unless and until all major powers agree to do this. It remains a prime objective of U.S. policy to end all nuclear weapons testing permanently and as quickly as possible. We firmly believe that negotiations on this matter must go forward, and we will do our best to see that these negotiations are continued until testing is ended.

This tenth session of our CENTO Council affords an opportunity for us to take stock of CENTO's accomplishments, to review our purposes and objectives, and to chart our course anew in the light of that assessment. I would venture to suggest that an alliance such as this is its own excuse for being and that its chief benefit to its participants is the security provided by CENTO's existence. I suggest that we keep in mind the essential fact that CENTO's existence is an asset upon which we should continue to build.

Over the years we have succeeded in establishing the credibility of our determination to resist jointly any incursions by a potential aggressor. We have clearly demonstrated our mutual interest in defense against Communist external and internal threats. We have also recognized that security involves not only military defense but also the promotion of our general welfare. In recognition of this the United States has undertaken large economic and military assistance programs in the regional member countries. While these programs are essentially bilateral in nature, they promote our multilateral objectives in providing added strength to the CENTO region.

At the recent tenth session of the CENTO Economic Committee in Washington, it was noted that the strength of CENTO consists of the strength of each of us and that our ability to cooperate in regional enterprises is thus dependent on the soundness of our domestic arrangements. To this I would only add that, in my view, CENTO's mutually cooperative efforts are something more than the sum of its parts. Through the interchange of ideas, techniques and experience contributed by each of us toward the accomplishment of some specific goal or project have come new stimulus and capacity different in both kind and magnitude. This new force has great potential benefit for the welfare of the peoples of the CENTO area.

In sum, we of the United States delegation believe that our mutual interest in providing for our security and welfare against the continuing threat of Communist aggression is well served through CENTO. In this Council session we look forward to constructive deliberations through which these accomplishments may be continued. I bring you the greetings and best wishes of

President Kennedy and of the American people. We are happy to be here among our friends and to work with each of you toward the high objectives which you have set for CENTO.

## Our Stake in India

. . . There have been irritations between us and India in the last several months. Two great countries in opposite parts of the world with different positions, different problems, are bound to have particular points in which they are in disagreement, and sometimes they disagree rather sharply.

But the point is, here is a country of 450 million people which is the largest constitutional democracy that the world has ever seen. More people going to the polls in free, orderly elections than we have ever seen anywhere, with basic commitments with which we are familiar, basic commitments that they borrowed in part from the same people from whom we borrowed them, namely the British, Anglo-Saxon tradition of constitutional government. They have maintained that democracy in the face of some great difficulties: 450 million people, adding about ten million a year; an average income of about $70 per capita; 25 per cent of them are illiterate; a dozen or more major languages . . . ; no common language throughout the country. And yet they have made a constitutional system work along democratic lines.

We have disagreed with them and they with us on certain issues like Goa, Kashmir and nuclear testing, but we and they both have joined to support the United Nations in the Congo. They and we joined to defend the United Nations against the troika attack by the Soviet Union. The Indian chairman of the Control Commission in South Viet-Nam joined with his Canadian colleague to call attention to the fact that it was the North

Excerpt from interview on "Issues and Answers," ABC-TV network July 8, 1962.

Viet-Namese intrusion into South Viet-Nam that had stimulated this fighting in the last two years.

We will disagree on certain subjects. There is no reason why we shouldn't. India is not a satellite of ours, and we are not a satellite of India. We are great countries with vital interests all over the world. So we will have our differences. But we also have great common commitments that are important; and it would be a great mistake, I think, if we did not take an active, even if only a small, part in the Indian development program.

I don't think people realize, for example, that in the Indian third five-year plan more than $24 billions of investment are going to be needed. More than $20 billion of that will come from India itself, and less than $5 billion will come from outside resources. We and other friendly countries in the West are providing a substantial amount of that, but we are only providing as much as others in the West provide.

Our investment there, while it is large in actual terms, is relatively small in Indian terms.

So these are the great historical stakes that we have—that there be in Asia, that there be in the subcontinent, this strong constitutional democracy. . . .

# XII. TRADE AND EXCHANGES WITH THE COMMUNIST STATES

*In this section Secretary Rusk explains our policies in regard to trade and cultural exchanges with the various Communist nations and why we have extended aid to Yugoslavia and Poland. In regard to trade with Communist nations, these facts may be noted: Since 1948 the United States had used export controls to keep strategic commodities from the Soviet Union and its European satellites. Since 1950 it has maintained a total embargo on trade with Communist China and North Korea; and somewhat later this embargo was extended to North Viet-Nam. In October 1960, the U.S. embargoed*

Testimony before the House Select Committee on Export Control, October 25, 1961.

*exports to Cuba, excepting food and medicines.*
*In controlling exports of strategic goods to*
*Soviet-bloc countries, the U.S. consults and*
*coordinates with fourteen other free-world in-*
*dustrial countries through a Coordinating*
*Committee, known as Cocom.*

. . . There is one question which is central to the subject
of U.S. East-West trade control policy. That question is: Why do
we permit any trade at all with the Soviet bloc at the present
time? My answer is that we believe that the national interest is
better served by permitting the continuation of some trade than
by cutting it off entirely.

Selecting the U.S. policy with respect to trade between the
United States and the Soviet bloc which best serves U.S. interests is a difficult and complicated task. It involves broad political
and economic considerations as well as study of a mass of technical details. It is necessary to balance and reconcile long-term and
short-term factors.

I suggest we can best get to the central issues by analyzing
qualitatively and quantitatively what is now going on. For the
present I should like to concentrate on the main issue—our trade
with the Soviet Union. Later I shall comment on special considerations which have influenced our trade policies toward some
other countries of the bloc.

### TRADE WITH SOVIET UNION

From a qualitative standpoint, to start with, no licenses are
granted for weapons or specialized military equipment or for
materials of military value in the field of nuclear energy applications. Nor are any licenses approved for materials or equipment specially adapted for the production of military equipment.

On the other hand, at the opposite extreme, individual licenses are not required at all for items whose normal use is so strictly limited to the most harmless form of civilian consumer convenience as to be freely exportable under general license.

This leaves, subject to case-by-case discretion in approving or denying individual licenses, two types of items. First is equipment and supplies which can have important military as well as civilian uses—such as heavy trucks or machine tools specially designed for use in the production of heavy trucks. Secondly, overlapping in some cases with the first category, is equipment not necessarily limited to military use which embodies technology more advanced than that believed to be currently available to the Soviet Union.

Assessment of the qualitative significance of our trade must also take account of its total volume. In 1960, U.S. exports to the Soviet Union amounted to $38 million. To put this figure into perspective, it was in fact considerably less than two-tenths of 1 per cent (0.14 per cent) of our total exports. While it is not easy to estimate Soviet gross national product figures accurately, our best guess is that in 1960 their gross national product was about $231 billion, or about 6079 times the value of the goods they got from us. During 1960 the Soviet Union to our knowledge shipped as economic aid to other countries, to be paid for over a term of years, $140 million worth of goods. Thus they were able to export without current payment, resources $3\frac{1}{2}$ times as great as the goods they got from us, all of which they had to pay for.

This last is a significant point. The U.S. economy, with underutilized plant and labor, could afford without any loss to export these goods; in fact, this trade added its small bit to the strength of our domestic economy and our tax revenues. And since we required immediate repayment in goods or cash, these exports took, out of the much harder pressed and poorer Soviet economy, goods, foreign exchange or gold they could not as easily spare. By the same token, we improved our balance-of-payments situation, whose weakness has been a cause of national concern. I do not suggest that these factors should cause us to abandon all control over our trade with the Soviet Union, but I do wish to make clear that the balance of advantages and disadvantages of such trade is composed of a number of factors which must all be weighed in determining where our national interest truly lies.

### WHY DO SOVIETS BUY FROM US?

From the data I have described, it would seem clear that the Soviet Union derives only the most marginal help in its economic development for the amount of U.S. goods it receives. Why, then, do the Soviets buy from us?

The answer of course lies in qualitative factors, some general and ill definable and some perhaps quite specific. It is in this area that difficult judgments, often having to be based on somewhat inadequate facts, must be made. In assessing the qualitative value of these exports to the Soviet Union, I think it is worthwhile to make a general comment about the nature of much international trade, which, I am sure, plays its role in Soviet purchasing policy.

The United States, United Kingdom and Germany all have very large and varied machine tool industries, each capable of making machine tools for performing any kind of metalworking operation. Yet the trade between them in machine tools is very large. In 1960 the United States exported $36 million worth to the United Kingdom and $35 million to Germany. Yet we imported in that year almost $8 million of tools from the United Kingdom and close to $14 million from Germany. This same two-way flow characterized the trade in machine tools between the United Kingdom and Germany. This pattern results from minor variations in quality and performance, delivery dates, financing terms, prices, traditional business connections, brand reputations and aggressive salesmanship. Each party to these transactions believes that he has gotten the better of the exchange, and it is in the nature of trade that in most cases each is undoubtedly right.

To some extent these same factors can explain some portion of U.S. exports to the Soviet Union. It is not that our goods cannot be produced in the Soviet Union or are indispensable. Rather, it is convenient or desirable for one reason or another for the Soviets to try to buy them here. By the same token, our refusal to sell any one item is unlikely to have any major effect on Soviet economic strength or the rate of Soviet economic growth.

In fact, failure to export may only accelerate the rate of expansion of Soviet capacity in a particular area and thus make her that much sooner independent of outside sources and hence less vulnerable to pressure in time of acute conflict.

There can be, of course, cases of items in this middle ground between clearly civilian and clearly military uses in which the sheer volume of an item sought from outside suggests a large and important deficiency. Filling such a gap may make a contribution to Soviet strength of greater value than our gain from making the sale and lead us to refuse the license, especially where this will effectively cut off supply, a difficult point to which I wish to return later.

There are, however, other types of cases where a Soviet purchase seems clearly designed to secure knowledge of an advanced design or new technology by importing a few prototype models. This is giving the Soviet Union something it might take the Soviets a long time and much effort to develop in the absence of information from abroad. In these cases the impact of the export could be substantial on Soviet economic power and indirectly Soviet military strength.

In these situations, as in the case of large volume sales of key items, the disposition should be to refuse the license on grounds of the relative advantage conferred if the export were made.

It is in these two types of cases that, in my judgment, controversy can legitimately arise about individual decisions. The facts are technically complicated and often not readily available. One must take what one is able to learn and make an overall judgment. Three kinds of facts must be weighed.

First, to what extent can the item contribute to military strength? A process for making socks more efficiently is less significant than one to produce a high-quality steel or a new electronic device. Is a large copper wire order likely to help expand civilian communications or an air warning system?

Second, to what extent does the item represent a really

short supply bottleneck in the Soviet Union or a technological breakthrough they have not achieved? As Soviet technology is advancing at a very rapid rate, it becomes increasingly difficult to be sure we are ahead of them in particular fields.

Third, to what extent, if we reject the license, can the Soviets avoid the effect of our refusal simply by getting it elsewhere? This involves a fairly simple determination if the item is unavailable because it is on the Cocom control list but often a very difficult problem of comparing qualities when it is not so controlled by other potential supplying countries.

### WHY CONTINUE TO EXPORT TO SOVIETS?

The bulk of the effort of our interdepartmental system is spent on answering these questions. It is in answering them that mistakes can be and perhaps are occasionally made, mistakes due to inadequate or faulty data. You may wonder why we do not avoid the chance of error and resolve all difficult cases in the negative. What do we have to lose?

This is a fair question but I firmly believe the course of action it suggests would not be in the U.S. national interest. There are several reasons.

1. As I have mentioned before, a significant factor to be taken into account, when the contribution of an export to Soviet strategic strength is slight or questionable, is its contribution to U.S. strength by providing employment to our resources and by earning us foreign exchange. I am convinced that, so long as the United States remains economically and politically and militarily strong and determined, we have no need to fear the Soviet Union. The maintenance of our strength must always be our first objective.

2. In nearly all these borderline cases, moreover, it will be true that our denial would not achieve its objective of depriving the Soviet Union of the items and hence that the loss of business to the United States has even less justification. For the items we might or might not license will be those which are not on the

internationally agreed Cocom list, and which therefore will not be subject to licensing control, if ordered in Europe or Japan. The technological progress of our associates in Cocom since the war has been so great that there are few items that they cannot also produce. We have of course tried to secure an international control list as close as possible to that which we would like to see controlled but due to the greater importance of trade to the other participating countries, and to differences in intelligence and technical evaluations, we have not completely succeeded. Our past efforts have so fully covered the ground that we nearly always will know that special additional efforts to secure agreement to join us in embargoing an item that is before the U.S. Department of Commerce for consideration will not succeed in all those countries which are possible sources. And since this is true, there is no compelling basis for our abandoning the benefits of the business by denying the license.

3. Furthermore, as a general consideration, I find it of value in dealing with the Soviet bloc to make much of one of our major points of difference with it; namely, to limit Government interference with the activities of American citizens, whether in trade or tourism or intellectual or cultural exchange, to the minimum consistent with national security. On this ground we should permit as much trading freedom as is possible without impairing our strategic needs.

4. There is a further important reason for not resolving all difficult cases through denial. The current Berlin crisis is but one in a series which have occurred between the West and the Soviet Union in the past fifteen years. Even if it is resolved, we can have no possible basis for believing that it will be the last. The existence of a reasonable amount of trade of value to the Soviets between us and the Soviet bloc, and even more extensively between our NATO allies and the bloc, leaves us the possibility of trade limitations as a credible demonstration of our solidarity and determination which would undoubtedly be embarrassing and disrupting to Soviet economic planning.

5. Finally, from a much longer range standpoint, I believe our policies must reflect the vital necessity to U.S. peace, safety

and wellbeing of doing what we can to influence the peoples of the Soviet Union toward a national attitude which will make their country a responsible and peaceful member of the community of nations. I have no illusions that this is apt to come about soon or that our trade policy can make a decisive contribution to it. But the means for reaching the Soviet people and affecting their attitudes are scarce and we must make the most of those few we have in promoting this most vital goal. Keeping open the channels of peaceful trade will, I believe, contribute to this goal in several ways. It may erode gradually the concept that conflict between us is inevitable and replace it with some recognition of the mutual advantages of closer economic relations. Seeing U.S. goods technologically advanced and performing well may do something to build respect for us and encourage an interest in knowing more about what the United States and its people are really like. For undoubtedly one of our greatest obstacles to a reduction in East-West tensions is the vast ignorance at all levels in the Soviet Union of the outside world, an ignorance that here as elsewhere breeds distrust, suspicion and fear, and more immediately of concern, miscalculation. And finally, trade can gradually get people in touch with each other to operate directly in removing the tangle of misunderstandings which threaten the great future of the American people and our way of life.

Although the basic principles which I have described have continuing validity, it is important to note that the implementation of our trade control policy has taken account of significant developments in East-West relations. There are thus elements of flexibility in the policy which we consider to be of great importance.

It is U.S. policy to encourage and assist bloc states to achieve and maintain national self-determination and independence. The objective of assisting "the people of the nations under domination of foreign aggressors to reestablish their freedom" is set forth in section 101 of the Battle Act. Controls under the economic defense program are so applied as to support the foregoing objectives, as exemplified in the cases of Yugoslavia and Poland.

YUGOSLAVIA

Yugoslavia, while subject to Communist rule, is wholly independent of the Sino-Soviet bloc. In 1948 the Yugoslav Government, under Tito's leadership, broke away from Soviet control and the international Communist movement. Since that time Yugoslavia has shown a determination to preserve its national identity and freedom from outside domination. To a considerable extent, Yugoslavia has resumed its earlier ties with Western peoples and institutions. It has also evolved an economic and political system which differs substantially from that of the Soviet Union. Yugoslavia's economy has undergone a process of decentralization with definite elements of competition and individual incentive. In this connection, it is interesting to note that Yugoslavia has achieved a rate of economic growth greater than is found anywhere in the Soviet bloc. Yugoslavia's independence of Soviet control has been emphasized by Yugoslavia's participation as member or observer in certain international organizations in which the Soviet bloc does not participate and which, in some respects, are obstacles to Soviet ambitions. These include the GATT, the OEEC and the new OECD.

Within the context of the cold war, Yugoslavia is a neutralist country and usually behaves as such. It frequently takes positions on international issues that are opposed to U.S. attitudes and interests, but this is equally true of other neutralist nations. In the U.N., for example, Yugoslavia's voting record corresponds closely with that of India.

The United States has a definite interest in maintaining Yugoslav freedom from Soviet control. In addition to our general interest in preventing the expansion of Soviet power and influence, the independence of Yugoslavia gives us certain special advantages. It has profoundly disturbed the political and ideological unity of the international Communist movement. It has definitely encouraged nationalist anti-Soviet tendencies among the populations of the Soviet-dominated states of Eastern Europe. The fierce Soviet and Chinese attacks on Yugoslav "revisionism" and "deviationism" have vividly reminded Marxist sympathizers in all parts of the world that the Sino-Soviet bloc is not satisfied with a mere triumph of ideological principles, but demands direct subservience to the policies of the bloc, as conceived in Moscow.

On the basis of the foregoing considerations, the United States has maintained a relationship with Yugoslavia generally similar to that maintained with other neutralist nations. We have pursued friendly and frank diplomatic contacts, have conducted extensive information activities in Yugoslavia, and have carried on a broad exchange program. Yugoslav requests for economic and technical assistance have been considered on their merits, and trade with Yugoslavia has been conducted as with any friendly European or neutralist country.

Whatever differences may exist between the United States and Yugoslavia, it is important that the United States never lose sight of its own basic interests. It is important to the United States that Yugoslavia remain independent.

POLAND

Poland, unlike Yugoslavia, is clearly a member of the Soviet bloc. It is bound to the U.S.S.R. not only through such formal instrumentalities as the Warsaw Pact, but also because of its exposed geographic position and its heavy economic dependence upon the Soviet Union. Even more important is the fact that Soviet troops are still present in Poland. The Polish position on international issues is rarely distinguishable from that of the Soviet bloc itself. In brief, Poland is a part of the Soviet bloc and U.S. policies must fully take account of this fact.

On the other hand, it is equally important to recognize that Poland reflects nationalist sentiments within the Soviet system. It differs from the other bloc members in a number of significant respects. First, since the establishment of the Gomulka regime in 1956, the Polish Government has enjoyed a measure of autonomy which, while limited, is nevertheless unique within the bloc.

The people of Poland have a longstanding antagonism toward Russian domination and a basic orientation toward Western civilization. Only a small part of Polish agricultural land has been collectivized. Essential freedom of worship exists in Poland, including the teaching of religion to children by the clergy and the operation of a university and seminaries by the Catholic Church. The Polish Government permits a diversity and expression in the arts which is unmatched elsewhere in the Soviet bloc, and intellectual activity is more vigorous than in Yugoslavia.

The Polish Government has also been more restrained in the exercise of police power, as evidenced by the relative absence of political arrests and greater freedom of movement within the country.

Finally, the Polish regime permits more extensive and active contacts with the West than is permitted by other satellite states. This is true in terms of scientific and cultural contacts, tourist travel and the immigration of large numbers of Poles to various Western countries.

Under the Gomulka regime, there has also developed a considerable expansion of relations with the United States. U.S. officials in Poland are able to maintain and develop broader contacts, both with officials and with private citizens.

U.S. volunteer agencies are able to administer food distribution programs which include full identification of the source of the distributed goods. VOA broadcasts are not jammed in Poland. Finally, the United States has been able to develop a far more extensive exchange program with Poland than with any other bloc country.

In developing U.S. policies toward Poland, it would be erroneous and dangerous to base such policies on the illusion that Poland is not tied to the Soviets within the bloc, or is likely to be detached from the bloc in the immediate future. On the other hand, it is apparent that Poland enjoys a significant measure of autonomy and thus affords an opportunity for U.S. initiatives that is not now available in any such degree in the rest of the bloc.

This necessarily implies the application of special policies to Poland in such fields as trade, economic and technical assistance and exchanges of persons. The application of these special policies inevitably involves uncertainty whether our efforts will lead to an ultimate result that can be achieved, at best, only over a long period of years.

For the reasons indicated, the United States has accorded Poland a considerable measure of special treatment since 1956, including preferential treatment in the export control field. This policy was never expected to produce any sudden or dramatic results. On the other hand, this policy has unquestionably brought some visible gains. It has helped to preserve the changes distinguishing Poland from the other bloc states, to keep the door open to wider American access to the Polish people, and to maintain the intrinsic Western orientation of the great mass of the Poles. This policy continues to provide a lever by which the United States can hope to influence the future destiny of Poland and to moderate the policies of other bloc states.

STRICTER CONTROLS FOR FAR EAST

While U.S. trade controls toward Yugoslavia and Poland show a relaxation in the application of the basic economic defense policy, not every move is in that direction. The serious threat to U.S. security interests which resulted from the spread of hostile Communist powers on the continent of Asia led to imposition against Communist China and other Far East Communist countries of more severe controls than are applied against the remainder of the Soviet bloc. There are two reasons for the continuation of such stricter controls. First, the complete embargo on trade and financial transactions with Communist China and North Korea is such a key symbolic element of the U.S. treatment of these two countries as outcasts, that a relaxation of that embargo would inevitably have adverse political repercussions in the Far East. Pressures could be expected to increase in many Asian countries, and especially in Japan, for greater commercial and political contacts with the Peiping regime. Second, if the United States were to relax its trade and financial controls against Communist China and North Korea to the level now applied against the Soviet bloc generally, it would significantly increase the capacity of Communist China to overcome its present domestic economic difficulties and to extend its aid and influence to the so-called uncommitted nations of Asia, Africa and Latin America. Communist China's trade pattern to date suggests that the new U.S. export opportunities which would materialize would be less in value than would be the new Chinese Communist exports to the U.S. market as exchange earners, thus providing the Peiping regime with additional net resources for activities abroad hostile to us and augmentation of their military potential.

For all practical purposes, North Viet-Nam has been treated on the same basis as Communist China and North Korea. A complete embargo exists on trade, but not on financial transactions; in practice, this has not been a significant omission in the U.S. system of controls against that country, because there have occurred few transactions in U.S. dollars that have involved North Viet-Nam. Even so, in view of North Viet-Nam's aggressive acts in Laos and South Viet-Nam, it may become advisable to extend the foreign assets control regulations, with their financial embargo provisions, to North Viet-Nam as well.

There is one specific reservation which I must attach to the foregoing explanation of our control policies. That is the possible impact of immediate world conditions upon our control policy. Present increased international tension connected with Berlin might require modification of established policies on economic relations with the Soviet Union and other members of the Soviet bloc. If the Soviet Government continues its threatening attitude toward vital interests of the United States and its allies, we may be obliged to reconsider all aspects of our relations, including economic, with the Soviet bloc. Export license applications for shipments to these areas are already being reviewed with special care to be certain that none are permitted which have even marginal strategic significance to the bloc under current conditions.

While U.S. trade restrictions apply mainly to countries of the Sino-Soviet bloc, they are not confined solely to those countries. In furtherance of foreign policy objectives in certain other areas of the world, the United States on occasion restricts exports to specific destinations. For example, such controls presently exist, to a very limited extent, on exports to the Congo and the Dominican Republic. Since October 1960, only shipments of foods and medicines have been permitted to Cuba.

### IMPORTANCE OF MULTILATERAL SECURITY TRADE CONTROL SYSTEM

I should like to conclude my testimony by emphasizing the importance which I attach to the present multilateral security trade control system. While our policy of control is a selective one and while we cannot expect to cripple Soviet bloc economic or military power through an export control system, we can accomplish something useful if we recognize that our objective must be a limited one. That objective is to delay the development of Soviet military capability in selected areas where a coordinated denial policy by Western suppliers may have an impact. We cannot hope to erect an absolute barrier to Soviet advancements in military production; we can make it more difficult or more time-consuming for the Soviets to make certain kinds of progress. From this standpoint, the trade control operation is closely akin to the basic objective of our national defense policies —namely, the preservation and if possible the widening of the margin of advantage in time wherever we enjoy it in military capability. It is this margin in ultimate military power which is the hope of the West in the near term, and whatever contribution the trade control system has made to its maintenance is valuable.

In addition and as a specific matter, we attach great importance to the existence of a multilateral organization in being— the Consultative Group—Coordinating Committee operation. It represents a forum where necessary measures in the control field can be agreed quickly and definitively. The value of this sort of standby organization was proven at the time of the Korean war when it made possible the adoption of special trade and shipping controls toward Communist China and North Korea. We want to be certain that it remains as a part of our total mutual defense system.

## THE UNDERLYING CRISIS

Mr. Chairman, if the committee would permit me, I would like to make a few informal remarks about the underlying nature of our problem with the Soviet Union and the Sino-Soviet bloc.

We have, I think, two elements in what I would call the underlying crisis of our period of history as it involves the Soviet Union.

The first is a pursuit by the Soviet Union of what probably can be called the national ambitions of the Russian state reflected in pressures around their borders, toward the warm water ports in the south, toward Western Europe in the west, policies which might well have been associated with a czarist Russia had that type Russia lasted into our own period.

But the far more threatening aspect of Soviet policy is that it embraces a doctrine of world revolution, a world revolution which they call historically inevitable, a world revolution which they are committed to backing with the means at their disposal in all parts of the world.

Anyone who listened to Mr. Khrushchev in Vienna in his talk with Mr. Kennedy, or who has read his January 6 speech of this year, or his recent thirteen-hour speeches to the Party Congress in Moscow can be under no illusions about what the long-term objectives of the Soviet system are.

This contest is not just between the Soviet Union and the so-called Western bloc with the neutrals caught in between. In fact, this is between the Soviet bloc, an agency which would like to make over the world in its particular image, and all those, whether allies or whether neutrals, who would like to see a kind of world come into being that is generally described in the U.N. Charter.

So in the most fundamental sense, the issues here are between the Soviet Union and all the rest.

When we consider what might be done to frustrate these ambitions of the Soviet bloc, ambitions which they confess openly, ambitions which are no secret, and ambitions which they clearly have been backing in action, then we come up against some of our most far-reaching problems.

Certainly we would agree that the United States and its allies must be strong, and I must say from the Department of State point of view, we were extremely gratified that the Congress moved promptly in the last session to provide the President with the additional military resources that he asked for as a part of the buildup of the alliance.

I think it is all too true we have a stake, as have others, in trying to build up viable, independent countries of a sort which would not be susceptible to blandishments from the Soviet bloc, or susceptible to their penetrations. A great deal can be done and is being done in what is generally known as the free world to fend off the kind of penetration which is coming out of the Sino-Soviet system.

I think there are things, however, which can be done within the Sino-Soviet bloc which are important. Some of them are short-term, some long-term.

I would think, for example, in the longer term, we ought to give encouragement as we can to forces or developments within the Soviet Union which have some chance of making some changes in their system.

### INCREASING CULTURAL EXCHANGE

I think an example is the multiplication of contacts between Soviet scientists and scholars with scientists and scholars in other parts of the world. I do not believe the Soviets have yet discovered how they are going to get over what might prove to be a fundamental dilemma for them, that is, if they are to compete they must free the minds of those who are to produce the knowledge and techniques they will need in order to compete on the one side, and on the other side, in freeing those minds they will free them to think about a great many things other than scientific. The growth of a large class of managers, of scientists, of technicians, professors, research people, may I think in due course impose some moderating influence on the Soviet system.

I think also that the growing pressures and demands from the consumer interest in the Soviet Union can serve to moderate the more difficult aspects of Soviet aggression abroad. I think this is something Soviet leaders cannot be indifferent to. I think it will over time impose a kind of inertia on their system which will make it uncomfortable for them to deny steady increases in consumer standards of living. I think it is not accidental they have gone to considerable lengths not to let their own people feel there is a growth in the possibilities of war. It is not an accident, I think, they have been hiding from them information on the nuclear testing that has been going on there in the last several weeks.

I think also, finally, that there are opportunities for us in other countries, non-Russian countries within the Sino-Soviet bloc. I do think any of us who had any contacts with the Poles or Hungarians in these past several years cannot help but be impressed with the persistence there of strong nationalist feelings in those countries. There is no question about the Communist character of their government, there is no question about the general orientation at the present time of their foreign policy. Nevertheless, they are people who come from a proud tradition in Central Europe, who dislike Russian domination and who would like to establish, or re-establish, their contacts with the Western world.

These contacts are not going to pay dividends promptly, but my guess is in the longer run these contacts will be important.

Trade and cultural exchange are part of that effort. Of course, these must be handled in terms consistent with national security, and certainly national security is a primary objective of American foreign policy.

I just want to point out these are complex questions on which judgments can differ, and we want to do the very best we can on them, taking into consideration all the factors involved. . . .

## CONTACTS WITH SOVIET SCIENTISTS

I would not be candid if I tried to tell you there are measurable results at this time which are specifically attributable to the exchange procedures.

But I think you will find as Western scientists and scholars meet with Soviet scientists and scholars in one session after another, they get more the impression these Soviet scientists are able to carve out within the Soviet system certain islands of freedom within which they can be scientists, and yet not come into direct conflict with the political powers that be on political questions.

I think, for example, this could be illustrated in contrasting their situation in two fields. In the field of space science, for example, I think we can assume that the Soviet Government has allowed its space scientists and technicians complete freedom insofar as space science and technology is concerned. When you get over into the field of agricultural science, you still find in that field the remnants of Lysenkoism on agricultural problems

I happened to have had some direct contacts with this problem, and it is quite clear that Soviet agricultural scientists by and large are behind Western agricultural scientists, and this is because of the doctrinal instruction given to the life sciences in the Soviet Union by the party, and the fact they have not yet created a completely free atmosphere in which these scientists can operate.

Mr. Khrushchev has an agricultural crisis which is from his point of view unnecessary. This is partly because they have not opened up the vistas of science for men who are working in this field.

You get many private remarks by Soviet scientists and scholars visiting abroad which indicate considerable skepticism of artificial dogma, and I am sure in the long run there is going on there an elbowing out of certain areas of freedom by elements in the Soviet population on which the Soviet Government, itself, is heavily dependent. I mention the managerial class and the scientists as two of the strongest elements in the group.

So far as the other Communist countries are concerned, I think it would be hard to overestimate the importance of what I have just said about Soviet scientists and add to that the impact of nationalism.

I happened to be in Budapest two months after the fighting

in Budapest a few years ago. I was there to see whether it was feasible to help to restore the medical facilities of the medical university there which had been destroyed, because that had been the center of the rebellion and it had been deeply damaged and the population of the city of Budapest was in serious trouble.

Nothing ever came of these discussions because the Kadar government came back into control and broke them off.

When I was talking about certain kinds of equipment I said to these officials in Budapest, "How do we know that these items will not be put on a train and hauled off to the East?"

They thought for a moment and said, "We cannot tell you for certain that that could not happen because there are Soviet troops here. What we can say to you is that if it does happen this will be the most valuable money you have ever spent because every Hungarian would know this within twenty-four hours."

I do not think we ought to be indifferent to or content with the status quo in these Eastern European countries. There are important reasons for us to maintain contact. Some of the contacts that have been established there produce really a very moving relationship and result.

On the question of trade, I do not want to exaggerate the importance of this trade factor, particularly for the United States, because of its almost insignificant quantity. However, we are concerned about efforts now being made in East Germany to free East Germany from the necessity of turning to West Germany for important products. In the nature of prewar Germany, East German factories became dependent on West Germany for spare parts, and so on.

To the extent that East Germany becomes freed from dependence upon West Germany, we lose influence on the East Germans. To the extent that the Soviets now are trying to make East Germany independent of the West, I think this is a move in the wrong direction. We ourselves cannot control it. If we could keep East Germany in a position of economic relations with West Germany, this would be an element of strength we would be glad to have. . . .

NEGOTIATING WITH COCOM COUNTRIES

. . . . We have had some differences of opinion within the Cocom countries on trade policy. The United States has consistently pressed for a somewhat more restrictive policy than most of the other members of Cocom would accept. We have had, therefore, to balance the advantages of maintaining the Cocom system in order that our influence might keep those restrictions as strong as possible, or letting that system disappear and finding that the Cocom controls might gradually wither away.

We have an annual review now of the Cocom arrangements and in the early spring we will be having the first full review that will have taken place since I became Secretary of State.

There were a few discussions which have been held over from this past year's review early this year. We shall be taking up those matters again.

There are some differences within the Cocom countries based, first, upon the importance of trade to them as a matter of national interest in their own economies. Most of them are more dependent upon foreign trade than we are.

Secondly, some of them take a different view concerning the possibilities of moving to what might be called normal relations with the Soviet Union in a relatively few years. We are very doubtful about the possibilities of early relations with the Soviet Union. We want to maintain some contacts, but this looks to us like a pretty grim battle around the world, so we tend to be more interested in slowing down the Soviet Union than some of our Cocom partners.

This is a judgment on which only history can produce the answer, I suppose, but because of those differences we have some difficult negotiations each year with the Cocom countries. . . .

Our interests and the interests of our allies are so much intertwined in so many ways in NATO as part of the entire Western community, in the growing help they are giving underdeveloped countries, in support which we get from the rest of our NATO partners that it is very difficult for us to press a matter of this sort in effect to the breaking point. There are so many other interests which are also involved that it is not easy to go to them and say, "Unless you do this then we will cut this off or we will have to, in effect, pull ourselves away a distance from you in general policy."

This is a trail which has some very dangerous endings in dealings with particular countries.

You would think in some situations we would be in a position to put on very great pressure but that would be true only if we were willing to break up, in effect, the intimacy of the alliance. At the moment this unity of the alliance is of the most urgent possible importance to us in dealing with the Berlin problem. . . .

# XIII. DISARMAMENT, A NUCLEAR TEST BAN AND SPACE

*Why We Seek Disarmament
and Arms Control*

*A compact basic analysis and report, delivered
the day after the eighteen-nation Committee on
Disarmament at Geneva recessed for one
month.*

. . . . The fundamental conviction of the United States is
that the awesome nature of modern armaments and of the war
which would be fought with these armaments is such that no responsible nation can regard the problem of disarmament and
arms control with anything less than the deepest seriousness. We
live today with a paradox: Although the nations of the world
are pouring more and more resources and skills into improving
armaments, they are, on balance, enjoying less and less security.

Address before the New Hampshire Council on World Affairs,
Concord, N. H., June 16, 1962.

The pace of weapons development since World War II has quickened exponentially. Weapons costs continue their upward spiral. As someone has grimly observed of modern weapons: "If it works, it's obsolete."

Let me illustrate. A key present problem is: How do you defend against missiles with nuclear warheads, traveling at 12,-000 miles an hour? Some scientists say this problem is insoluble. Others say not and that the stakes are so large you must not say it is insoluble until you give it a full try; therefore the investment of vast talent and billions of dollars. Suppose you succeed. Then the problem becomes: How do you develop a missile system that will penetrate such a defense? If you succeed in that, how do you develop a defense system that will take care of that much more elaborate missile system? And so both sides go on and on, using huge resources at a level of technical requirement which is already pressing the ceiling of the mind of man. And all the time each side lives under the risk that the other side will make a significant breakthrough, injecting new elements of instability into the world situation.

### COMMAND AND CONTROL PROBLEMS

The command and control problems associated with the weapons in today's arsenals, particularly missiles, are already extraordinarily complex. The possibilities of war by accident, miscalculation or human failure grow as these weapons increase and proliferate to a widening circle of nations.

This is a situation that modern man must view with becoming gravity. Historically, the purpose of our maintaining a military establishment has been to preserve and protect our national security. This will continue to be necessary in the absence of safeguarded disarmament. But it behooves us, at the same time, to draw upon every effort of will and imagination to find an alternative system which will preserve and enhance the national security of the United States, along with that of other nations, and which involves less danger and less instability. This is a major challenge of our time.

This is the standpoint from which the United States approaches disarmament and arms control. We believe that disarmament negotiations should be pursued not as propaganda, nor as a game in which the nations seek to secure some advantage over one another, but as a serious effort stemming from a shared conviction that a continued arms race is not the answer in the search for national and international security in a nuclear age.

## SOVIET OBSESSION WITH SECRECY

The United States entered the Geneva negotiations which began last March with a resolve to explore any pathway which might lead to progress. Upon our initiative eight new members—Brazil, Burma, Ethiopia, India, Mexico, Nigeria, Sweden and the United Arab Republic—were added to these negotiations in the hopes that their influence would help find ways to break the deadlocks which had beset us in the past. The participation of these new members has been useful. They have let it be known they are more impressed by serious negotiation than by cold-war sallies. And yet, despite their presence, we have found ourselves facing once more the same impasse which we have confronted before: the question of inspection.

More than any other single factor, the attitude of the Soviet Union on the problem of inspection and control has been responsible for the failure to report any significant progress in the quest for disarmament. The Soviet Union has charged that inspection is tantamount to "espionage."

In the negotiations on banning atomic tests the British and we went to great lengths to meet the Soviet obsession with secrecy. Under the U.S.-U.K. draft treaty, control posts would be immobile units with fixed boundaries. No site would be chosen for a control post in the U.S.S.R. without the specific consent of the Soviet Government. Within the post, one-third of the technical staff and all of the auxiliary staff would have been Soviet nationals, nominated by the Soviet Government. In these circumstances nothing taking place at the post could remain unknown to the Soviet Government.

The procedures for conducting on-site inspection were equally circumscribed with protection against misuse for espionage. The area to be inspected would be predetermined on the basis of objective seismographic recordings. There would have been no random selection of the geographic site. To get to the site the teams would have to use transport provided by the Soviet Government. In addition the Soviets would be able to assign as many observers as they wished to check on the activities of the inspection team. Finally, it is noteworthy that, under the U.S.-U.K. proposals, less than one part in 2000 of Soviet territory would be subject to human inspection in any one year.

And yet the Soviet Union persists in calling all of this "espionage."

But this is not the only Soviet position which has blocked progress in this vital question. In the general disarmament negotiations the Soviets have taken the untenable position that inspection in the disarmament process can be applied only to the arms actually destroyed and not to provide assurance that agreed levels are not exceeded.

The United States cannot accept a disarmament agreement which, in the words of Aristide Briand, could leave us dupes or victims. We ask nothing of the Soviet Union which we ourselves are not willing to accord the Soviet Union. But if we were willing to rely on good faith alone, disarmament would not be necessary. Until there is a change of Soviet attitude on this question, the prospects for disarmament are not bright. Unilateral disarmament is a completely unacceptable alternative, since this is a guarantee of surrender.

### U.S. PROPOSES PROGRESSIVE ZONAL INSPECTION

In the negotiations in Geneva the United States has made a major new proposal for solving the impasse created by Soviet opposition to inspection and control.

Our proposal for progressive zonal inspection should meet every legitimate objection that the Soviet Union could have to inspection. This proposal relates the amount of inspection to the amount of disarmament which takes place, while still providing an acceptable measure of assurance that agreements reached are being lived up to.

Let me describe quite briefly and in broad outline how this proposal would work. According to our inspection proposals, a country—either the United States or the U.S.S.R.—would divide its territory into an agreed number of zones of more or less equal military significance. At specified time periods during the disarmament process, say at the end of each successive step, an agreed number of zones would be selected for inspection by the other side. At the beginning, therefore, there would not be extensive intrusion by the inspectors into the territory of any state. The percentage of a state's territory subject to inspection would, of course, increase with each step, and we would envisage that the amount would, roughly, parallel the amount of disarmament. In a sense this would be a form of sampling, which, when combined with inspection of declared production facilities and of the armaments destroyed in each step, would give satisfactory assurance of compliance.

This imaginative new concept should have opened new pathways to success in the disarmament negotiations. We still hope that this approach will be acceptable to the Soviet Union. Only one breakthrough is required: The Soviet Union must realize that it cannot eat the cake of disarmament and keep the cake of secrecy. The choice is clear. It is our hope that the Soviets will come to realize that secrecy is a dangerous anachronism in a nuclear age.

The United States and its free-world partners do, I believe, have a common interest with the Soviet Union, in that both sides desire to preserve their mutual security against the dangers of the arms race. I hope this common interest will become increasingly apparent in the period ahead.

DANGERS COMMON TO EAST AND WEST

There are four specific dangers which the East and West now share which could be the basis for early action in the disarmament field, while we continue the more complex negotiations relating to general disarmament.

First, there is the danger which arises from the proliferation of nuclear weapons under the control of an increasing number of individual nations. As more and more nations come to possess their own nuclear stockpiles, the danger of a nuclear conflagration also increases.

Secondly, there is the danger of outbreak of war by accident, miscalculation or failure of communications. This danger grows as modern weapons become more complex, command and control difficulties increase, and the premium is on ever faster reaction.

Thirdly, there is an increasing danger that outer space will become man's newest battlefield. Steps must be taken at this early stage to keep outer space from being seeded with vehicles carrying weapons of mass destruction, further reducing the security of all of the inhabitants of our planet. This is preventive disarmament, for such nuclear weapons are not now deployed in space.

Fourthly, there is the danger that mounting proportions of our national resources, skill and treasure will have to be diverted to the business of developing newer and newer armaments. Neither the United States nor the U.S.S.R. has so many schools, hospitals and highways—or so many scientists, engineers, scholars and artists—that we could not put to better use the funds and energies and talents which go to make our warships and tanks and missiles.

These are four areas of potential common interest that are tangible and real. Disarmament negotiations should build upon these areas of interest and achieve concrete agreements which can lessen the dangers that they pose.

U.S. CONTINUES QUEST FOR AGREEMENT

The United States has offered specific proposals for such concrete action. We will continue to negotiate and to seek effective ways, consistent with our security and that of the nations which associate with us in mutual defense, to turn downward the competition in armaments.

On April 18 of this year in Geneva the United States presented a major new proposal—an outline of basic provisions of a treaty on general and complete disarmament in a peaceful world. This plan is a detailed and specific blueprint for disarmament and security.

This program has been presented for negotiation—not as a take-it-or-leave-it proposition. We believe it is a good basis for negotiation. I have already spoken of the new inspection feature of this program.

This plan, if put into effect, would contain and reduce the nuclear threat.

It would reverse the upward spiral of destructive capability which, if unchecked, could by 1966 be double what it is today.

It would quickly reverse the trend toward diffusion of nuclear weapons capability to additional nations.

It would put into effect measures to reduce the risk of war by accident, miscalculation or surprise attack.

It would insure that general and complete disarmament is matched by the strengthening of the world's institutions for keeping the peace, else there could be no safety in general disarmament.

At Geneva we seek the widest possible area of agreement on a general disarmament program. Our goal, of course, is agreement upon the entire process, but we recognize that this will take time. We would hope, therefore, that, in addition to early action in the fields of the four danger areas I mentioned earlier, we and the Soviet Union could agree upon balanced measures that could start the disarmament process while we continue negotiations on some of the more difficult problems that arise in connection with the later phases of a general disarmament program.

We continue to hope for a treaty banning nuclear weapons tests. President Kennedy has said that he has had no greater disappointment since he assumed office than the failure to achieve a test ban agreement. Such an agreement inevitably would improve the prospects for success in broader disarmament efforts. It would also end one significant element in the arms race and help to prevent the spreading of nuclear weapons among more and more nations.

The Soviet resumption of nuclear weapons tests last fall left the United States with no option but to resume testing. The decision was undertaken only after the most soul-searching examination, for the President views with great concern the further acceleration of the competition in developing newer and more destructive weapons. However, in the absence of a safeguarded agreement, we could not hold back further in the face of unacceptable military risks for the United States and the entire free world.

### NEED TO NEGOTIATE IN GOOD FAITH

The United States will not abandon its quest for a safeguarded agreement which will put an end to nuclear weapons testing for all time. Under the pressure of world opinion and with an awakening to the need for responsible statesmanship, we hope the Soviet Union will turn from its present negative posture and agree to resume negotiations for an effective test ban agreement.

We are preparing to go up and down the range of negotiation, seeking agreement wherever possible. And we are determined to make only those proposals which we ourselves are prepared to live with. It is important that these negotiations be conducted in good faith and not as propaganda moves.

Let me say in passing that many other countries could well think about this. Everybody is happy to vote for disarmament resolutions in the United Nations—for those which seem particularly applicable to the great powers. But not all the nations which vote for them show the same interest in curbing their own arms races with their neighbors—or in settling the disputes which give rise to these other arms races. I'd like to see a United Nations meeting in which it would be out of order for any delegate to say what somebody else ought to do about disarmament, in which each would state quite simply what he is prepared to contribute to disarmament.

The United States wants disarmament. We have set forth comprehensive proposals for achieving disarmament. We believe that disarmament in balanced steps would increase the security of the whole world, including ourselves.

We will insist, however, that disarmament take place in a peaceful world. If we are to be realistic, we must not expect that in the near future such a "peaceful world" will mean a world without rivalries. But it must mean a world where competition between systems is conducted within ground rules which preclude the use of force to impose change. If the Soviet Union and other Communist states wish general disarmament, and through it the removal of the present terrible dangers of the arms race, they must be prepared to await the verdict of history—and of peoples—as to the merits of political systems; that verdict must not be imposed. If there is to be agreement that we will both await that verdict and that we are going to gain control of the arms race, then we must be prepared to work together to better keep the peace.

## WHERE DISARMAMENT NEGOTIATIONS STAND

Where do the disarmament negotiations stand now? The negotiations at Geneva have been temporarily recessed for a month. Up to now there has been no major progress. However, the conference is to be resumed on July 16.

Despite the discouraging history of disarmament negotiations, we cannot give up hope. The objective is too important. We intend to keep on pressing. We are moderately optimistic that in time other states, including the Soviet Union, will come to see that an unrestrained arms race poses a threat which requires all of us to change traditional modes of thinking and to cooperate in the prevention of a great war.

There is some basis for hope, although our hopes may remain, for a time, greater than our realistic expectations. For the first time we have been able to identify some of the main problems in talks with the Soviet Union. The joint statement of agreed principles worked out last summer by Mr. [John J.] Mc-

Cloy and the Soviet delegate, Mr. [Valerian A.] Zorin, have been accepted as the basis of the Geneva negotiations. While these eight principles are quite general, they have made it possible to begin discussion with a more nearly common language.

By contrast with past performance, the manner of work of the present conference has been encouraging. The atmosphere is businesslike, with somewhat less polemics than usual. The eight new members, chosen to represent the other geographical areas of the world, are making a responsible contribution. The management of the conference by the United States and Soviet co-chairmen and the practice of holding informal meetings have also substantially reduced well-known tendencies toward propaganda abuses.

We cannot underestimate the obstacles created by international distrust. We cannot give way to wishful thinking nor overlook the frustrations of the past. This time, however, I think we are farther along the road by virtue of common recognition of the specifics of danger and the creation of a more effective forum for discussion.

The road to disarmament and arms control is a long and hard one at best. Negotiations must be pursued uninterruptedly, patiently and persistently. We must mobilize all of our efforts, resources, and imagination to explore new approaches. Above all, we must not allow ourselves to become discouraged or to abandon a worthwhile objective because its achievement does not seem to be in sight.

I decline to conclude that what man has invented he cannot control.

## Disarmament—the U. S. Position and Some New Proposals

*This was Secretary Rusk's initial address to the disarmament conference, which convened that day.*

. . . . All of us will agree, I am sure, that this conference faces one of the most perplexing and urgent tasks on the agenda of man. In this endeavor we welcome our association with delegates from countries which have not previously been intimately involved with earlier negotiations on disarmament. The dreary history of such negotiations shows that we need their help and fresh points of view. The presence of these delegations reminds us, too, that arms races are not the exclusive concern of the great powers. Countries situated in every region of the world are confronted with their own conflicts and tensions, and some are engaged in arms competition.

### DISARMAMENT A WORLDWIDE RESPONSIBILITY

We are not here dealing solely with a single struggle in which a few large states are engaged, with the rest of the world as spectators. Every state has a contribution to make in establishing the conditions for general disarmament in its own way. Every state has a responsibility to strive for a reduction of tension, and of armaments, in its own neighborhood.

This means that each of us will bear personal responsibility for what we do here. Every speech and every act must move us toward our common objective. At the same time, every one of us brings to the search for disarmament a separate fund of experi-

Statement at the Second Plenary Meeting of the eighteen-nation Committee on Disarmament at Geneva, Switzerland, March 15, 1962.

ence relevant to our problem. The United States, for example, has established a major new agency of government to mobilize its skills and resources to seek out and study every useful approach to arms reduction.

What is needed is immediate reduction and eventual elimination of all the national armaments and armed forces required for making war. What is required most urgently is to stop the nuclear arms race. All of us recognize that this moment is critical. We are here because we share the conviction that the arms race is dangerous and that every tool of statecraft must be used to end it. As the President stated on March 2, the United States is convinced that, "in the long run, the only real security in this age of nuclear peril rests not in armaments but in disarmament."

Modern weapons have a quality new to history. A single thermonuclear weapon today can carry the explosive power of all the weapons of the last war. In the last war they were delivered at 300 miles per hour; today they travel at almost 300 miles per minute. Economic cost skyrockets through sophistication of design and by accelerating rates of obsolescence.

Our objective, therefore, is clear enough. We must eliminate the instruments of destruction. We must prevent the outbreak of war by accident or by design. We must create the conditions for a secure and peaceful world. In so doing we can turn the momentum of science exclusively to peaceful purposes and we can lift the burden of the arms race and thus increase our capacity to raise living standards everywhere.

A group of experts meeting at the United Nations has just issued an impressive report on the economic and social consequences of disarmament which should stimulate us in our work. The experts, drawn from countries with the most diverse political systems, were unanimously of the opinion that the problems of transition connected with disarmament could be solved to the benefit of all countries and that disarmament would lead to the improvement of world economic and social conditions. They characterized the achievement of general and complete disarmament as an unqualified blessing to all mankind.

This is the spirit in which we in the United States would deal with the economic readjustments required if we should achieve broad and deep cuts in the level of armaments. The United States is a nation with vast unfinished business. Disarmament would permit us to get on with the job of building a better America and, through expanded economic development activities, of building a better world. The great promise of man's capacity should not be frustrated by his inability to deal with war and implements of war. Man is an inventive being; surely we can turn our hands and minds at long last to the task of the political invention we need to repeal the law of the jungle.

### LAYING BASIS FOR DISARMAMENT

How can we move toward such disarmament?

The American people bear arms through necessity, not by choice. Emerging from World War II in a uniquely powerful military position, the United States demobilized its armed strength and made persistent efforts to place under international control the use of atomic energy, then an American monopoly. The fact that the story of the postwar period has forced increased defense efforts upon us is a most grievous disappointment. This disappointment teaches us that reduction of tensions must go hand in hand with real progress in disarmament. We must, I believe, simultaneously work at both.

On the one hand, it is idle to expect that we can move very far down the road toward disarmament if those who claim to want it do not seek, as well, to relax tensions and create conditions of trust. Confidence cannot be built on a footing of threats, polemics and disturbed relations. On the other hand, by reducing and finally eliminating means of military intimidation we might render our political crises less acutely dangerous and provide greater scope for their settlement by peaceful means.

I would be less than candid if I did not point out the harmful effect which deliberately stimulated crises can have on our work here. In the joint statement of agreed principles for disarmament negotiations published on September 20, 1961, the United States and the Soviet Union affirmed that, "to facilitate the attainment of general and complete disarmament in a peaceful world it is important that all States abide by existing international agreements, refrain from any actions which might aggravate international tensions, and that they seek settlement of all disputes by peaceful means." Yet we are confronted by crises which inevitably cast their shadows into this meeting room.

The same can be said for the failure of our efforts, so hopefully begun, to conclude an effective agreement for ending nuclear weapon tests. There is an obvious lesson to be drawn from these considerations. The lesson is that general and complete disarmament must be accompanied by the establishment of reliable procedures for the peaceful settlement of disputes and effective arrangements for the maintenance of peace in accordance with the principles of the United Nations Charter. For the rule and spirit of law must prevail if the world is to be disarmed.

As we make progress in this conference, we shall have to lay increasing stress on this point. A disarmed world must be a law-abiding world in which a United Nations peace force can cope with international breaches of the peace. In the words of the joint statement: "Progress in disarmament should be accompanied by measures to strengthen institutions for maintaining peace and the settlement of international disputes by peaceful means."

Fortunately there is one sign which can give us hope that this conference will in good time lay the foundation stones for a world without war. For the first time a disarmament conference is beginning its activities within an agreed framework—the joint statement of agreed principles—which all our governments have welcomed along with every other member of the United Nations. The United States considers the joint statement as its point of departure. Our objective is to build on that foundation and to give practical application to the principles.

The United States program for general and complete disarmament in a peaceful world, introduced in the United Nations on September 25, 1961, was presented to give life to the agreed principles. It is comprehensive in its scope and in its description of the subjects suitable for action in the first and subsequent stages of the disarmament process. It is framed so as to avoid impairment of the security of any state. It aims at balanced and verified disarmament in successive stages. It is not immutable, however. It is designed to serve as a basis for negotiation.

This conference also has before it another plan, presented by the Soviet Union. A comparison of the two plans will show some areas of agreement. We believe it is the task of the conference to search for broader areas of accord leading to specific steps which all can take with confidence.

At this meeting the United States wishes to put forward some suggestions and proposals regarding the course of our future activity, first as to objective and procedure, then as to a program of work for the conference.

We believe that the ultimate objective should be the working out in detail of a treaty or treaties putting into effect an agreed program for general and complete disarmament in a peaceful world. To bring this about we propose that all of our delegations agree to continue our efforts at this conference without interruptions, other than those we all agree to be desirable or necessary for our task, until a total program for general and complete disarmament has been achieved.

As for procedures we propose that we find means of achieving maximum informality and flexibility. We do not believe that the best way to make progress is to concentrate our time and efforts in protracted or sterile debate. Accordingly the United States will propose that, as soon as ample opportunity has been allowed for opening statements, the schedule of plenary meetings be reduced so that issues and problems can be explored in informal meetings and in subcommittees more likely to produce agreement.

### U.S. PROPOSALS FOR WORK OF CONFERENCE

Let me turn now to proposals regarding the work for the conference.

The first proposal is that the conference work out and agree on an outline program of general and complete disarmament which can be included in the report due to the United Nations Disarmament Commission by June 1. The United States believes that, to fulfill this first objective, the initial aim of the conference should be to consolidate and expand the areas of agreement and to reconcile the differences between the United States and Soviet disarmament plans. This should result in working out a single program of general and complete disarmament which all could support. This agreed program might well take the form of a joint declaration which could be presented to the United Nations by all the states represented here. Such a program could be a framework for the treaty or treaties which would put the agreed total program into effect.

But of course our aims must be more ambitious than this. We should begin at once to fill in the outline of the total program. Wherever possible we should seek specific commitments that could be put into effect without delay. This need not await agreement on the outline as a whole. Nor should it impede the development of an overall program. Wherever the common interest permits we can and should put into effect defined, specific steps as quickly as possible.

As a first step toward filling in the details of such a program the United States makes the following proposals:

One, we propose that a cut of 30 per cent in nuclear delivery vehicles and major conventional armaments be included in the first stage of the disarmament program. We propose that strategic delivery vehicles be reduced not only in numbers but also in destructive capability. We estimate that, given faithful cooperation, this reduction might be carried out in three years. Similar reductions can, we believe, be achieved in each of the later stages. It is recognized, however, that, in the words of the agreed principles, "All measures of general and complete disarmament should be balanced so that at no stage of the implementation of the treaty could any state or group of states gain military advantage and that security is ensured equally for all." But agreement on such a reduction and the measures to carry it out would be a significant step forward. It would reverse the upward spiral of the arms race, replacing increases with decreases, and men could begin to gain freedom from the fear of mass destruction from such weapons.

Two, the United States has proposed that early in the first

stage further production of any fissionable material for nuclear weapons use be stopped. We propose now that thereafter the United States and the U.S.S.R. each agree to transfer in the first stage 50,000 kilograms of weapons grade U-235 to nonweapons purposes. Such a move would cut at the heart of nuclear weapons production. The initial transfers should be followed by additional transfers in the subsequent stages of the disarmament program. Resources now devoted to military programs could then be employed for purposes of peace.

Three, the United States proposes that the disarmament program also include early action on specific worldwide measures which will reduce the risk of war by accident, miscalculation, failure of communications or surprise attack. These are measures which can be worked out rapidly. They are bound to increase confidence. They will reduce the likelihood of war.

We will be prepared to present concrete proposals for action in the following areas:

(a) Advance notification of military movements, such as major transfers of forces, exercises and maneuvers, flights of aircraft, as well as firing of missiles.

(b) Establishment of observation posts at major ports, railway centers, motor highways, river crossings and airbases to report on concentrations and movements of military forces.

(c) Establishment of aerial inspection areas and the use of mobile inspection teams to improve protection against surprise attack.

(d) Establishment of an International Commission on Measures To Reduce the Risk of War, charged with the task of examining objectively the technical problems involved.

Four, the United States proposes that the participants in this conference undertake an urgent search for mutually acceptable methods of guaranteeing the fulfillment of obligations for arms reduction. We shall look with sympathy on any approach which shows promise of leading to progress without sacrificing safety.

We must not be diverted from this search by shopworn efforts to equate verification with espionage. Such an abortive attempt misses the vital point in verification procedures. No government, large or small, could be expected to enter into disarmament arrangements under which their peoples might become victims of the perfidy of others.

In other affairs, accounting and auditing systems are customarily installed so that the question of confidence need not arise. Confidence grows out of knowledge; suspicion and fear are rooted in ignorance. This has been true since the beginning of time.

Let me make this point clear: the United States does not ask for inspection for inspection's sake. Inspection is for no purpose other than assurance that commitments are fulfilled. The United States will do what is necessary to assure others that it has fulfilled its commitments; we would find it difficult to understand why others cannot do the same. We will settle for any reasonable arrangement which gives assurances commensurate with the risks. We do not ask a degree of inspection out of line with the amount and kind of disarmament actually undertaken. Our aim is prudent precaution, in the interest of the security of us all, and nothing else.

We are prepared jointly to explore various means through which this could be done. It might be possible in certain instances to use sampling techniques in which verification could take place in some predetermined fashion, perhaps in specific geographic areas, thus subjecting any violator of a disarmament agreement to a restraining risk of exposure, without maintaining constant surveillance everywhere. This is, I repeat, one example of ways in which recent progress in verification techniques can be adapted to the needs of participating states. We would hope that this conference would make a thorough study of every practicable method of effective verification.

The four proposals I have just described are new and realistic examples of the specific measures which we contemplated in the first stage of the United States plan of September 25. We can recall that that plan had other specific proposals:

That the Soviet Union and the United States reduce their force levels by many hundreds of thousands of men, to a total of 2,100,000 for each.

That steps be taken to prevent states owning nuclear weapons from relinquishing control of such weapons to any nation not owning them.

That weapons capable of producing mass destruction should not be placed in orbit or stationed in outer space.

## CALL FOR EARLY ACTION OF TESTING

Finally, we call for early action on a matter that should yield priority to none—the cessation of nuclear weapons tests. Here we stand at a turning point. If a treaty cannot be signed, and signed quickly, to do away with nuclear weapon testing with appropriate arrangements for detection and verification, there will be further tests and the spiral of competition will continue upward. But if we can reach such an agreement, this development can be stopped, and stopped forever. This is why the United States and the United Kingdom have invited the Soviet Union to resume negotiations to ban all nuclear weapons tests under effective international controls. We shall press this matter here at Geneva and make every reasonable effort to conclude an agreement which can bring an end to testing.

I had expected that a number of representatives might express here their regrets that the Soviet Union and the United States had resumed nuclear testing. But I had supposed that there was one delegation—that of the Soviet Union—which could not have found it possible to criticize the United States for doing so. The representative of the Soviet Union has spoken of the possible effect of United States weapons testing on this conference. The statement of agreed principles and this conference were born amid the echoing roars of more than forty Soviet nuclear explosions. A 50-megaton bomb does not make the noise of a cooing dove.

Despite the Soviet tests of last autumn, nuclear weapons testing can stop—now and forever.

The Soviet Union has spoken of its readiness to accept inspection of disarmament, though not of armament. We hope that it will agree that the total, permanent elimination of nuclear testing is disarmament and will accept effective international control within its own formula.

## ACHIEVING CONSENSUS ON FIRST STEPS

I have presented the United States proposals for early disarmament action in this conference. We shall have further suggestions, and so, I am sure, will others. The conference will need to single out those points it regards as most susceptible of useful treatment, or most pressing in terms of the common danger, and to take them up at once.

We believe that, as soon as agreement is reached on the specific measures to be included in the first stage, we can develop the specific steps for the second and third stages. In these stages further reductions of armaments will move hand in hand with the strengthening of international institutions for the maintenance of peace.

Our plan of work must achieve what this conference is charged to do in the joint statement of agreed principles. Let us define the overall shape of the program. Let us develop in more detail the component parts which must be fitted together within the program. Let us do as much as we can as fast as we can.

Let us, then, apply ourselves to the task of this conference soberly, systematically and realistically. Let the need for disarmament provide the momentum for our work. Let us follow every promising path which might lead to progress. Let us with all deliberate speed reach a consensus on what can be done first and on what should be undertaken on a continuing basis.

And let us not permit this conference, like its predecessors, to become frozen in deadlock at the start of its deliberations. Surely it need not do so. The obstacles to disarmament agreements—the forces tending to divide us into rival aggregations of power—might at long last begin to yield to the overriding and shared interest in survival which alone can unite us for peace.

# The U. S. Still Hopes for a Nuclear Test Ban Agreement

*A résumé of U.S. efforts to obtain a ban on atomic tests and a plea to the Soviet Union to agree.*

. . . . Let me say that the United States deeply regrets, that it is not possible to report progress toward a treaty for the discontinuance of nuclear weapon tests, because the United States regards and will continue to regard a safeguarded end to nuclear testing as a major objective of its foreign policy. It also regards this as a major problem for consideration by this conference.

The reason is obvious. The moratorium which for almost three years has halted nuclear weapon tests was wrecked by the sudden resumption of testing by the Soviet Union last September. The President of the United States has announced that the United States will resume testing in the atmosphere late in April, if by that time a safeguarded test ban treaty has not been signed. The reasons for this decision were set forth in his speech of March 2, which we are asking be circulated as a document of this conference. The time is short, and this conference will understandably wish to be sure that every possible effort is made to prevent a further intensification of the race to produce more and more deadly weapons of mass destruction.

I have asked for the floor this morning to comment on the interim report which the conference subcommittee on nuclear weapons testing has made to the conference. Unfortunately that interim report indicates that no progress has been made toward the conclusion of an effective treaty to prohibit nuclear weapon tests. The Soviet Union appears to be adamantly opposed to any international system of detection and verification which could

Statement to the Geneva Disarmament Conference, March 23, 1962.

disclose clandestine testing and thus serve to place an obstacle in the way of a potential violator of a test ban treaty.

We hope we have not yet heard the last word of the Soviet Union on this matter, though I must confess that we see little ground for optimism at the moment.

Because of the United States Government's great desire to put an end to all tests of nuclear weapons, we are willing to sign a safeguarded treaty, with effective international controls, even though the Soviet Union conducted over forty tests last fall. However, we are willing to ignore these tests only if, in return, we can be assured that testing will actually be halted. We will not again make our security subject to an unenforcible and uncontrolled moratorium, whether this be in the form of a verbal pledge or a pseudotreaty such as the U.S.S.R. proposed on November 28, 1961.

What we need above all in this field is confidence and not fear, a basis for trust and not for suspicion. To get this is the major purpose of our insistence on effective international arrangements to insure that nuclear weapon tests, once outlawed, do not, in fact, ever occur again.

You will remember that the atmosphere for agreements on disarmament questions was not too favorable in 1958, especially after the collapse of lengthy negotiations in London during much of 1957.

Accordingly, in the search for a more promising approach to the issue of a nuclear test ban, the United States, the United Kingdom and the Soviet Union decided to try to resolve the technical questions first before proceeding to a consideration of political questions. This path led to a conference in Geneva in July and August 1958 among the scientists of eight countries, i.e., of the three then existing nuclear powers plus France, Canada, Poland, Czechoslovakia and Rumania.

On August 21, 1958, these experts unanimously agreed on the details of a control system which would be technically adequate to monitor a treaty ending all tests of nuclear weapons. Before September 1, 1958, the recommendations of the scientists had been accepted *in toto* by the Governments of the United States, the United Kingdom and the Soviet Union. Essentially these same technical provisions form the basis of the draft test ban treaty presented by the United States and United Kingdom on April 18, 1961.

## TECHNICAL ASPECTS OF CONTROLLING TEST BAN

I believe it would be helpful to review some of the technical aspects of controlling a test ban.

The words "detection" and "identification" are the key to an understanding of the technical aspects of verification. A great many methods have been devised by scientists to record the innumerable happenings of a geophysical nature which take place around us. Earthquakes are registered by seismographs; hydroacoustic apparatus records sounds in the oceans.

I have mentioned these two particular types of instruments because they, along with various other devices, also happen to be capable of registering signals which are emitted by nuclear detonations. What we call detection is merely the capturing of these diverse signals.

Detection, however, is only half of the story; in fact, it is rather less than half. The primary concern is to know exactly what has been recorded or detected. For example, the signal received on a seismograph from an underground nuclear explosion looks like the signals received on a seismograph from many types of earthquakes. Signals which may come from a small nuclear detonation in the atmosphere may be difficult to detect. In each case the overwhelming difficulty confronting any control system monitoring a nuclear test ban is how to differentiate among the various recordings or detected signals, how to tell which is a natural phenomenon and which is a nuclear explosion.

This was exactly the issue that faced the scientists in Geneva in mid-1958. It is the very same issue that faces us on control today. The answer of the scientists was that, where doubt existed, the only way to clear up the mystery was to utilize some form of on-site inspection. This is still the only answer available to us.

In regard to underground tests, except for quite large ones like the Soviet blast of February 2, 1962, the technical situation is unchallenged by anybody and was even readily admitted by the Soviet Government on November 28 last when it put forward its new test ban scheme based on existing monitoring systems. For these underground events which are detected but which cannot be identified by expert interpretation of the seismic recording, the only way to determine what has happened is to send an investigating team to the spot. The events could be earthquakes or secret nuclear tests. And there could be some hundreds of such events per year in the United States and the Soviet Union.

There is no scientific method not involving inspection that can identify positively a seismic event as a nuclear explosion. If our Soviet colleagues have reason to believe otherwise, they should come forward with their new scientific evidence.

This technical situation provides a further important reason for including the Soviet Union in the worldwide control-post network. The spacing between the control posts in the Soviet Union should be exactly the same as it is in the rest of the world. In order to have the best chance to eliminate a seismic event from suspicion without conducting an inspection, that is, by means of the interpretation of the seismic recording itself by experts, it is essential to have readings from control posts on a global basis, including those within the United States and the U.S.S.R. Without instruments in the U.S.S.R.—one-sixth of the landmass of the globe—many more seismic events in that country become suspicious.

In connection with atmospheric tests, the conclusive means for identifying the true nature of a detected event is to acquire a sample of the air near that event. If the event was man-made this will show up during a chemical analysis of the air sample. For medium and large atmospheric nuclear detonations, the radioactive debris will become part of air masses that are certain to move beyond the boundaries of the country concerned. This method is not reliable, however, for small atmospheric tests.

In recognition of this the 1958 scientists recommended the installation of air-sampling equipment at every control post. Even then they anticipated that in certain instances some question of identification would still remain, and for this they proposed the use of special aircraft flights conducted over the territory of a specific country to capture air samples. Naturally, to the extent that control posts within a country did not exist where radioactive air sampling could take place, there would be just that much greater need of special air-sampling flights.

Although American scientists have for the past several years been actively seeking new methods of detection and, even more, of identification of possible nuclear explosions, and although there are some promising avenues of investigation which may be proven in the next few years, the fact is that very little has been discovered up to date to justify any significant modification of the conclusions and recommendations of the Geneva scientists of 1958. Soviet scientists essentially agreed with this at our last joint meeting with them on a test ban during May 1960 in Geneva. Therefore, when we contemplate the cessation of nuclear weapon tests by international agreement, we must still look to international control arrangements similar to those proposed in 1958 to give the world security against violations. But the faster we have tried to move toward the Soviets in these matters, the faster they seem to move away from their earlier positions.

The draft treaty which the United States and the United Kingdom proposed in April 1961 reflected the recommendations of the 1958 experts. It also incorporated into its terms a large number of political and organizational arrangements for the test ban control organization on which the three powers had already come to agreement at the test ban conference or which went far toward meeting previous Soviet demands. Eastern and Western nations were to have equal numbers of seats on the Control Commission, which also had places for nonaligned nations, and there were detailed provisions for an equitable division by nationality of the international staff, as the U.S.S.R. had sought. The fact that many of the administrative and organizational provisions for the future International Disarmament Organization, as set forth in the Soviet document tabled here on March 15, are similar to the provisions of the Anglo-American draft test ban treaty of last year demonstrates that the Soviet Union can have no serious objection to large portions of our proposal.

## NO BASIS FOR FEAR OF ESPIONAGE

Indeed, when all is said and done, the fundamental Soviet complaint about the test ban control system to which it seemed to agree in 1958, 1959 and 1960, and which its own scientists had helped to devise, is that it would facilitate Western espionage against the Soviet Union. But the facts are otherwise. The proposed system would not have any potential for any espionage which would be meaningful in terms of present-day military requirements.

The truth is that under the United States–United Kingdom draft treaty control posts in the U.S.S.R. would be immobile units with fixed boundaries. No site could be chosen for a control post in the U.S.S.R. without the specific consent of the Soviet Government. No foreign personnel on the staff of any control post would have any official need to leave the boundaries of the post (except when entering and leaving Soviet territory), and it would be up to the Soviet authorities to decide whether such personnel should be permitted to leave the post. Within the post one-third of the technical staff and all of the auxiliary staff would be Soviet nationals, nominated by the Soviet Government. In these circumstances surely nothing taking place at the post could remain unknown to the Soviet Government.

The situation concerning on-site inspection teams would be equally devoid of espionage possibilities. The area to be inspected would be predetermined on the basis of seismographic recordings. There would be no random selection of the geographic site. To get to the site of the inspection the teams would have to use transport furnished by the Soviet Government. They could only carry specified equipment related to their immediate job. Although there would not be any Soviet national members of the inspection team, half of the team would be nationals of nonaligned countries and the Soviet Government would be invited to assign as many Soviet observers as it wished to verify the activities of the inspection team.

I should also stress that the size of the inspectable area would, in any event, be limited to the territory within a radius of about eight or, in some cases, thirteen kilometers from the point, the so-called probable epicenter, where the unidentified seismic event was presumed to have taken place. This radius would involve an inspectable area of 200 or, in some cases, 500 square kilometers. The Soviet Union has territory of over 21 million square kilometers. Therefore it can readily be seen that, even if there were twenty inspections per year in the U.S.S.R. and even if each of these inspections operated within a 500-square-kilometer area, less than one-twentieth of 1 per cent of Soviet territory, i.e. less than one part in 2000, could ever be subject to inspection in any one year.

Finally, no espionage would be feasible on the occasional special air-sampling flights which might take place over Soviet territory. The plane and its crew would be Soviet, and Soviet Government observers could be on board. The only foreigners would be two staff technicians from the control organization who would manage the equipment taking the air samples and who would insure that the plane actually flew along the route previously prescribed.

I have recounted these matters in some detail because it is easy to make generalized charges over and over again about the dangers of espionage in a test ban control system.

It takes careful explanation to show why such charges are completely groundless, even though it stands to reason that the U.S.S.R., which was just as sensitive about espionage in 1958 as in 1961, would never have accepted such a control system in principle in 1958 if it had then believed that the system could have had the slightest real espionage danger for the Soviet Union.

It should be clear now that the explanation for Soviet behavior on the issue of a test ban must be sought elsewhere. There is no rational basis for Soviet concern about misuse of the control system for espionage purposes. There is no scientific basis for the Soviet desire to abandon the still indispensable control system which was recommended by the scientists in 1958 and approved by the governments of the then-existing nuclear powers. There is no political basis for any of us to believe that a test ban is any less urgent now than it was in 1958 or that the benefits which it would bring in improving the international climate would be any less.

## U.S.S.R. URGED TO REVIEW POSITION

My Government, therefore, is at a loss to understand the Soviet position unless it be that the U.S.S.R. has decided that it is still overwhelmingly important for it to be free to continue its nuclear weapon tests. This was what the Soviet Government said last September, when it referred to the tense international situation as a justification for its test resumption, and it may be that the U.S.S.R. feels a military need for another test series. If this is the case, then it is true that the easiest way for the Soviet Union to remain unhampered by a test ban treaty is to offer one which contains no provisions whatsoever for effective control and which the United States and United Kingdom could accept only at grave risk to their national security and to that of the free world.

I cannot urge the Soviet Government too strongly to review its position and to return to the previously agreed basis of negotiation, namely, the experts' recommendation of 1958. We ask the Soviet Union to cease its attempts to have the international community distort sound verification procedures to accommodate one state which is obsessed by a passion for secrecy. We call upon the Soviet Union to enter into genuine negotiations in the three-nation subcommittee set up by this Committee to consider the test ban problem.

There is today an interim report of this subcommittee. But, unfortunately, there are no grounds for encouragement. I should like to comment briefly on the events of the past few weeks which have led us to this point.

## RECENT U.S. PROPOSALS TO ACHIEVE TEST BAN

The President of the United States on March 2 stated in referring to our conference here that:

. . . we shall, in association with the United Kingdom, present once again our proposals for a separate comprehensive treaty—with appropriate arrangements for detection and verification—to halt permanently the testing of all nuclear weapons, in every environment: in the air, in outer space, under ground, or under water. New modifications will also be offered in the light of new experience.

In fulfillment of this pledge the United States presented to the Soviet Union, first in an informal meeting on March 15 and this week in the subcommittee, new proposals of the kind indicated. We have indicated clearly in both formal and informal discussions that the United States is prepared to grant a point to which the Soviet Union has apparently attached great importance, namely, to drop the 4.75-degree threshold and to make the treaty from the outset complete in its coverage—banning from the beginning all tests in the atmosphere, outer space, underground and in the oceans. We will do this without increasing the number of inspections or the number of control posts in the Soviet Union. We would seek, by common agreement, to allocate the quota of inspections in such a way that most would be conducted in a few areas of high seismicity and only a few would be allowable in a large region in the heart of the Soviet Union, where there are normally few seismic noises which would require investigation.

These moves have been made possible by increased experience and increased scientific knowledge. But our experience has also shown the need for provisions for safeguarding other states against the consequences of preparations for testing. This would consist, in large part, of periodic declarations on the parts of heads of state that there will be no preparations for testing, and agreed rights to inspect a certain number of times per year equal numbers of declared sites on each side.

Experience has also shown the need for provisions to shorten the time spent before the beginning of the inspection process. This would primarily be a question of the way the Preparatory Commission functioned and agreement to cooperate in speeding up, by all possible means, the establishment of detection facilities, including temporary control posts.

The United States has made clear that it still stands by its original treaty proposal of April 18, 1961, plus the amendments proposed in 1961, and will sign that treaty. It has also made clear that it is willing to negotiate along the lines I have described to update the treaty if the Soviet Union prefers.

The response of the Soviet Union thus far has not given us any hope. The Soviet delegation has told us that the U.S.S.R. will not accept a treaty with or without the amendments we propose. We are still confronted with the unmistakable reversal of the Soviet position which took place a few months ago after the Soviet Union had for four years asserted its willingness to accept a controlled test ban agreement and after seventeen articles and two important treaty annexes had been negotiated. The roadblock to a cessation of tests is this reversal of the Soviet attitude. The U.S.S.R. was prepared to accept controls before the recent test series. Now, after forty or more tests, it is not ready to do so. It is difficult for us to understand the reason.

The problem cannot really be espionage. For over two years in the test ban conference, as I have outlined in detail, we negotiated arrangements which would insure that the modest amount of control and inspection contemplated could not be misused for espionage purposes.

The problem also cannot be that the verification system is overly burdensome. As I have said, the system which we worked out was directly based on the estimate of the minimum technical requirements which was the product of an agreed analysis by Soviet and Western scientists. The technical basis for this system has never yet been challenged on scientific grounds by the Soviet Union.

The U.S.S.R. now seems to be telling us that under existing circumstances the idea of international verification is wholly unacceptable in any form whatsoever. It seems to be telling us that verification is not even necessary—that it is an insult to request it, even though this is a measure of disarmament. Unnecessary? Merely necessary to end nuclear testing. It seems to be telling us that there can be no impartial investigation, even when there has been a signal recorded from within the Soviet Union and when it is impossible, without such an investigation, to ascertain whether the cause of the signal was a phenomenon of nature or a man-made nuclear explosion.

We recognize that there are risks in any disarmament measure because no control system can give 100 per cent certainty. But a study of our draft treaty with our proposed modifications will indicate that the United States and United Kingdom have been willing to accept a very considerable degree of risk. However, we cannot move to a treaty which is based on no adequate controls at all but solely on pure faith. We do not ask the Soviet Union to trust the word of other nations, and other nations cannot be asked to trust the Soviet Union's word on matters of such far-reaching significance.

In President Kennedy's words of March 2, "We know enough now about broken negotiations, secret preparations, and the advantages gained from a long test series never to offer again an uninspected moratorium." The same could equally be said about an unverified treaty obligation such as the U.S.S.R. is now proposing. We do not intend to be caught again as we were in the autumn of 1961, and there is no reason why we should have to be caught again by a unilateral Soviet decision to resume nuclear weapon tests. This is a risk to national and international security which the United States cannot and will not take. A test ban, or any disarmament measure, will be acceptable to us only when it is accompanied by adequate measures of verification.

INTERNATIONAL VERIFICATION ESSENTIAL

In summary the essential element on which we must insist is that there be an objective international system for assuring that the ban against testing is being complied with. This means that there must be an international system for distinguishing between natural and artificial events. The April 18 treaty provided for such a system. Last week the U.S. and U.K. made some modifications of the proposed treaty in a way calculated to meet Soviet objections. These proposed modifications were rejected almost immediately by the Soviets on the grounds that international verification was not necessary. This refusal to accept any form of verification strikes very hard at our efforts to guarantee the world against resumption of nuclear tests. The key element in the U.S. position is that there must be effective international verification of the obligations undertaken in any such treaty.

Let there be no misunderstanding in this Committee. A nuclear test ban agreement can be signed in short order. There are no hidden difficulties; there are no mysterious obstacles in the way. No time-consuming negotiations need be required. The groundwork has all been laid. Only one element is missing: Soviet willingness to conclude an agreement.

The United States will consider any proposal which offers effective international verification, but the United States cannot settle for anything less.

We urge the Soviet Union to reconsider its attitude and join in putting an end to nuclear weapon testing—a total end, a permanent end.


## A Safe Total Environment


*Excerpt from address at Davidson College, Davidson, N. C., February 22, 1962.*


. . . . We can be safe only to the extent that our total environment is safe. By environment, I mean not only the land and waters and air of the earth but the adjoining areas of space, as far out as man can project instruments capable of influencing significantly the life and affairs of the planet. . . .

# New Frontiers of Science, Space and Foreign Policy

. . . . I congratulate the citizens of Seattle and of the State of Washington on a magnificent concept, nobly executed. These new frontiers of architecture cannot help but open new horizons of awe and wonder to every visitor.

What would your own legendary frontiersman of the nineteenth century have thought? How would Paul Bunyan have measured your Space Needle, the highest edifice west of the Mississippi? I think he would say that his beloved Pacific Northwest had performed a great service for the nation and the world at large. I think he would approve and urge us to get on with building larger space capsules—large enough for him.

My guess is that we are not looking here at Century 21 but at the decades immediately ahead, for the pace of change is so dazzling that our imaginations cannot grasp what four more decades will bring. And all who come here must pause for some still moment of contemplation on what this is all about, what man's progressive mastery of his physical environment really means, and what kind of a world their children will inhabit and form.

The new frontiers of science forecast at this fair are not excursions of the imagination into fairyland, unreality or science fiction. They will come to pass—most of them in this century. We cannot foresee a time when science and technology will cease placing new insights, new data, new tools and new capabilities at the disposal of society. Man's problem is how to use them—in his physical environment and in his social environment of family, nation and international community.

### NEW FRONTIERS FOR SCIENCE

If we look toward Century 21, what are some of the frontiers which science will breach? Among the prospects held out to us by the scientists are these:

Portion of address at Seattle World's Fair, May 25, 1962.

New sources of food, water, power and natural resources.

Desalinization of ocean waters, enabling deserts to bloom; cultivation of crops in the seas; control of the growth of living organisms in the oceans; control of the weather to extend growing seasons in some regions; alas, perhaps balanced meals in capsule form, that can be gulped down in a couple of seconds.

The mining of mineral nodules on the ocean floor; abundant supplies of magnesium extracted from sea water; harnessing of the tides and ocean currents for power.

Immense quantities of power from other sources as well—electric, nuclear and solar; power plants of type and size to meet almost any contingency on almost every location on earth; greatly enlarged and improved power storage facilities.

A vast proliferation of labor-saving devices.

Continuing revolutions in construction through plastics.

The wizards of electronics offer us, through communications satellites, the physical ability to talk to any place on earth, and to almost any person, at low cost. They also hold before us the prospect of beaming television anywhere. But the possibility of instantaneous visual and oral communication with anyone, anywhere and in privacy, has a certain appeal to a Secretary of State. My opposite numbers in other governments and I now have to spend a good deal of time traveling in order to talk directly and intimately to each other. We speak of a shrinking world. But a recent trip, covering 26,900 miles, reminded me that, even at jet speeds, the earth is still a pretty big place.

In the field of medicine, we may expect progress—perhaps deep breakthroughs—in control of such diseases as cancer, the great varieties of viruses and the biochemical imbalances which affect many vital tissues, including the brain. Biochemistry, genetics and electronics will give us new tools for the diagnosis and handling of human disease.

Science, we are told, may make it possible for us to get on with less sleep at night. (I know some Government officials who, of necessity, have already made considerable progress on that front.)

The behavioral scientists will find out more about how the two most complex mechanisms on earth—the human brain and body—think, feel and react. They may be expected to establish new ways of keeping thought processes and the emotions in balance. With greater freedom from mental disease, we will surely make a net gain in constructive and congenial personal relations. We shall almost certainly trespass nearer to those frontiers which guard the secret of life.

And, to mention still another frontier of special importance to foreign affairs, the social and behavioral sciences may improve our ability to communicate with and understand nations and peoples whose cultures are radically different from our own.

### PUTTING SCIENTIFIC PROGRESS TO GOOD USE

Life on earth will be affected by each of these advancing frontiers I have mentioned. But it will be improved only to the extent that men put them to good uses.

For example, the potential of worldwide vocal and visual communication can be either good or bad. As Edward R. Murrow, in whom the State of Washington can proudly claim a special interest since he received part of his education in this state, recently pointed out: A communication system is totally neutral; it has no conscience, no principle, no morality; it can broadcast falsehood as loudly as the truth.

We of the atomic age are starkly aware of the ability of the physical sciences to outstrip man's practical mastery of political and social affairs. Sixteen years ago the United States had the vision to present to the world through the United Nations a plan to place all atomic enterprises under international control. If that plan had been adopted, there would have been no nuclear arms race, there would be no nuclear weapons today, and the power of the atom would be devoted solely to bettering the life of man.

What a tragedy it was that the Soviet Union called that plan "atomic blackmail" and refused to take it up seriously! And what a tragedy it is that, owing to the persistent refusal of the Soviets to permit the most minimum international supervision and verification, we have thus far been unable to make a start on the reduction of armaments and to obtain a treaty banning atomic tests!

Despite sixteen years of Soviet disagreement, we have not given up hope. We have presented a comprehensive plan for reductions in armaments leading to general and complete disarmament. This is not a piece of propaganda but a plan which we most earnestly hope will be adopted. Likewise we continue to seek a test ban treaty and are prepared to sign it the instant that the Soviets agree to it with the essential minimum of international verification to assure compliance.

### EXPLORATION OF SPACE

Now we are in the earlier stages of another scientific, technical and human adventure, as staggering to the imagination as the unleashing of the atom—and as challenging to man's ability to organize his affairs with at least a modicum of good sense. I refer of course to the exploration of space. I have no doubt that we shall reach the moon and explore it. I am told that, after the moon, Mars is the most likely target of exploration, unless we are unexpectedly lucky with Venus. Dr. Willard Libby says there is a 95 per cent probability of finding some form of life on Mars. I have little doubt that we shall eventually reach Mars and somehow set foot on it, with results in expanding knowledge that none of us can now predict.

Meanwhile, within the nearer regions of outer space, we will perfect communications, television and navigational satellites. We will probe the mysteries of weather and learn something of how to control it. We will resolve some of the ambiguities of the earth's magnetic field. We will recover new, and perhaps rare, metals from the heavenly asteroids. We will progressively press closer to some of those secrets of the universe which man has always yearned to know.

But let us take a more somber look at what could happen. The frontiers of space might be pierced by huge nuclear-propelled dreadnaughts, armed with thermonuclear weapons. The moon might be turned into a military base. Ways might be found to cascade radioactive waves upon an enemy. Weather control might become a military weapon. Man, in short, can put outer space to uses which might in the most real sense imperil civilization and even life on this earth of ours. All this seems possible.

## U.S. GOALS IN OUTER SPACE

We fervently hope that the exploration of space will not augment the dreadful perils which hang over the heads of mankind. We earnestly seek international arrangements to assure that this great venture outward from our planet benefits the human race and redounds to its credit.

Our goals are simple and straightforward:

First, we think that outer space should be free for use by all nations as long as the use is consistent with the principles of the United Nations Charter.

Second, we think that the regime of law obtaining among the nations on earth must be extended and improved as it pertains to outer space.

Third, we think that there must be devised a clear and recognized means for the identification of rights and the adjudication of disputes as between nations conducting activities in outer space. We require, for example, mechanisms to assist in the rescue of astronauts who land unexpectedly in foreign territory and for the determination of liability for injuries or damage caused by objects returning from outer space.

Fourth, we think that useful applications of space technology, such as communication and meteorological satellites, should be available to all nations, particularly the less developed nations, commensurate with a realistic assessment of their needs and their ability to commit resources to the use of these applications.

Fifth, we stand for the proposition that opportunities to participate in outer space activities should be open to all nations commensurate with their ability and willingness to cooperate constructively.

And sixth, we have proposed, as part of our disarmament proposals now being discussed at Geneva, that, under adequate inspection and control, the placing in orbit of weapons of mass destruction be prohibited.

Our activities in outer space are consistent with these goals. Many of these principles are embodied in a resolution of the United Nations which the United States supported. They are our frame of reference in discussions now under way for cooperative outer space programs with the Soviet Union and for implementation of programs already in effect with many of our European allies, with countries in South America and Africa and the Far East.

We hope that these principles will continue to be embodied in reliable and enduring agreements which in the future will concern all nations. The right time to subject activities in space to international law and supervision is now, before possibly untoward developments occur.

## A Call for Action

Mr. Chairman and distinguished colleagues: As others have pointed out, it was four months ago that the foreign ministers met here in Geneva to begin this supreme effort to achieve a breakthrough on the disarmament front. Our presence here at that time was meant to show the world that each state represented at the disarmament conference considered an effective solution to the problem of the arms race to be of the utmost importance for the future of our world.

Although it is the conclusion of an international agreement on the future status of Laos that has brought some of us here

Remarks made at the Sixtieth Plenary Session of the Conference of the eighteen-nation Committee on Disarmament at Geneva, Switzerland, July 24, 1962.

to Geneva at this time, those of us serving the nations participating in this disarmament conference have the additional pleasure of attending this session of this eighteen-Nation Committee.

I have not been present myself for conference meetings since those first few weeks, and my stay here necessarily is of brief duration, but we have in no way altered our assessment of the importance of this disarmament conference. The United States considers that progress in disarmament is a practical goal and a practical necessity. This is a continued conviction of my Government.

I believe we all realize that the conference now finds itself deeply involved in a large number of complicated factors and details directly connected with attaining a satisfactory disarmament agreement. The reaching of such agreement therefore requires both a persistent attention to the exploration of matters in depth and an intensive preoccupation with the very broad subject of general and complete disarmament.

Such labors are necessarily in the province of the permanent heads of delegations, who need not be, and indeed should not be, distracted by daily concern for other pressing international problems. This does not mean, of course, that foreign ministers themselves will be any less concerned with what goes on with respect to disarmament. Indeed, I can assure you that at any appropriate time I will be available to reassemble with the other foreign ministers to assist the Committee to overcome specific difficulties of prime importance or to carry through final agreement on questions which appear to be on the way to resolution. For foreign ministers cannot stray far away from the proceedings of these meetings, nor can we fail to be intimately connected with all of the preparations and the policy decisions that accompany participation in this conference.

The discussions of the first three months have carried us more deeply into a thoughtful consideration of the many facts as well as the many difficulties of this subject, more so than any previous disarmament conference. The nature and location of the real hurdles which block the achievement of disarmament are now evident to most of us. The fact that we now see where our problems lie demands that we push forward our efforts and that we concentrate on these troublesome points.

### EFFECTS OF OTHER EVENTS AND TROUBLESOME ISSUES

It is clear, also, that we cannot deal with the problems of disarmament in a vacuum. Problems which arise between states and the resolution of those problems, even though they are far removed geographically from these council chambers, have made and will continue to make their effects felt here.

I need only point out, as Mr. Gromyko [Soviet Foreign Minister Andrei A. Gromyko] has pointed out, that the agreement signed yesterday on the future status of Laos is a welcome sign. Its signature and its effective carrying out could, by improving the international climate, contribute to the work of the nations meeting in this conference to reach their objective of general and complete disarmament in a peaceful world.

Unfortunately we cannot overlook or set aside or forget other events and troublesome issues, for their effects on this disarmament conference are in the opposite direction. They tend to retard rather than push forward our vital work here. I need not at this moment mention or debate each of the specific areas which I have in mind. But I am quite sure that you are all aware of the situations where contention prevails over agreement, where difficulties beset our relations, and where conflict rather than harmony appears the order of the day.

But surely we all understand that persistent pressures against the vital interests of others cannot prepare the way for disarmament. Surely we all understand that disdain for solemn agreements concluded in the recent past breeds distrust about agreements on disarmament which ought to be concluded in the near future. Surely we all understand that repeated declarations that a particular socialist system is destined to dominate the world, and that it has programs of action to bring that prediction into reality, are not a useful introduction to a disarmament discussion.

International tensions often generate military forces. And to the extent that these tensions are reduced or eliminated, it becomes easier to view with less passion and worry those questions relating to the elimination of military establishments which are at the center of all disarmament negotiations.

This conference faces many complex problems, but it can also be the seedbed for agreements of incalculable value. My Government is prepared to press patiently and urgently these potentials for accord—for each agreement in this area will serve to pave the way to still broader and more significant accomplishments. As in the past, so now too, we are convinced that one of the areas where it should be possible to reach early agreement is on a sound and safeguarded agreement to ban nuclear weapons tests now and on a permanent basis.

The regrettable announcement by the Soviet Union over this past weekend that it feels constrained or forced or compelled to follow the recent round of Soviet and United States nuclear tests with still further weapons experiments of its own only makes it more urgent that our efforts in this field succeed. I don't know where the expression came from that "there is a right to test last" —surely from imagination.

But memories tend to be very short. After the Soviet Union last year abandoned the moratorium and conducted a series of more than forty tests, I suppose that it felt that it had a right to test last. Be that as it may, members here will remember that even after that series of more than forty tests the United Kingdom and the United States made proposals for the stoppage of testing at that point, and forever—the principal price for which, in terms of assurance, was that international inspection be permitted to look at less than one part in two one-thousandths of Soviet territory in any given year. After that series of tests (before the recent U.S. series of tests) even that farthing was not paid to bring this testing to an end.

But, as has been recently announced, the United States is in the midst of re-evaluating both the technical aspects of the problem and its own past proposals to see whether further moves which might facilitate agreement can properly be made. This is a matter on which Ambassador Dean [Arthur H. Dean, chairman of the U.S. delegation] will, in the very near future, have more to say, in the light of new technical data which have been derived from recent tests, and we hope thereby to advance the possibility of agreement.

### OBSESSION WITH SECRECY

But let us not be mistaken; an obsession with secrecy locks the door of disarmament. Reference was made to information which the Soviet Union does not need about the United States. They don't need it because they have it. Secrecy and disarmament cannot live together, as Lord Home [British Foreign Secretary] so effectively pointed out in his remarks. Let me repeat what I said here last spring: There is suspicion. There is suspicion about what might be going on in the vast reaches of the Soviet Union when the rest of the world is open for all to see. There is suspicion that even a tiny bit of international inspection involves espionage affecting the security of the Soviet Union. But surely we can find some way not to have to deal with this problem of good faith: arrangements which make it irrelevant; arrangements which provide assurance; arrangements upon which confidence can be built in the light of experience, as we move forward.

And, of course, while pressing forward with subjects where agreement may be somewhat easier to achieve—and I agree with most of what my colleague Mr. Green [Howard C. Green, Canadian Foreign Secretary] said on that point—we cannot neglect the exploration beyond the present limits of our understanding to the other more challenging and more difficult areas that have been opened up for discussion in this disarmament conference. Lord Home has referred to the remaking of human nature. It may take some time, but even before that we are talking about the transformation of the political structure of international life. And that, too, will take some thought, some imagination, some creative statesmanship, some patience and, I suspect, some time. But within my own Government detailed studies continue as a matter of urgency on all aspects of disarmament, and new possibilities are continually under the most careful consideration.

The United States delegation can go forward, under the able leadership of my very distinguished friend and colleague, Ambassador Dean, with a detailed consideration of the possible provisions of a treaty on general and complete disarmament. We hope the same is true of other governments. For our goal is perhaps the most ambitious, but, certainly, it is the most essential of the items on the agenda of mankind. That goal must be sought in a spirit of fairness and reciprocal accommodation during the negotiations which the forum of this conference makes possible. Attempts to attain propaganda gains and short-sighted or limited tactical maneuvers will get us nowhere and will only engender further mutual suspicion, which is to be avoided. For disarmament is much too important to humanity for such a divisive and a diversionary approach.

I should like to thank each of the eight new members of the conference for their cooperation and understanding. They have made some extremely useful contributions to this subject, both in general and with regard to specific details. And I earnestly hope that we will find in all of the other delegations to this conference a readiness to continue to work with us in a cooperative spirit.

## U.S. READY TO MOVE FORWARD

We shall always state our positions frankly, and we shall put forth only those positions which we expect to be accepted—with which we think the world can live—and not positions based purely upon the basic tactics of public opinion. But we will be reasonable and forthcoming and imaginative to the limit of our ability in seeking ways to overcome difficulties.

We will be ready to share certain risks in disarmament. We are not trying to insist upon foolproof arrangements, because we understand, as others around this table, that an unlimited arms race itself is also risky. We should like to find ways to reduce these risks through arrangements which do provide for the growth of confidence. For we must, as the statement of agreed principles indicated, move forward, but with prudent concern for security and peace and also for the security interests of all signatories to these arrangements.

It is, I am confident, an encouraging sign that, during the presence of a number of foreign ministers here, the co-chairmen were able to reach an agreement, which is before you, about the general procedures which are to govern the Committee's work in the next months on preparing a treaty on general and complete disarmament. I think we should be grateful to Ambassador Zorin [Valerian A. Zorin, chairman of the Soviet delegation] and Ambassador Dean for the patient, skilled work which went into that negotiation. This agreement allows full scope for the consideration in plenary sessions of all of the many detailed problems of stage one, which must be resolved before an accord on treaty language can be reached. It also puts on the two co-chairmen the responsibility for drafting such treaty language.

I can assure you that no government is more anxious than the Government of the United States, from President Kennedy on down, to assume the responsibilities which go with the drafting, the signature and the execution of a sound and safeguarded treaty on general and complete disarmament.

# XIV. THE UNITED NATIONS

## *Why We Support the United Nations*

It is a high privilege for me to be here. As a mere man, I have not been so outnumbered since I taught at a woman's college many years ago. But that experience caused me to treat your invitation as a command. I do not claim that, as a teacher of young women, I came to understand them. But I can confess that I was deeply impressed by them.

One reason was their disconcerting practicality about public affairs. I found that women students insisted upon moving rapidly from the general to the particular, from the abstract to the tangible, from the global to the personal implication. I found them skeptical about the artificial and dangerous games they suspected men were prone to play with words, concepts, myths, and pretense on such important matters as war and peace. And I found them deeply interested in how the story is going to come out in the end, in the building of a decent world order, in arrangements which could make life tolerable for individuals and families, homes and local communities.

Indeed, foreign policy is not a remote abstraction, having only to do with entities called "states," notions like "sov-

Portion of address at the Assembly of the United Church Women, Miami, Florida, October 11, 1961.

ereignty," and formal arrangements called "protocol." In this
climactic period of history foreign policy involves every citizen,
lays its hand upon every home, and embraces our personal aspirations for the kind of world in which we hope our children can
live.

We in the Department of State are deeply interested in what
United Church Women think about the major issues of foreign
policy. We follow your reports, appreciate your support when
you feel you can give it, and pause to reflect if policy fails to com-
mend itself to you. I am grateful, therefore, for an opportunity
to comment upon certain matters upon which you have passed
resolutions at this meeting.

### THE UNITED NATIONS

The first has to do with our support for the United Nations.
The United Nations, of course, has its enemies—those who
fear cooperation among nations, even though science has made
this a world in which we must cooperate or die. The United Nations has its fair-weather friends, who cheer loudly when things
go well but abandon ship if the sea gets rough.

Then there are those who have the patient courage to support the United Nations year in and year out as an indispensable
instrument of peace. Your resolutions over the years have spoken
for your steadfast support, and you represent, I believe, the great
majority of the American public.

I happened to be present at the birth of the United Nations
in San Francisco more than sixteen years ago. I was with it in
New York during the crisis brought on by the tragic death of that
hero of peace, Dag Hammarskjold.

The story of the United Nations during the intervening
years tells us a great deal about the world in which we live. It
also enables us to appraise realistically the present capabilities of
the Organization. I think we should be quite clear about what
the United Nations can do and cannot do, what it is and what it
is not.

Obviously the United Nations has not fulfilled the hopes of

some of its most devoted advocates in 1945. But it is more than a debating society, although debate, even when it does not lead to action, may serve as a safety valve for national passions and helps to clarify issues. We must recognize also that many of the problems put before the United Nations are extremely difficult; they go there because they have not been solved somewhere else.

The United Nations has not banished war. But it has reduced and averted threats to peace—in Iran, Greece, Palestine, Suez, Lebanon and the Congo.

The United Nations has not created unity in a divided world. But it has organized concerts of nations to do together the things upon which they can agree.

The United Nations has not bridged the gap between the world of coercion and the world of free choice. But it provides a bridge between the Northern Hemisphere and the Southern Hemisphere, where most of the new nations are found and where most of the peoples of the non-Communist world are struggling to throw off their burden of poverty.

The United Nations has not ushered in the millennium. But it has laid the foundations for a world community through a wide range of international institutions. Some, such as the World Bank and the International Monetary Fund, have grown into powerful, mature organizations; others are still finding their way. Some do such undramatic but important tasks as working out common technical definitions and allocating frequencies for radio transmission. Some have such dramatically humanitarian tasks as the elimination of malaria and the inoculation of millions of children against the disfiguring and crippling disease of yaws. Others are pioneering in new fields, such as planning a world system of weather reporting. Over the years the United Nations has created the framework for doing more and more of the world's business on the basis of voluntary cooperation among sovereign states.

Within this family of United Nations organizations the United States cooperates with most of the non-Communist world —despite Soviet obstruction, despite the veto, despite threats to peace, despite severe budgetary problems, despite the passion of such subjects as colonialism, despite the inexperience of new members and the inertia of old ones, and despite the inclination of us all to look upon our own views with parochial attachment.

The United Nations is the symbol and the primary substance of the kind of world which the United States seeks to build. Its charter contains an expression of our deepest ideals. We are committed firmly to supporting and strengthening the United Nations. We earnestly wish to extend its writ, its influence, its capacity to act. We look forward to a time when the Soviet Union will join the United Nations in spirit, as well as in name, when it, too, will abide by the principles of the charter and cooperate genuinely in strengthening the great international organization and its agencies.

### REGIONAL ORGANIZATIONS

The United Nations is not the only channel for United States foreign policy. We support various regional organizations. In Western Europe we have lent our encouragement to the formation of a great common market of nearly 300 million relatively prosperous and highly skilled peoples, the second greatest industrial complex in the world. We are working actively to create new institutions for economic cooperation throughout the North Atlantic community.

We take part enthusiastically in the maturing complex of Western Hemisphere institutions. We welcome the trend toward common markets and other forms of cooperation in South and Central America. We salute the new Alliance for Progress. We would like to see durable new forms of regional organization in Southeast Asia. We would welcome progress toward regional cooperation in the Arab world and in tropical Africa.

These new institutions for regional cooperation are not alternatives to the United Nations. Indeed, they are specifically anticipated and authorized in the charter.

We have a vital interest in our system of defensive alliances against those who boast that they will make the world over in their own image. Against threats to freedom, the free must be firm and united.

Many aspects of our foreign policy must be handled on a bilateral basis.

Thus our foreign policy and overseas operations are conducted through a variety of United Nations, regional and nation-to-nation arrangements. These instruments are not mutually exclusive. All are essential, and each complements the others. They must be used simultaneously. For our choice is not among standing firm in our direct confrontation with the Soviets, or building an Atlantic Community, or working with the United Nations. All three, and many other lines of action, help to preserve and develop the kind of world in which free peoples can live in peace and can flourish. . . .

## The Troika

*This was in response to Mr. Khrushchev's renewal of his demand that the Secretary-General of the U.N., then Dag Hammarskjold, be replaced by three persons, each representing one of the principal groups of states.*

Throughout history men have dreamed of a world organization capable of preserving the peace. After World War I the League of Nations was established for this purpose but failed because of internal weakness and defiance by aggressive powers. After World War II the United Nations was created to preserve the peace and security which are now essential as the alternative to the destruction of civilization.

It is therefore particularly regrettable that Chairman Khrushchev persists in his assault on the United Nations. In Moscow

Statement for the Press, July 14, 1961.

this week he stated flatly: "To preserve the situation which now exists in the United Nations means to pave the way to the ruin and death of that international organization."

No one else wants the "ruin and death" of the United Nations. The reason he objects to the United Nations, as he said, is "the situation which now exists" there.

The basic situation "which now exists" in the United Nations is that the Organization has acquired a capacity to act to preserve the peace and security of the smaller nations which make up the great majority of its membership. This does not appear to suit the plans of the Soviet Union.

Mr. Khrushchev contends that he wants an organization in which "all countries belonging to the United Nations have equal rights and enjoy equal opportunities." This is what we have now —and what he does not like. To destroy these equal rights and opportunities, Mr. Khrushchev last year launched his proposal for a three-headed Secretary-General, which he repeated on Monday.

Under this proposal, the executive organ of the U.N. would not be administered by international civil servants but by "three persons *representing the three principal groups of states.*" This reflects Mr. Khrushchev's pretension that the world is divided into three "blocs." There is only one bloc in the United Nations which takes its orders from a single authority: the Communist bloc, which represents 10 per cent of the members. The other 90 per cent are free to think and decide for themselves although they tend to group themselves by cultural and political sympathies and common interests.

The so-called "troika" proposal flies in the face of everything we know about effective administration. But the real point of it is that a majority of the members of the United Nations— countries in Asia, the Middle East, Africa and Latin America— would have a total of one vote among them in the executive direction of the U.N.—and that vote could be nullified by a veto. The United Nations would be powerless to act on any proposal that did not suit the purposes of the Soviet Union.

Thus Mr. Khrushchev's assault against the United Nations is, in reality, an attack on the "equal rights and equal opportunities" now enjoyed by all members of the General Assembly—and the protection afforded them by the U.N.'s peace-keeping machinery.

An impressive majority of the members already has answered Mr. Khrushchev's assault on the integrity of the United Nations when they rejected his outrageous demand, during the Fifteenth General Assembly, to replace the Secretary-General with a three-headed directorate. Mr. Khrushchev made it very clear on Monday that he will continue to press his attack. There is no way that the Soviet Union can impose his proposal. This would mean an amendment of the charter, which requires the consent of the United States and other permanent members of the Security Council. We would not consent, nor would the necessary two-thirds of the General Assembly. The United Nations will not destroy itself.

## The Succession to Dag Hammarskjold

*The death of Dag Hammarskjold, U.N. Secretary-General, in an airplane crash in Africa, threatened to paralyze the executive arm of the U.N. during a critical period in the Congo and gave the Soviet Union a new opportunity to press its "troika" proposal. By a veto in the Security Council, the Soviet Union could prevent the selection of a new Secretary-General. The U.S. took the position that the General Assembly itself could and should immediately*

Remarks at the Foreign Press Association Luncheon, New York City, September 22, 1961.

*designate an Acting Secretary-General. In this talk, Secretary Rusk dealt specifically with this question as well as with the broad commitments of U.S. foreign policy.*

We meet today at the beginning of a General Assembly, which itself is meeting in a climactic period in world affairs. There will be some ninety-six or more items on its agenda. It is not my purpose today to try to comment on those items but to speak briefly on certain aspects of the problems of the United Nations—to speak briefly in order to prepare the way for your questions within the time which is available. I shall try not to filibuster in order to shut off your questions.

But these ninety-six items include some of the most far-reaching, complex, dangerous, important problems before mankind, such as the nuclear arms race, as well as administrative questions such as a staff pension plan.

Some of these items are hardy perennials. You have seen them before. You will undoubtedly see them again. They will remind us that not all questions are solved promptly. Some questions are handled over time, and perhaps some issues can be improved and made less dangerous by applying the poultices or the processes of peaceful settlement represented in the United Nations. But I would suggest to you that no item on the agenda is really unimportant. Some of them will involve attempts to settle difficult and dangerous disputes, but others, and many others, will be involved with the process of building a decent world order.

And, if I might have the privilege of making a recommendation to my colleagues of the press, I would hope that you would help us bring to the attention of the peoples of your countries the great unseen, unsung work of the international community which is going on every day, every week, throughout the world, trying to bring into being a dream which man dared to dream at a time when he was chastened by the bitterest war of our history.

Today I should like to comment on four central threads of

United States policy, which will help us and perhaps you in understanding some of our reactions to the almost hundred items on the agenda of the United Nations. Let me say at the beginning that I know that, when I speak of these central threads of United States policy, there will undoubtedly be some questioning, perhaps a trace of cynicism, some doubts, because one can think of instances where these policies do not appear to be carried fully into effect. May I remind you that—to use the language of the baseball field—at this period of history the United States by and large is expected to bat 1.000. The center of world attention, in a position of leadership at a time when influence on United States policy is a primary object of most foreign offices throughout the world, at a time when we inevitably find ourselves involved in problems throughout the world, therefore in the middle of many disputes, whether of our own making or not, it is not easy for a great power such as the United States to be always entirely simple, entirely clear, even in the application of its most profound commitments. What we can say is that we are determined to work hard, persistently, and in the best means available to us under the circumstances, to give effect to these commitments.

#### COMMITMENT TO THE UNITED NATIONS

I would suggest, if I may without presumption, that our first commitment with respect to an agenda such as we have in front of us is our commitment to the United Nations itself. If I were advising a foreign correspondent or a new ambassador reporting to Washington about how he could best predict the long-range, instinctive reactions of the American people to particular situations, I would suggest that he look first at the preamble and articles 1 and 2 of the United Nations Charter, because I am deeply convinced that in those sections are accurately and succinctly reflected the long-range foreign policy of the American people. I believe that that charter describes the kind of world we should like to see come into being. I believe that charter was drawn to describe that kind of world when men's feelings were disciplined by a war, when their hopes were elevated by the prospects of peace, when men sat down quietly and with patience and dared to think about the kind of world we ought to have.

The most immediate matter in front of us in regard to our commitments to the United Nations is of course the problem of the Secretary-General, brought about by the death of the great man to whom we have just paid tribute, for the United Nations is at a critical crossroads as a result of the unexpected and tragic death of Secretary-General Hammarskjold. The United Nations is now engaged in urgent peacekeeping action in the Congo, in the Middle East and elsewhere throughout the world. Its widespread activities—political, economic, social and humanitarian —demand strong, uninterrupted executive leadership. The Secretariat must continue to be directed with vigor, confidence, and integrity.

It is unfortunately clear, however, that an immediate agreement cannot be expected on the naming of a permanent Secretary-General. The United States therefore believes that action must be taken now to assure that the functions of the office of the Secretary-General are performed effectively and fully while agreement is sought on the appointment of a new Secretary-General.

An outstanding world leader should be named immediately to perform the functions of the office of the Secretary-General for a temporary period, during which efforts to elect a permanent Secretary-General should proceed in accordance with article 97 of the charter.

The authority of the office of the Secretary-General must not be compromised. A "troika" or a panel in any form and at any level of the Secretariat would paralyze the executive of the United Nations and weaken it irreparably. Whoever is appointed should perform the full functions of the office.

The General Assembly, we believe, has full authority to make such a provisional appointment. By the terms of the charter the Assembly has the power to regulate appointments in the Secretariat. That power necessarily includes provisional arrangements for carrying on the functions of the Secretariat's chief officer in emergencies. It has used that power before on at least two important occasions.

The first of these was in 1946 prior to the formal election of a Secretary-General, when the General Assembly adopted the proposal of its President that the Executive Secretary of the United Nations Preparatory Commission be authorized to carry on the duties of Secretary-General pending the appointment of the Secretary-General.

The second occasion was in 1950, when the Security Council was deadlocked in attempting to choose a successor to the first Secretary-General, Mr. Trygve Lie. In November of that year, by a vote of 46 to 5 with 8 abstentions, the General Assembly decided that the present Secretary-General should be continued in office for a period of three years.

The vital interests of the members of the United Nations are heavily involved in this question. The Assembly must move rapidly to fill the void. Events cannot permit drift and indecision in the leadership of the United Nations. We must not allow the prestige and authority of the Organization to be dissipated by delay or by diminution of the effectiveness of an office which has become one of the United Nations' unique contributions to the peace of the world.

#### COMMITMENT TO GROWTH OF LAW AMONG NATIONS

I have spoken of our commitment to the United Nations as the first of the central threads of American policy. I should think a second central thread would be our commitment to the growth of law in relations among nations. We believe that the history of man has shown that the development of law enlarges and does not restrict freedom. In our own personal affairs we understand that we as individuals pass in the course of a single day through hundreds and sometimes thousands of legal relationships, some of them active, many of them latent, some called into play by our own action, others called into play by the action of government or by the conduct of others. But in the mystery and majesty of the operations of law, each of us finds it possible to go through our eccentric orbits with a maximum amount of personal freedom.

That process of law is steadily going on in the international community. On every working day throughout the year, in meetings all over the world, on almost every imaginable subject, arrangements are being reached across national frontiers which make it possible for us to enlarge our respective areas of freedom and to get on with the world's work with harmony.

### COMMITMENT TO FREEDOM

The third commitment and central thread of American policy is our commitment to freedom. This commitment is a part of an ancient dialogue of the human race, a discussion of the political consequences of the nature of man. In the late eighteenth century those who came before us articulated it in the proposition that governments derive their just powers from the consent of the governed. I believe that the American people deeply believe that simple proposition. And we find it important that, when you look through the present membership of the United Nations, you find more than sixty independent members who have traveled the path of national independence—including the United States, of course—and that, looking back on the history of the independence of those sixty members, one can find the sympathy and the support, the influence and the help, of the American people expressed in many different ways.

This commitment to freedom causes complications because it is worldwide, because it has to do with the nature of man. It explains our instinctive reactions to certain issues in the colonial field. It explains our concern about what is going on in areas where the people live under dictatorships. It explains why we are more comfortable with close, democratic friends than with other forms of government. It explains why our consciences are disturbed when we are not able to perform within our own society in full accordance with our own deepest commitments.

### COMMITMENT TO ECONOMIC AND SOCIAL ADVANCEMENT

Our fourth thread of policy is our commitment to economic and social advancement deeply written into the charter of the United Nations and drawn out of our own national experience.

Indeed, we believe that there is an intimate link between economic and social advancement on the one side and freedom on the other. In our own history these two have come together. Indeed, the institutions of freedom were strengthened and enlarged to permit more rapid economic and social advancement. We believe that free institutions provide the machinery, the impetus, the inspiration, through which the resources of men can be mobilized for such advancement and that authoritarian forms cannot properly claim to have special advantage in the speed of development.

To us these are four important commitments. We shall be saying a great deal about them in the United Nations in the weeks and months ahead. When we come to the end of the Assembly, the right question to ask, it seems to me, will be: Has the 16th session of the General Assembly moved us a few steps further along the way toward the kind of world society to which we all are committed under the charter? These words—committed or noncommitted—come in for a great deal of discussion these days. As far as the United States is concerned, we do believe that there are basic common interests between us and all those governments and peoples who understand their own basic commitments to be to the charter and to the principles inscribed in that charter.

Man has lived through some rather dreadful events. He has been seeking his way up a rather slippery glacier for centuries. He has been trying to reach a level of civilized condition which accords with the dignity of man himself. He has chipped out fingerholds and toeholds, sometimes with extraordinary skill, and he can be proud of his accomplishments. But below there remains the abyss, and a few slips can plunge him back again to the jungle out of which he has tried to rise.

These are the issues that underlie the work of an Assembly such as the 16th Assembly. I believe myself that there is great strength in the charter, in the commitment of men to the charter, in the common interests which tie us together. I believe that we can move ahead with confidence and with courage and without fear of those particular storm clouds which are now on the horizon and which must, of course, be somehow dispersed.

*Many of the U.N. members who opposed the troika were reluctant to proceed without prior agreement between the U.S. and the U.S.S.R. Seven weeks of negotiation ensued. On November 3, 1961, the Security Council recommended unanimously that U Thant of Burma be appointed as Acting Secretary-General for the remainder of Mr. Hammarskjold's previously fixed term, ending April 10, 1963. The General Assembly voted unanimously this appointment.*

# XV.  EDUCATION, INFORMATION AND CULTURAL AFFAIRS

*The Community of Science and Scholarship*

. . . I am deeply moved and I am grateful for your receiving me today and giving me this very high honor. These are troubled times. There are problems; there are also great promises and great hopes. But one who is your servant and serving our President and thinking about the world which is shaping itself for the future cannot help but appreciate the kindness and the confidence of his own neighbors here in Atlanta. I will not have time to make what the trade calls a policy speech, but I can't refrain from expressing my respect to a fine university; for a fine university is really a wondrous thing. And one who is in-terested in our relations with the rest of the world cannot help but have the liveliest interest in what a university means.

We think of foreign relations as essentially a governmental matter. And, indeed, relations among governments are—it is almost a truism—handled through governmental channels. But among peoples who are free, among open societies, the foreign relations of the peoples themselves are by no means limited to

Major portion of remarks at Emory University, Atlanta, Georgia, after receiving honorary LL.D., April 20, 1961.

government. Indeed, only a fraction of their relations are handled through official channels. There are a number of great international communities, formed by the people themselves, which spin the threads of common interest and agreement across national frontiers. One of the greatest of these is the international community of science and scholarship, a community formed indeed long before there were national states as we know them today, a community of scholars who have prevailed despite the most awful happenings in the military or the political field, a community that either has known no national frontiers or rejects national frontiers, a community which accepts no language barrier because it learns language and has, to begin with, a community of discourse.

This community of science and scholarship is united by an insatiable curiosity and a thirst for knowledge. And it has an interdependence among its members, among its scientists and scholars, because of the very nature of knowledge. For the building blocks of human knowledge are added one by one to create the mansions of knowledge, by many scholars in many countries, each doing what he can, each cheering and rejoicing in the accomplishments of his fellows, each striving to do his own small part.

In the political field and in formal international relations, we talk sometimes of sanctions. Here is a community which has, though it has no organization, the most subtle, the most powerful, of sanctions one can imagine; for this community enforces its standards of integrity and its expectations of cooperation. Its accolades are awarded on merit. Its esteem is given to those who have added something to the glory of the human race. Few communities are so adept at discovering fraud, and few communities are so ruthless in rejecting it.

Understanding requires knowledge. We need more than passing amiability if we are to understand other peoples and other cultures. The university was invented to understand. And the great world's universities make up a great community of increased understanding. I have no doubt that these great institutions will play an increasingly larger role in the decades ahead in shaping the world and in the structure of our formal relations. The complexity of international relations, the demands being made for talent, the interlocking of the societies of the earth, inevitably will draw universities more and more into the scene—first, by simply being universities, for the greatest contribution such an institution can make is to start by being a fine university in every respect; secondly, by developing the talent we shall need in growing numbers.

In many fields of human activity, in almost every aspect of our own society, certainly in the attempts to build institutions in countries in all parts of the world, it is evident that there is a great shortage of talent. There are less men than money. There are things which cannot be accomplished by money because the men and the women to carry them out are simply not there. And so the universities face the need to train this ever increasing flow of leadership, to take on the complex responsibilities which a growing, unifying world will need, to enlarge the frontiers of knowledge. How often when we stare problems in the face, whether in government or in private life, we must fall back upon the knowledge that we are a rather tiny species, homo sapiens, lost in a mighty universe, learning more and more about the physical universe and, too, about the human universe, but recognizing that there are still great areas of ignorance which may be critical to the survival of man.

But this great adventure is on. It is an exciting decade in which we are living, because a world we have known is passing from view, and a world which is on the horizon is just coming into being. The vast changes of our time are historical changes . . . We have an opportunity now to take our part in building and shaping a new world, a new world based upon those things which universities are joined to discover, the common interests of the human race. This is a great task. It is one which can be accomplished by knowledge, first, by persistence, by hope, of course, by faith, by effort.

## *Education and Development*

. . . the American people have had from the beginning what some people have called an inordinate national interest in education. From the very beginning we emphasized on these shores a strong attachment to the educational process. First it was to educate ministers and our other professional manpower. But something very important happened in the middle of the nineteenth century, which is directly related to our topic today. Because we then were a rapidly developing country, we had great potential of resources, great shortages of trained manpower. We had a continent to open up and develop.

Next year we shall be celebrating the hundredth anniversary of what we call our land-grant college system. Those land-grant colleges and universities were invented in essence to assist in the process of development. They did not phrase it that way at the time, but that in fact was the purpose which underlay our interest in agricultural, mechanical colleges, and that indeed has been the role played by these great institutions.

Alongside of them have been hundreds of private institutions and indeed tax-supported collateral-type universities, which have played more traditional roles. But for us in this country education is not something which is a luxury which can be afforded after development has occurred; it is an integral part, an inescapable and essential part of the developmental process itself.

### "PEOPLE ARE THE BOTTLENECK"

I would suggest that the bottleneck in development today right around the world is not exclusively money or capital resources; a crucial bottleneck continues to be people.

Major portion of remarks at the meeting of the Organization for Economic Cooperation and Development (OECD), Washington, D. C., October 16, 1961.

During the years when I was working for the Rockefeller Foundation, more often than you will imagine, funds were marking time because there was not the qualified manpower either on the giving side or on the receiving side to make those funds profitable on the other end.

I think if we look at the problems of development in country after country outside the West we shall find that people are the bottleneck, and this means that education has a crucial role to play. And this I suspect is the great difference between the possibilities of a program like the Marshall plan and the problems of the developmental programs in the non-Western parts of the world which we see at the present time.

So today in this country we recognize that education has a variety of roles to play. The democratic institutions cannot exist without education, for democracy functions only when the people are informed and are aware, thirsting for knowledge, and are exchanging ideas.

Education makes possible the economic democracy that raises a social mobility, for it is education that insures that classes are not frozen and that an elite of whatever kind does not perpetuate itself.

And in the underdeveloped economies education itself stimulates development by diplomatically demonstrating that tomorrow need not be the same as yesterday, that change can take place, that the outlook is hopeful.

Even in developed economies, education is a key to more rapid and more meaningful economic growth. The old adage has never been more true than today that there is plenty of room at the top. Advanced education is the base on which research and development rests and the foundation of technological progress.

But it is through mass education that the discoveries of the laboratory are applied in the production process, insuring more rapid growth than could occur merely through interest in the acres of land or the number of machines and the total number of man-hours worked.

Knowledge can be found by the few, but it must be applied and distributed by the many.

## *Education—Do It Right*

. . . . The chart of American economic and social development and the chart of American educational development would show approximately the same curve. We did not wait in our educational development until we were rich enough to afford it. We could not have become rich enough to afford it unless we had built education in, with a major effort, at our very beginnings. And we have to be a little careful as Americans in trying to translate our experience into other countries.

My guess is that we might be well instructed to try to think back for a generation, or even fifty years, to look at some of our own problems in education somewhat earlier, if we are to be directly responsive and relevant to the situation that we find in many other countries.

I gather that we have about 2000 institutions of higher education in this country, including junior colleges.

. . . . Our system of higher education is made possible by the enormous resources of the country that are already here. Now, when we turn to other countries that are somewhat nearer the beginnings of their educational effort, we have to remember that it's easier to build a building than it is to build a faculty, that a university cannot inject an educational system downward, that a university caps an effective educational system which provides men and women ready for, prepared for, a university education. And . . . despite the generality of our own experience in this country, there could be such a thing as effective cooperation among educational institutions, some division of labor, some sharing of responsibility, some regional cooperation, in order that the resources which can be made available can be used to the best advantage. . . .

. . . . In this aspect of the matter, private organizations and government play an inseparably linked role of partnership. You

Portion of remarks at National Conference on International Social and Economic Development, Washington, D. C., December 1, 1961.

will be talked to this afternoon about the role of private organizations in this field of education.

Without pointing my finger at you, I should like to suggest to all of us, whether in government or in the private field, that when we are talking about education, and particularly when we are talking about bringing young people from other countries to the United States for training, the emphasis had perhaps better be on the quality of the job rather than the numbers of those who might be somehow involved.

I may leave my colleagues in the Department of State some explaining to do, with these remarks, before the afternoon is over, but let me put it this way: Two halves don't make a whole in this matter. Two ill-prepared or half-prepared young people going back to their country cannot make the contribution which one well-prepared person can make. And if you have six young people who come here for training, who go back disappointed or frustrated or with a sense of failure, there may be six young people who had better not have come in the first place.

And so I would urge both those of us in government and those of us in private organizations to take this business of playing with the lives of people with the greatest of seriousness. And if we involve young people abroad in this process of education by any effort of ours, [let us] do so determined to do it right, whatever the numbers involved. Fewer done well will be far more effective and important and satisfying than a larger number done less well. . . .

## On Knowing What America Stands For

. . . . I can conceive of few subjects more timely for study these days by a wide American audience than the character of our Government.

Remarks on "Continental Classroom," NBC TV, September 25, 1961.

At this moment the philosophy upon which that Government rests is being challenged in many places around the world, yet it is still the most powerful influence in the world because men take seriously the simple notion that governments derive their just powers from the consent of the governed. Or, to put it more simply, men just do not like to be pushed around too much.

In such a time of continuing conflict, it is imperative that we Americans not merely recognize by name and by instinct the values which we are defending, but that we thoroughly understand them. These values find their expression in the nature of our Government as it has developed from our own revolutionary manifesto, the Declaration of Independence, and through the Constitution and the Bill of Rights, and through many decisions in courts of law, so that we have a government of the people, by the people, and for the people which we believe we have succeeded in providing in ever greater degree.

Millions of people in other countries think of America as a place where no one need go hungry, where children have shoes, where workingmen own automobiles. It is sad but true that many of these people believe it is these material conditions that we have in mind, rather than any climate of political and social principle, when we speak of our way of life.

It is equally sad, but I think true, that we have ourselves in part to blame for this. We are very apt to fall into ways of thought and speech in which the values of our system are defined in terms of per capita income or tons of steel. How can other peoples understand if we ourselves forget that it is not our material welfare by itself, but the fact that we have been able to achieve it alongside of and because of individual liberties, which constitutes the glory of our American system?

No Soviet citizen who crosses the borders of the Communist world is unschooled in the dialectic of Marx and Lenin, of Stalin and Khrushchev. The Soviet student who comes to this country under our exchange program and finds himself pressed in argument by the Americans he meets is crammed to his fingertips with answers to the questions which challenge his Communist faith. They may be wrong answers to us, but he believes them. He has been schooled in these answers from the nursery. But sometimes our own students, and older travelers as well, find themselves at a loss under similar cross-questioning by a Soviet group.

How can this happen? It happens ironically because our own free system does not insist that every citizen be competent in political theory, even in the theory of the Government of his own country, because our own free citizens sometimes have not themselves thought through these basic questions. Such questions as: What is it in this country that is really of enduring value? And why are we proud to be what we are, Americans? The fact is that we take for granted a great deal which is taken for granted by few other people.

For example, we have recently come peacefully through a great national election which found the nation divided in almost equal halves over issues on which millions on both sides had deep convictions. We take this peaceful outcome for granted, regardless of which candidate or party we voted for, and we know it will be just as orderly next time. But in many countries in the world no one knows when he will have an opportunity to make a free electoral choice, and in many others the next election when it does come will be the certain signal for much violence, for military plots and efforts to determine the outcome by force. Those who live as we do, secure in the expectation of peaceful political change, are a small minority among people.

Just as we take our elections for granted, so we are apt to take for granted other manifestations of those rights which we hold to be inalienable but which relatively few governments in any era, in any time, have had both the will and the power to assure. The ideas upon which our nation was founded and upon which it continues to grow are our most precious national resource; and ideas, like other resources, are valid only so long as men and women use them and live by them. Ideas need exercise if they are to continue strong.

To be an American today, more than ever, is to know the ideas that have made America what it is, to know what it is that we stand for in this time of worldwide conflict. Few of us can fail to gain from a study of our Government today, and I think that most of us can gain a great deal. . . .

## The Voice of America

. . . . Information has been an ancient arm of diplomacy, growing with the means available and with the increasing role of ordinary citizens in the course of public affairs.

Diplomacy today has many dimensions—economic and technical assistance, military aid, and information and cultural activities among them. Today we proudly mark the twentieth anniversary of the Voice of America, one of the oldest of the modern American ventures in international information.

I say "modern" because periodically through our history we have sought to explain ourselves to the people of the world as well as to their leaders. Our first efforts, in fact, date back to the very beginnings of this nation, when our Declaration of Independence noted the American desire for a "decent respect to the opinions of mankind."

Although we made a small effort during the First World War, it was not until World War II that we Americans fully realized how much our country's security and stature depended on what ordinary people everywhere thought of us, our institutions and our intentions. In 1942, at the high-water mark of enemy advance, President Roosevelt launched the Voice of America and shortly thereafter asked the celebrated radio news analyst Elmer Davis to head an Office of War Information and tell America's story to the world.

After the war the United States for the first time made information activities a permanent part of our work abroad. Today we in the State Department consider the information program an indispensable dimension of American diplomacy. The Voice of America and our other information activities demonstrate our respect for the opinions of people as well as their governments.

We in this country define responsible government as that which is responsible to, and periodically accountable to, the people in whose name it acts. However, not every government ac-

Portion of remarks at ceremonies marking the twentieth anniversary of the Voice of America, February 26, 1962.

cepts this definition. And yet, even in these countries, public opinion is not a negligible factor in the considerations of their rulers. It is precisely in those countries in which public partici- pation is the smallest where the greatest precautions are taken to control the information reaching the public.

If, then, the public in countries controlled by dictatorships can exercise a moderating influence on their government officials, we must see to it that the public knows the facts. It must have more information than its own governments are willing to make available. This is an important part of the job of the U.S. Infor- mation Agency and its Voice of America.

Thus the first responsibility of the Voice of America is to broadcast the news, fully and fairly. This the Voice is doing, and it should not be otherwise. In its commentaries the Voice of America should explain clearly the policies and views of the United States Government. This the Voice is doing, and it should not be otherwise.

These days VOA commentaries deal with the most impor- tant subjects of current affairs: the Berlin crisis, and our deter- mination that this city shall remain free and accessible; disarma- ment, and our determination to reach agreement on an effective program of general and complete disarmament; the United Na- tions, and our determination that this peacekeeping body shall be strengthened, not weakened; man's desire to choose his own future, and our determination that freedom of choice shall be cherished and extended; and the efforts of newly developing na- tions to modernize their economies and societies, and our deter- mination to help them.

Now twenty years old, the international information pro- gram is a full-fledged partner in the conduct of American foreign affairs. I welcome and appreciate this opportunity to participate in these ceremonies marking the twentieth birthday of the Voice of America. My colleagues in the State Department at home and abroad join me in wishing this voice of freedom many happy re- turns of the day.

With confidence in the future of our country and free men everywhere, I am certain there will be many more such happy anniversaries.

# XVI. TOASTS AND TRIBUTES

*Bataan and Corregidor*

*On this occasion two short streets in Washington were renamed respectively Bataan Street and Corregidor Street.*

. . . . Some twenty years and four months ago the waves of aggression swept through the peaceful Pacific—in the Philippines, in Hawaii, in Southeast Asia. It was a war unwanted, unprovoked and for which we were not prepared. Once again we learned that peace-loving peoples who neglect their arms can tempt the ambitious who make the mistake of confusing democracy's desire for peace with a willingness to submit. Our friends in the Philippines were moving rapidly toward the complete freedom which a free people in America had pledged to them in full measure. The land was bright with the promise of dreams about to be fulfilled.

But in those months of early 1942, freedom was hanging by the sheerest threads in Europe, the Middle East and Asia. The human spirit was called upon to provide, in gallantry and cour-

Portion of remarks at exercises commemorating Bataan Day, Washington, D. C., April 9, 1961.

age, what slender arms could not accomplish. The final victory of free men was assured by what was revealed on Bataan and Corregidor, by the Filipino and American men and women who fought with General MacArthur and General Wainwright. It was their splendor which gave the ring of true prophecy to the words, "I shall return." The enemy flag was finally hoisted on Corregidor but it was only occupied, not conquered. The courage of the regiments which were overcome there became the courage of individuals who continued the fight, singly and in small groups. The war continued within the Philippines until MacArthur and his forces came ashore to link up with those who had been carrying the struggle and to bring it to a prompt and victorious end. The march to Philippine freedom was then resumed and a great democracy arose from the consuming fires of those bitter years.

Today, Mr. Ambassador, the Filipino and American peoples are joined with us here in Washington. In every state of our union are homes which shared with yours the glory and the suffering of Bataan and Corregidor. Both in your land and in ours the wounds of war will heal, for reconciliation is a great source of hope in the tragic story of man. But we shall not forget our comrades, and the personal friends, who reminded us that freedom is not cheap, but is for the strong in spirit.

Bataan and Corregidor make up another inspiring chapter in the history of freedom. It is a history not fully told, filled with great deeds by individuals and nations, who staked all they had on the hard choices which had to be made. Here was an entire people denying to mere power a privileged intrusion upon the dignity of man. Here might have been a judge, throwing his arm around a prisoner at the bar, saying to a despotic King that the King must do no wrong. In another place it was a writer or an orator who proclaimed at great hazard the simple truth that man was born to be free. Bataan and Corregidor are a part of the greatest story written by man, a story not yet finished, but a story which can have only one end because the nature of man will have it so.

It is a great privilege for me to be here today to speak for the President and for the people of the United States in sending our greetings to President Garcia and the people of the Philippines and to pay tribute to those we remember as we establish here in Washington a perpetual reminder of their gallantry in the naming of Bataan and Corregidor Streets.

## To the President of the Republic of China

*This is the first of three examples of Mr. Rusk's toasts to visiting dignitaries, following dinners given by him and Mrs. Rusk in the State Dining Room on the eighth floor of the New State Department Building.*

Mr. Vice President, we are deeply grateful for this opportunity to bid you welcome. We are especially grateful that you have brought with you a distinguished body of colleagues, including your Foreign Minister and other associates in your Government, your Ambassador to Washington and your able and veteran Ambassador to the United Nations in New York. These are old friends, these men whom you bring with you, and we welcome them. But you have given us a special treat this evening because of the charming and gracious ladies who are members of your party. I wonder if I might ask the ladies from China who are present please to rise and let us greet them.

Thank you very much.

One of the elementary principles of good international relations is the principle of reciprocity. Mr. Vice President, it is perfectly obvious to all of us, I am sure, that our guest list this evening was prepared on the basis of the loveliness of our ladies who could join us here. . . .

Portion of toast given at a state dinner honoring Chen Cheng, Vice President of the Republic of China, and Mrs. Chen, August 1, 1961.

It is difficult, Sir, to speak just with the mind about China, because Americans who think of China and speak of China must do so with their hearts as well. There are many speeches about China which could be made on an occasion like this by any American. We could speak, for example, of the more than a century of affection for China and the Chinese people, an affection which endures in this country. And if we have been disturbed, distressed, upset, appalled by events in that great country, part of it is the feeling that a lover has gone astray; because every American child has grown up with a sense of respect and affection for your great country.

We could make a speech about our comradeship in war, the service we had together in uniform; you, Sir, and I, myself, and many hundreds of thousands of Americans were engaged in that great struggle. We can recall General Chennault's flyers, who wore on their jackets a message in Chinese which, in effect, said that this is an American flyer who is helping China fight the enemy and that it is the duty of every Chinese to risk his life to bring this flyer back to his base. And the heroism shown in that process is something which Americans shall never forget.

I, myself, Sir, can remember in Burma how difficult it was for me as an American officer to shave in front of a mirror hanging on a bush without two or three Chinese soldiers standing around, fascinated by this mysterious operation. And I can remember, after the war, reflecting with my Commanding General upon our experiences in China and Burma, when he remarked, "You know, the only things we did not like about the Chinese were their American characteristics."

We could make a speech, Sir, about the great debt which we owe to your country, its traditions, its art, its philosophy, its contribution to the enrichment of American life and culture. Anyone who has seen that stunning exhibit in the National Gallery in recent weeks will have a full appreciation of what we mean.

But apart from the past, we could make a speech about the promise and the future of China, about what you and your colleagues have done on the Island which is now your primary responsibility; the revolution in the life of the people which has occurred under your leadership, the demonstration that economic and social development can occur quickly and that American aid can make its contribution to a total effort which revolutionizes the life of an entire people.

And we can speak of the future in longer range terms. We can think of that China of which you are the spokesman; we can think of the day when the Chinese people will once again be free. So, Mr. Vice President, our hearts are full, if our tongue is halting, with all that China means to the American people. We appreciate your being here. The President and the rest of us have greatly benefited from the discussions which we have had. It has been an inspiring, a fruitful and a frank discussion of the sort which can take place only among close friends.

So, ladies and gentlemen, it is with deep honor that I ask you to rise to join in a toast to the President of the Republic of China.


## To the Shah of Iran

Your Majesty, it is a very great pleasure to welcome you here in the Department of State and to the United States. . . . It is just possible that you have wondered how it can be that a people who are so stubbornly republican in their tradition could be so enthusiastic about a visiting monarch. I will try to tell you, sir. In the first place, I think I would have to confess that there is just a little streak of royalist in each one of us. And I think also, when we know of the elan and gallantry which you have brought to the public life of your country, we cannot help but recall that phrase out of our own literature, "every inch a king." When we think of what you are doing for your country, it reminds us of a phrase which comes out of our own tradition of royalty, from many generations back, "Ich diene," I serve. And may I say that Her Majesty, the Queen Empress, has in the most literal sense won the hearts of the American people.

Given at a state dinner for the Shah of Iran and the Empress Farah, April 13, 1962.

The American people react with, I think, sir, considerable understanding about people in other parts of the world, and we know that there are kings and kings. We remember, for example, the remark in our tradition that when the king announced at mid-day, "what a beautiful night," everyone else said, "and how lovely the stars." We know, sir, that you are not that king because we know that your crown is deeply rooted in the affections of your people, that your dreams are dreams on behalf of your people. . . .

You assumed responsibility at the head of your great nation at a most difficult period, and you have brought it through some very horrendous events: war and crisis and disturbance. You have injected into the life of your country an element of repose and stability and confidence, at the same time a demand for progress and achievement. You have put before your people the vision of the future which it is in their hands to accomplish. You are a people's king. You are a sovereign whom we greatly admire because of the commitments which you have made. We have been deeply impressed, sir, in your conversations here in this capital in this most recent visit, by the eloquence with which you have voiced your aspirations, and the simplicity with which you have demonstrated your basic purpose. Ladies and Gentlemen, may I ask you to join in a toast to His Imperial Majesty, the Shah-in-Shah of Iran?

# To the President of the Republic of the Ivory Coast

Mr. President, Madame Houphouet-Boigny, distinguished guests from the Ivory Coast, distinguished members of Congress, Mr. Justice Reed, Mr. Bowles, ladies and gentlemen:

Given at a state dinner honoring President and Mme. Felix Houphouet-Boigny, May 23, 1962.

I know, Mr. President, that you would wish our guests to join with us in thanking our friends in the Navy Band and the Marine Band and the Army Chorus for having made our evening very gay. . . . Thank you very much, gentlemen.

Mr. President, you know already from President and Mrs. Kennedy and from the people of New York and Washington how welcome you and your party are to the United States. It is a great occasion for us, and we hope it will be one which you, also, will remember. If I were to tell the exact truth, sir, I would have to say that, by and large, the American people have not known a great deal about your country. This is for historical reasons. But I would also have to say to be truthful, that they have a consuming appetite to know more about your country, and that we are most receptive to the efforts of your distinguished ambassador and other representatives of your country to teach us more about the Ivory Coast. Your own personal reputation, sir, has preceded by some years the knowledge of most Americans about your country. But, nevertheless, there are deep ties, which, upon reflection, bind us together.

The first of these ties, Mr. President, lies at the very center of our own tradition. We represent that tradition here in this building and here in this city. We are meeting this evening in the Benjamin Franklin Room. You received our guests in the Thomas Jefferson Room. From the balcony after dinner you can look to the East and see the lighted Capitol of our Congress, which gives tangible representation to the simple idea that governments derive their just powers from the consent of the governed. And your eye will sweep across the Washington Monument, the Jefferson Monument, the Lincoln Memorial. This great tradition of freedom is one which you and we have shared, even though with a slight difference. If John Locke and Thomas Jefferson articulated these ideas in English, Montesquieu and Rousseau and others articulated them in French, and brought to life those flaming words, "Liberty, Equality, Fraternity." You, sir, have drunk deeply of this tradition, and have made your own contribution to it. This is a tradition which is universal, which goes beyond what we in the West have had to say about it.

There is another tie which links our two countries. We have

here many millions of citizens who came from West Africa. We are not proud, sir, of the way in which their forefathers came here, but we are very proud that they are here. We know that there is unfinished business before their contribution reaches full flower, but we also know that we would be a poorer nation materially and spiritually were they not with us to help us live out in this continent this common chapter in the great story of the freedom of man.

And, finally, sir, we share a great tie in our dreams for the future. You have in your heart, at the top of your mind, at the top of your anxieties, the need for the economic and social development of your country. This is a need which we recognize and for which we have the deepest, affectionate interest, because what is sometimes forgotten about this country is that we, too, were undeveloped through vast areas of our own country during the lifetime of people in this room. We know what life without science and technology, without public health, without education, is, and we have seen, within the framework of free institutions, a dramatic development within a short period, which can transform the life of peoples. So we are not discouraged by these problems of development which you face, sir. We feel your ally in these problems, because they touch upon an experience which is deep in the hearts of many American citizens at the present time. We share this vision of the future, and that, perhaps, is the most important of all the ties which bind us together, because the world which is coming into being is even more important to us and to our children than the worlds which have gone before. And on that tie we are necessarily and easily, congenially and comfortably, in the closest association.

And so, Mr. President, what we do not know about each other is of passing importance. What we do know about each other is entirely fundamental. It is a great privilege for me, therefore, to ask ladies and gentlemen present to rise and drink a toast to His Excellency, the President of the Republic of the Ivory Coast.

## *To John Foster Dulles*

### *John Foster Dulles, Secretary of State, 1953-1959, died May 24, 1959.*

. . . . John Foster Dulles brought to his post a rich experience of preparation. Not many of us here will live to hear the final verdict of history upon his role as a great leader of our country. Future historians will enjoy the luxury of being able to tell more precisely how things turned out, but he was confronted with the task of looking through the swirling fog to perceive events before they occurred, to help shape them where possible, and to move on with his task. But we need not await the final verdict of history—those of us who have worked with him—to recall important things about him and to recognize his stamp on ourselves, his colleagues.

I think first of personal dedication, a stern sense of duty, a capacity to commit himself totally, selflessly, to his task. You have heard something about the hours he kept, his work with the churches, his public life. I recall times when we assigned staff officers to him in rotation because one officer alone could not keep up the pace. He was a man who never spared his energy, a man who never was diverted by triviality from the job at hand, a man who brought his total resources to the task which he had undertaken.

I recall a man of peace, but a special kind of peace: a just and durable peace. A peace with a quality to it, not just a peace of submission; a peace of which men have dreamed since man began to articulate; a peace to be worked for because building a peace is hard, a peace to be ordered because law must permit change to occur without violence; a peace which in moments of crisis might have to be fought for.

Portion of remarks at John Foster Dulles Memorial Service, New York City, May 22, 1961.

Peace is directly related to a continuing search for the things which unify. The headlines talk of the things which divide. But the builder is looking for the foundations of peace, and these are often the little noticed, the apparently unimportant, the undramatic, the quiet ways in which men from different parts of the earth set about their daily tasks through common interest and common practical advantage.

I recall a man who cherished freedom; who studied deeply the unfolding of the great story of the freedom of man; who knew something of the great forks in the road where decisions had to be made which embarked upon one great course rather than another; who understood two thousand years of effort to establish freedom under law, to bring tyranny under the rule of constitutions, and to provide peaceful processes for settling disputes within societies as well as outside national states; who knew what it took to transform the doctrine that the King can do no wrong to the practice that if it is wrong the King must not be permitted to do it. The great revolution of freedom is deeply rooted in human nature and is still the fermenting force of the world in which we live. It is a revolution in which we find allies in all parts of the earth and which history will surely not turn back.

He was a man who had great love and respect for his own country. He was not unduly boastful of its successes, not unduly proud of its great achievements. But he was also not unduly apologetic of its failures, because he understood something of the pathetic story of man, the efforts which have gone into this great nation, and the promise which lies ahead, the never-ending struggle for the perfection of a democratic society.

John Foster Dulles thought of his own nation as a part, an honorable and active part, of the great commonwealth of man. He never hesitated to suggest that a particular national interest might be fused in the common interest with others to build toward that great commonwealth. He was a man of courage derived from deep faith, and of the joy which comes from that kind of courage. For him, life was not always a succession of triumphs. There were disappointments, there were defeats. But he took these without losing stride, or blinking an eye, or diverting himself from the great tasks ahead. And these are matters of great public record: his role as a founder of the United Nations—an organization which has not quite lived up to our hopes, perhaps, because our hopes are high—but an organization which has served as a "near miss," the nearest miss we have had so far in giving institutional life to the great dream of men.

We recall the extraordinary feat of reconciliation he negotiated with our former enemies in Japan, as well as the steps he took to bring another enemy, Germany, back as an eminent member of the great Atlantic community. We also remember his efforts to bind those who were committed to freedom into strong associations all over the earth because it was important that those who were free should be determined to remain so. But perhaps my warmest recollection is that of his deep sense of individual responsibility both as an official and as a citizen. He was, as are many people in public life, frequently asked as he traveled around: "What can I as a citizen do?" I remember on one occasion he said, "Don't ask me the answer to that question. Look around you—you are surrounded by opportunities. Think about them, take hold of them, make use of them, rise to meet them."

*Statement on dedication of the John Foster Dulles Library of Diplomatic History at Princeton University, May 15, 1962.*

I am deeply distressed that overriding duties, of the sort with which John Foster Dulles was entirely familiar, make it impossible for me to be present for the dedication of the John Foster Dulles Library at Princeton University.

It is entirely fitting that Princeton University should be the repository of his papers. Those of us who knew him as a friend knew of his devotion to his alma mater. It was while a Princeton undergraduate that he undertook his first diplomatic mission—at the second Hague Peace Conference in 1907. Thus began more than a half century of dedicated service to his country in the foreign policy field.

The Dulles Library at Princeton and the Eisenhower Library at Abilene will be invaluable sources for the historians of the future. The papers themselves, standing alone, will not tell the complete story; they can only be clues to the story. For John Foster Dulles was Secretary of State at a time when United States policy was pursued in an utterly complex world and in a period when events moved with breathtaking speed. Only a fraction of what was in his mind, and in the mind of the President he served, was inscribed in formal documents. The historian, if he is to be accurate, must try to reconstruct the context—the total context —which surrounded what was written down. Today was not yesterday, and tomorrow would be different, too. To recapture the changing scene and what Mr. Dulles thought about it will be the historian's delicate and painstaking task.

Accident, mystery, the surging events in a hundred countries in every continent were all a part of his daily fare. And he was building toward a decent world order not on the basis of exact blueprints, mathematically guaranteed, but in the light of a future but dimly perceived, as through a fog. For the statesman must move from facts which can never be quite complete into a future which, perhaps mercifully, cannot be surely known.

But out of the papers stored here in Princeton will come a picture of a dedicated man, deeply committed to the peace and wellbeing of his own country and deeply, as well, aware that the fate of his own country was linked to that of peoples in the remotest parts of the world. It was a privilege to serve with him as friend and colleague and to share both his satisfactions and his disappointments as he tried to shape the course of events to accord with the aspirations of the American people and his own commitments to peace and freedom.

## To Diplomacy

There is a corporate sense in diplomacy . . . something beyond the passing temporal interest of each particular state. And this corporate sense is related to the aspirations of all mankind. . . .

Diplomacy works for the elimination of the accidental irrelevancies in relations among states. That is why we try to be formal and correct and civil and polite despite the vigor and the depth of our occasional differences. In diplomacy we understand that it is the duty of a diplomat to represent earnestly and vigorously and actively the interests of his own country. But in the great business of diplomacy, there is that constant search for the common interest, for the possibilities of the resolution of disputes, for the possibilities of the small steps or the large steps upon which peace can be built. For the diplomat knows it is never too early to try to prevent a crisis from arising, and it is never too late to attempt to prevent a catastrophe.

Excerpts from toasts at two state dinners for members of the diplomatic corps given by Secretary and Mrs. Rusk, Washington, D. C., December 8 and 19, 1961.

# XVII.   OUR GOAL:
## A WORLDWIDE   VICTORY
## FOR FREEDOM

. . . . All of us, of course, are deeply concerned about our country's future; but there is something special about that concern among men and women who have worn the uniform of their country in times of trial. For us, words like "war" and "peace" have a special meaning. We know, as veterans, that foreign policy reaches into every home and into every community. We know the price when statecraft fails. We know why it is important to seek peaceful solutions wherever possible, consistent with basic principle and vital interest.

I know I don't need to prove to you that we live in a world of turmoil and change. I know I don't need to emphasize to you that we live in a time of danger and that the primary cause of this danger is the existence of powerful forces which are determined to destroy our free way of life.

The global struggle for freedom and against Communist imperialism is our main business in the State Department. My colleagues and I give intensive attention, day by day, to Communist strategy and tactics.

No one has to convince us that when Khrushchev said com-

Major portion of address at convention of Veterans of Foreign Wars, Minneapolis, Minnesota, August 13, 1962.

munism will bury us he was proclaiming not just an alleged historical inevitability but an objective toward which Communists work relentlessly by all the means they deem effective. No one has to convince us that "peaceful coexistence" means to them a continuing attempt to spread their system over the earth by all means short of the great war which would be self-defeating. No one has to convince us that the contest between Communist imperialism and freedom is for keeps.

### ACHIEVING A PEACEFUL WORLD COMMUNITY

We have a simple but transcendent goal. It has been stated many times and in many ways. It is, in President Kennedy's words, "a peaceful world community of free and independent states, free to choose their own future and their own system so long as it does not threaten the freedom of others."

This goal of ours—and of most of the nations of the world—and the Communist goal are incompatible. This global struggle will continue until freedom prevails. It goes without saying that our purpose is to win.

One hears now and then that we have a "no win" purpose or policies. That is simply not so. Of course we intend to win. And we are going to win.

And who makes up the "we"? Not only 185 million Americans, but most of the rest of the people of the world. And what is the worldwide victory we work for? Not the victory of one nation over another or of one people over another, but a worldwide victory for freedom.

To win this worldwide victory we must achieve:

a world free of aggression—aggression by whatever means;

a world of independent nations, each with the institutions of its own choice but cooperating with one another to their mutual advantage;

a world which yields continuing progress in economic and social justice for all peoples;

a world which provides sure and equitable means for the peaceful settlement of disputes and moves progressively toward a rule of law which lays down and enforces standards of conduct in relations between nations;

a world in which, in the great tradition shared by peoples in every continent, governments derive "their just powers from the consent of the governed";

a world in which the powers of the state over the individual are limited by law, practice and custom—in which the personal freedoms essential to the dignity of man are secure.

Our hope and purpose is to win without a great war and the damage which the weapons of today would inflict upon the human race. For we will defend our vital interests and those of the free world by whatever means may be necessary, but a military climax to this struggle is to be prevented if possible.

## PRIMARY PURPOSE OF U.S. MILITARY STRENGTH

The primary purpose of our military forces is to make resort to force by our adversaries unprofitable and dangerous. Our forces have been greatly strengthened in the last eighteen months. Our nuclear deterrent has been amplified, and a rising proportion of it is relatively invulnerable to attack. We have the capacity to inflict massive destruction upon any nation that would be so irrational as to attack us or our allies.

Our conventional forces, too, have been strengthened. They are being modernized and made more mobile—not as a substitute for our nuclear capacity but to cope with more limited requirements.

In addition we have been improving our capacity to deal, and assist our allies in dealing, with guerrilla warfare, a form of aggression which the Communists, in their inverted jargon, call "wars of national liberation." This is the form of the present aggression against South Viet-Nam. And it will not be allowed to succeed.

Thus, as my colleagues in the State Department and I go about our business, we have at our backs a formidable array of military strength under the command of a resolute President. This strength, with that of our many allies, is capable of de-

fending the vital interests of the free world. When President
Kennedy says that we and our allies have vital interests in West
Berlin—vital interests which all free peoples share with the
brave inhabitants of that city—"vital interests" means just that:
interests to be protected as a matter of elementary safety for free
men. We are prepared to discuss ways and means for reducing
tensions in Central Europe and to search for more permanent
solutions to those problems, but we will not be forced, harassed
or squeezed out of West Berlin. We are determined to see that
West Berlin thrives in freedom. And we have other vital interests in common with the free peoples of Latin America, Europe,
Asia, the Far East and elsewhere, which we are also resolved to
maintain.

### SEARCH FOR AREAS OF POTENTIAL AGREEMENTS

At the same time, despite bitter and far-reaching differences,
we seek continually areas of common or overlapping interest—
areas of potential concrete agreements. In June 1961, at Vienna,
Mr. Khrushchev and President Kennedy agreed that both favored an independent and neutral Laos. Last month at Geneva
an agreement was signed by fourteen nations providing for the
independence and neutrality of Laos. If the agreement is faithfully executed, all foreign troops will leave Laos and the Laotians
will be left alone to control their own affairs and Laos will cease
to be an avenue of supply and reinforcement for the Communist aggression against South Viet-Nam. I underline the need that
the agreement be faithfully executed. We on our side shall do
everything possible to see that it is. We believe the Government
of Laos will do its best, and we expect all others to do the same.

There is another matter in which, objectively examined,
all the great powers have a genuine common interest. I refer
to the halting of the upward spiral of the arms race. Let us be
clear about what this means and what it does not mean. We have
a security interest in turning the arms race downward; otherwise the path ahead means increasingly vast diversions of re-

sources away from the unfinished business of mankind as well as increasing dangers for all concerned as weapons systems tax or exceed the capacities of the mind of man. But disarmament measures cannot be unilateral; surely the free world learned that lesson from the demobilization after World War II. Disarmament must be achieved by steps consistent with the security of all concerned and with fully adequate assurance that agreements are faithfully carried out. In today's world such agreements cannot rest upon blind faith; but arrangements can be worked out under which confidence can rest upon knowledge and not mere trust. In limited fields, such as nuclear testing, improved techniques and instrumentation may permit somewhat more efficient and less costly arrangements. But the need for verification remains. We see no way in which the abolition of all nuclear testing can be achieved unless the Soviet Union is ready to abandon its obsession with secrecy. And the rest of the world cannot disarm without knowing what arms are being concealed in those vast and closely policed areas in the very heart of the Eurasian landmass. We hope that self-interest and the yearning of the Soviet peoples for a better life will cause the Soviet Government to reconsider and sit down with the rest of us to work out practical steps which will begin to reduce the burdens and dangers.

### PROGRESS TOWARD OUR GOAL

Now how are we getting along in this great struggle for freedom? A Secretary of State, watching the daily flow of cables from a world in rapid and far-reaching change, cannot afford to be an easy optimist. But I believe that a measured appraisal leads to the conclusion that the historical forces of freedom are writing fresh chapters of achievement and confidence.

With regard to the industrially advanced countries of the free world, a new industrial revolution has swept over the free countries of Europe in this postwar period. Everywhere there are new factories, new jobs, new buildings, growth and prosper-

ity. Strong new economic and political links have been forged,
and still others are now taking shape.

The notion that we in America somehow resent or regret
this new vitality and confidence in Europe is plain nonsense.
This new era has been an objective of our own hopes and policy;
it is, among other things, the rich harvest of the massive efforts
which the Europeans and we made together through the Marshall Plan. We applaud the result thus far and warmly support
the prospects for an even stronger and more unified Europe.

For let us not underestimate the importance of these developments to the worldwide struggle for freedom. A vigorous Atlantic partnership will mean closer political consultation to build
the strength and unity of the free world as a whole. It will mean
an ability to share more broadly the larger economic responsibilities for development beyond the Atlantic community. Already Europe is approaching the magnitude of effort of the
United States in responding to the urgent needs of the developing countries.

And under the strenuous conditions of a still unsettled
world, this partnership can provide the military strength, both
conventional and nuclear, necessary to defend the peace and to
sustain a steadily growing rule of law. In a period of lively discussion within the NATO alliance about next chapters in the
organization of our common defense, it is inevitable that there
would be speculation which sometimes misses the point. NATO
is not a limited liability company. For us, and for our allies, the
defense of NATO requires whatever means are necessary. We
have taken important steps, through the sharing of information, the frank discussion of strategic problems, and consultation on multilateral NATO nuclear forces, to emphasize that we
consider that the safety of NATO as a whole is critical to our
own security. If there is a ferment of discussion within the alliance, this has nothing to do with the underlying commitments
to which we all pledged ourselves when NATO was born. "What
is past is prologue." What is present is the takeoff point of the
future. The ferment comes out of the creative discussion of next
steps, of which the Common Market and those negotiations are
only the most immediate.

Beyond the Atlantic community are others joining in similar efforts—nations such as Japan and Australia, whose contributions are large and growing.

The prospect among all these nations is for vigorous economic growth and the steady expansion of trade. Let me point out that according to Marxist-Leninist dogma this could not occur. According to that fanciful doctrine, the industrialized nations should be ripped by ever deepening economic crises and by fighting among themselves. Instead, they are working together in ever closer cooperation and are enjoying levels of well-being undreamed of a generation ago.

### PROGRESS WITHIN THE UNDERDEVELOPED WORLD

Equally dramatic changes are taking place in that vast portion of the non-Communist world that is less advanced industrially. Never before in history have so many new, independent states been born in so short a period of time. And all of them, as well as the older but still underdeveloped nations, are determined to modernize their societies and improve the standards of living of their people.

One by one, new nations and their leaders are experiencing the sobering influence of responsibility. They are learning, sometimes painfully, that independence is by itself no panacea for their ills. Independence alone does not feed hungry mouths nor turn the wheels of industry; nor does it alone find markets for excess production or automatically build schoolhouses or homes or communications.

But some have managed the transition from revolutionary struggle to peaceful construction with great skill and statesmanship. Within the last few years a number of underdeveloped countries have made solid economic and social advances. And many others have made promising starts.

Some are still floundering. Some are devoting time and energy and resources to questionable adventures. But, on the whole, there is progress within the underdeveloped areas of the non-Communist world. All the free nations have a vital interest in assisting this progress.

### NEW PARTNERSHIPS DEVELOPING IN FREE WORLD

As for us, we have rejoiced in the arrival of the peoples of Asia and Africa to the "separate and equal station to which the Laws of Nature and of Nature's God entitle them." This is well understood in the new nations. Most of their leaders are familiar with our history and the great and enduring ideas expressed in our Declaration of Independence.

Nearly all of them also appreciate our readiness to assist them and understand well that our only purpose is to help them maintain their independence and improve the wellbeing of their people. And nearly all understand that the United States stands not for a sterile *status quo* but for vigorous progress.

As President Kennedy said in Venezuela last December:

We do not merely talk of slogans, of democracy and freedom; it is our function here in this hemisphere in 1961 to make it possible for all the people not only to be free but to have a home and educate their children and have a job for themselves and in security. And that is what we are determined to do.

President Kennedy spoke of this hemisphere, but the goal he set applies to other regions as well.

New ties are being created almost daily between us and the new states of Asia and Africa. In Latin America the Alliance for Progress has breathed new life and vigor into an old and valued relationship. We must expect change to create tension; but we and our Latin American partners must insure that change and tension mean movement toward a free society.

We are not interested in maintaining a dole or giveaway program. We are pledged to help most those who do most to help themselves bridge the wide gap between what they have and what they need to provide their people with a decent life.

For the most part, the transformation of the old empires into independent states has proceeded in an orderly manner. In some places resentments still linger from the old colonial era. These the Communists try to inflame. But on the new and better basis of political and social equality, new partnerships are developing between the industrially advanced free nations and the underdeveloped areas.

### DIFFICULTIES IN COMMUNIST BLOC

There are other reasons for quiet confidence, and these come out of the Communist world itself. The sterility of their original doctrine has long been exposed. Marxism first offered a fictitious debate between a communism rejected by its own disciples and a capitalism which has long since disappeared if it ever existed at all. And in recent decades the Communists themselves have, in a curious left-handed way, recognized the overwhelming strength of the great tradition of freedom throughout the world. They have done this by their insistent efforts to capture the great words of that tradition and turn them to their own ends.

They have spoken of "peace" to conceal the use of force; they have spoken of "liberation" to conceal an effort to capture; they speak of "people's democracy" to avoid the free consultation of the people themselves. Conversely, the people of Germany who want self-determination are "revanchists." Free peoples determined to defend themselves are "militarists." And, oddly enough, those the Communists like most to call "imperialists" or "colonialists" are exactly those who have ushered into the United Nations row upon row of independent nations since World War II.

This tactic is increasingly transparent all over the world. So too is the emptiness of such phrases as "classless society," "workers' paradise" and "great leap forward."

There is no question but that the Soviet Union has achieved some notable successes in certain directions, for example, in space science and technology, in mass education, in public health and in selected sectors of industry. But it is interesting to note that their successes have come where they have permitted science and technology to move forward without doctrinal blinders and where substantial freedom of action is given to those responsible for the particular enterprise. In other sectors, for example in agriculture, there are serious difficulties throughout the bloc from East Germany to North Viet-Nam. Nature itself has imposed certain limitations, but this cannot be the answer throughout so vast an area. Limitations are imposed by organization, by official stultification of scientific freedom, and by failure to mobilize the most productive element in the history of agriculture, namely, the incentive and individual initiative of the farmer himself. The desperate situation in mainland China cannot advertise successfully the promised paradise of communism.

Other adjustments are having to be made within their bloc because of powerful ideas which long preceded the Communist revolution. A sense of national pride and desire for national independence, yearnings for more freedom for the individual himself, and the desire for higher standards of living and security for family and home have forced certain changes in the monolithic structure of the authoritarian system. And these changes, in turn, have produced sharp differences within the bloc itself— differences of doctrine, of organization, tactics and priorities.

Successful societies do not have to build walls and string barbed wire against their own people. The Berlin wall, erected a year ago today, is a monument to failure—the failure of a "competitive coexistence" that dared not compete.

### THE WINDS OF FREEDOM

No quick or easy victory for freedom can be promised. But those who are committed to freedom have less to worry about than those who would reverse this centuries-old history of man. As I have said on another occasion:

It is not for us to fear the great winds of change that are blowing today. They are the winds we have long known and sailed with, the winds which have carried man on his unending journey, the winds of freedom.

. . . America at her best is admired and trusted; and America is at her best when she is true to the commitments we made to ourselves and to history in the Declaration of Independence. These are the ideas and ideals which give us allies, spoken or silent, among men and women in every corner of the earth. They are part of the unfinished business which is a part of our story. This is the basis of our confidence; this is the scope of our task.

The revolution of freedom, which we have so proudly nurtured and fought for in the past and to which we pledge today, as in 1776, 'our Lives, our Fortunes and our sacred Honor,' is the true, enduring revolution, because it springs from the deepest, most persistent aspirations of men. History says this revolution will not fail.

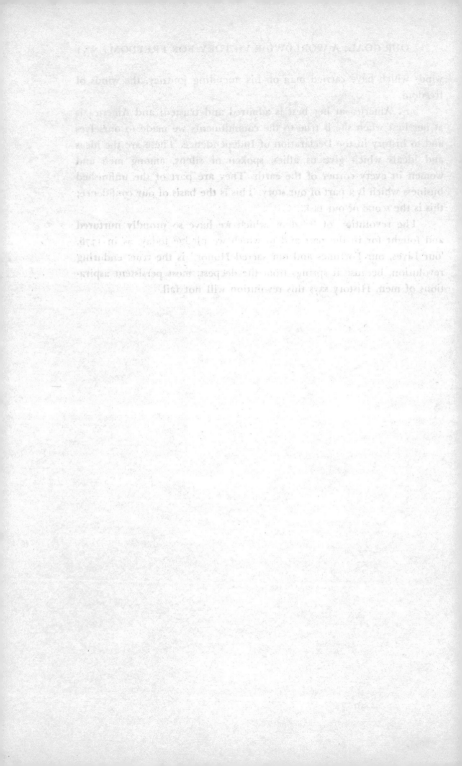

# Index

# INDEX

Abilene, and Eisenhower Library, 338
Acheson, Dean, 200
Acton, Lord, quote, 21
Adams, John, 2
Adams, John Quincy, 28
Adoula, Cyrille, 224-225
*Adventures in Ideas* (Whitehead), quote, 80-81
Africa, interview in *U.S. News and World Report*, 1962, 226-228; 2, 4, 5, 28, 30-33, 43, 51-55, 99, 118-120, 132, 221-228, 247, 306, 348
Agency for International Development (AID), 53-54, 93, 117, 123, 125
aid, international, 17, 92-97, 203-204, 209-211, 225
Akers, Anthony B., 206
All-India Institute of Medical Sciences, 209
Alliance for Progress, address at Johns Hopkins University, 1962, 149-157; 17, 33, 52, 55, 99, 116, 122, 123, 124, 145, 146, 149-157, 304, 348
allies, Western, *passim*
ambassador, an, 28, 65, 76, 83

America: Central, 304; Latin, 2, 30-33, 43, 51-54, 99, 100, 118-120, 127-149, 247, 306, 344, 348; North, 3; South, 304
American Geographical Society, 205
ANZUS, 55, 197-212, 231; signatories, 197
Antartica, 57, 205
Arab world, 304
Argentina, 152
Arms Control and Disarmament Agency, 57
arms race, 25, 57-58, 231, 264, 267, 268, 291, 299, 308, 344
Asia, 2, 4, 5, 30-33, 36, 43, 51-54, 99, 132, 234, 246, 247, 306, 327, 344, 348; South, 120; Southeast, 31, 36, 38, 51, 177-195, 201, 202, 304, 327
Athens, 169, 231
Atlanta (Georgia), 19, 315
Atlantic Community, 34-35, 116, 175, 305, 337, 347
atomic, see nuclear
Australia, address at parliamentary dinner, 1962, 197-205; 51, 103-106, 177, 197-205, 231, 347
Austria, 92, 185

Baghdad Pact, 228
Balubas, 227
Ban Padong (Laos), 183
Bangkok, 181
Bataan, 327-329
Battle Act, 242
Bay of Islands (New Zealand), 205
Beale, Sir Howard, 199
Belgium, 49, 119, 174, 222
Bemis, Samuel Flagg, 27-35
Berendsen, Sir Carl, quote, 207
Berlin, statement for the press, 1961, 167-168; 21, 23, 25-28, 29, 37, 44, 132, 133, 142, 159-173, 241, 247, 255, 350; West, 16, 19, 26, 29, 57, 344
"Big Four," 160, 171
Bill of Rights (U.S.), 1, 322
Bogotá, 137; Act of, 118, 123
Bolívar, Simon, 141; quote, 130-131
Bolivia, 152
Bonn, 35
Bowles, Chester, 70, 332
Brazil, 259
Briand, Aristide, 260; quotes, 18, 25
Britain, 3, 37, 50-51, 160, 168-169, 226, 233. See also: United Kingdom
Budapest, 252
Bunyan, Paul, 289
Burma, 259, 330
Byrd, Admiral Richard, 206

Calwell, Arthur A., 197
Cambodia, 177
Canada, 49-51, 98, 119, 174, 213, 233, 278
Canberra, 198
Capitalism, 16, 92, 133, 349
Castro, Fidel, 131-149
Central Treaty Organization (CENTO), address at CENTO, 1961, 228-230, address at

CENTO, 1962, 230-233; 55, 109, 228-233; signatories, 228
Charlemagne, 86
Chayes, Abram, 164
Chen Yi, 184; quote, 185
Chennault, General Claire, 330
Chile, 152
China, news conference, 1961, 217-218; Communist, testimony before House Foreign Affairs Committee, 1962, 219; 9, 51, 217-219, 235, 243-244, 248, 350; Republic of, toast at state dinner honoring Chen Cheng and Mrs. Chen, 1961, 329-331; 51, 109, 217-219, 329-331
*China Quarterly, The,* quote, 6-7
Christchurch (New Zealand), 206
Christmas Island, 208
Colombia, 152
Colombo Plan, 55, 180, 203, 209
colonialism and South Africa, 227-228
colonies: British, 3; American, 85, 96
Committee and Conference on Disarmament at Geneva, 1962, 257-288, 294-300
Common Market, 202-203, 346-347. See also European Economic Community
Commonwealth, British, 2, 55, 102-106
Communism, Communists, *passim;* 30-37, 235-255. See also: Sino-Soviet bloc; U.S.S.R.
Communist Party Congress, 140, 249
Congo, the, statement before Senate Foreign Relations Committee, 1962, 221-226; 31, 77, 83, 120, 142, 221-226, 248, 303, 307, 310
Congo Economic Program, 125
Constitution (U.S.), 1, 322

Consultative Group—Coordinating Committee, 248
Control Commission, 233, 281
Cooper, John Sherman, 61-62
Coordinating Committee (Cocom), 236, 241, 254-255
Coral Sea, Battle of the, 200
Corregidor, 327-329
Costa Rica, 152-153
Council of Ministers, 176
counterrevolution of coercion, 42-43
Cuba, 31, 127-149, 236, 248
cultural exchanges, 235-255
Curtain: Bamboo, 7, 96; Iron, 7, 42, 57, 96, 136, 166
Czechoslovakia, 223, 278

Davis, Elmer, 324
Dean, Arthur H., 297-300
Decade of Development, 52, 55, 93, 213
Declaration of Independence (U.S.), 1, 2, 3, 5, 10, 38, 322, 324, 348; quote, 206
Declaration of the Rights of Man of 1789, 3
democracy, 5-6, 32-33, 319
Democracy in America (Tocqueville), quote, 206
Denmark, 174
Detroit, 89
development, 51-56, 122, 124, 129, 146, 149-157, 166, 180, 189-190, 229-230, 234, 318-319, 345-347
Development Assistance Committee, 120
Development Loan Fund, 93, 110, 113, 118
diplomacy, state dinners for members of diplomatic corps, 1961, 339
Disarmament, address before New Hampshire Council on World Affairs, 1962, 257-266, statement at Committee of Disarmament at Geneva, 1962, 267-276, address at Davidson College, 1962, 288, remarks made at Committee on Disarmament, 1962, 294-300; 18, 22, 25, 257-300
Disarmament Agency, 25
Disarmament Commission, 169, 271, 272
Djilas, Milovan, 133
Dobrynin, Anatoly F., 169
Dominican Republic, 120, 146
Dorticós, Osvaldo, 136
Dulles, John Foster, remarks at John Foster Dulles Memorial Service, 1961, 335-337, statement on dedication of John Foster Dulles Library of Diplomatic History, 1962, 337-338; 200, 335-338

East: Far, 55, 120, 124, 209, 246-248, 344; Middle, 30-33, 55, 120
Economic Commission for Asia and the Far East (ECAFE), 55
Economic Committee, 232
Economist, London, quote, 107
education, remarks at Emory University, 1961, 315-317, remarks at Organization for Economic Cooperation and Development, 1961, 318-319; remarks at National Conference on International Social and Economic Development, 1961, 320-321, remarks on "Continental Classroom," 1961, 321-323; 52-53, 94, 116, 152-153, 315-325
Eisenhower, Dwight D., 222; quotes, 54, 113
Eisenhower Library, 338
Ethiopia, 259
Europe, remarks made outside of White House, 1961, 166-167; 36, 223, 225, 241, 327, 344-346; Cen-

tral, 165, 166, 251, 344; Eastern, 9, 23, 33, 36, 243, 253; Western, 2, 3, 8, 9, 23, 36, 87, 98, 103, 133, 141 172, 202, 211, 249, 304

European Atomic Energy Community (EURATOM), 98, 103

European Coal and Steel Community, 98, 103

European Economic Community, 49-51, 87-91, 98-102, 102-106. See also: Common Market

Evans, Reg, 200

Expanded Technical Assistance Program, 124

Export-Import Bank, 113

Federal Deposit Insurance Corporation, 113

Food and Agriculture Organization (FAO), 210

Food for Peace, 93

Foreign Assistance Act of 1961, 123, 125-126

Formosa, 36, 219

Fosdick, Raymond, quote, 24-25

Fowler, Henry H., 164

France, 49, 51, 92, 119, 160, 163-165, 168-169, 174, 177, 226, 278

Franklin, Benjamin, 85

freedom, address at National Press Club, 1961, 11-19, address to Veterans of Foreign Wars, 1962, 312, 341-351; free society, 131

Frost, Robert, quote, 4

Garcia, Carlos, P., 328

General Agreement on Tariffs and Trade (GATT), 55, 100, 105, 203, 243

Geneva, 18, 31, 162, 168-169, 173, 188, 191, 195, 201, 219, 230, 257-288, 294-300, 344; Accords, 187, 194, 201

Georgia (U.S.), 8, 198

Germany, news conference, 1961, 161-163, news conference, 1961, 163-165, news conference, 1961, 168-171, news interview, Radio Free Berlin and North German Radio, 1962, 171-173; 23, 49, 119, 159-176, 238, 337, 349; Federal Republic of (West), 9, 159-173, 253; German Democratic Republic (East), 9, 29, 57, 131, 132, 159-173, 210, 253, 350

Gizenga, Antoine, 224

Glenn, Colonel, 205

Goa, 233

Gomulka, Wladyslaw, 244, 245

Graham Land, 205

Greece, 3, 23, 109, 173, 175, 179, 303

Green, Howard C., 298

Gromyko, Andrei A., 168-169, 170, 296

Guadalcanal, 199

Guevara, "Che," 132

Habana, 134

Hague Peace Conference, 1907, 337

Hakone (Japan), 212, 214

Hamberg, 89

Hamilton, Fowler, 117, 120

Hammarskjold, Dag, 223, 302-314

Hanoi, 31, 194

Harriman, W. Averill, 73, 190

Hawaii, 327

Herter, Christian, 28

Hickenlooper, Senator, 147

Hiroshima, 22

historian, 27-29, 39, 338

Historical Association, American, address before, 27-39

Hitler, Adolf, 37, 159

Hoang Van Chi, 7; quote from article "Collectivization and Rice Production," 6-7

Hobbes, Thomas, quote, 24

Holyoake, Keith Jacka, 197
Home, Lord, 184, 193, 298
Hong Kong, 36
Houssay, Dr. Bernado, 152
Hughes, Charles Evans, 28
Hull, Cordell, 45, 50, 55; quote 58-59
Hungary, 23, 251

ICFTU, 224
Iceland, 174
Ikeda, Hayata, 212, 213
Indian Peninsula, 36
India, interview on "Issues and Answers," 1962, 233-234; 118-119, 120, 209, 233-234, 243, 259
Indus Basin Trust Fund, 125
Indochina, 181
Institutions of democratic government, British, 3
Inter-American Defense Board, 139, 146
Inter-American Peace Committee, 136, 145
International Commission on Measures To Reduce the Risk of War, 273
International Conference on Laos, 1961, 182-191; 1962, 191-193
International Control Commission (ICC), 183, 186, 192
International Cooperation Administration (ICA), 118
International Court, 22
International Bank, 55
International Development Association, 55
International Disarmament Organization, 281
International Monetary Fund, 55, 303
Italy, 49, 92, 174
Iran, toast at state dinner for Shah of Iran, 1962, 228, 303, 331-332

Ivory Coast, Republic of the, toast at state dinner for President and Mme. Felix Houphouet-Boigny, 1962, 332-334

Japan, statement at Joint U.S.-Japan Committee on Trade and Economic Affairs, 1961, 212-214, remarks to Japanese cabinet ministers, 1961, 214-215; 9, 36, 49-51, 53, 98, 100, 103, 119, 152, 211-215, 241, 246, 337, 347
Jefferson, Thomas, 2, 28, 45, 141, 333; quote, 42
Joad, C. E. M., 37
Johnston Island, 208
Joint Chiefs of Staff, Chairman, 49, 121

Kadar, Janos, 253
Kasai (the Congo), 221
Kasavubu, Joseph, 222-224
Kashmir, 233
Katanga (the Congo), 221, 223-226, 227
Kennedy, John F., passim; quotes, 2, 5, 25-26, 26, 30, 45, 114, 164, 175, 185, 195, 284-285, 342, 348
Khrushchev, Nikita, 58, 79, 132, 133, 160-163, 169, 171, 185, 222, 249, 252, 305, 307, 322, 344; quotes, 15, 100, 140, 170, 306
Kitona (the Congo), 225
Kohler, Foy D., 164
Korea, 23, 36, 51, 93, 179, 198, 248; North, 4, 235, 246, 248; Republic of (South), reply to Prime Minister of Republic of Korea, 1961, 215-216

land-grant college system, 100th anniversary, 53, 155, 318
Laos, statement at International Conference on Laos, 1961, 182-191, remarks at International

Conference on Laos, 1962, 191-193, interview on "Washington Conversation," 1962, 193-194; 31, 37, 142, 169, 177, 180, 182-191, 193, 201, 247, 294, 296, 344; King of, quote, 185-186
League of Nations, 305
Lebanon, 303
Lenin, 322
Léopoldville, 222
Lewis, Charles, quote, 83
Libby, Dr. Willard, 292
Lie, Trygve, 311
Lincoln, Abraham, 5, 53, 141
Locke, John, 333
Lumumba, Patrice, 222
Luxembourg, 49, 174
Lysenkoism, 252

MacArthur, General Douglas, 328
McCloy, John J., 19, 20, 265-266
McDowell, Harris B., Jr., 219
MacLeish, Archibald, quote, 82
Magna Charta, 3
Manila, 177
Mao Tse-Tung, 132
Mars, 292
Marshall, John, 28
Marshall, George Catlett, 20, 109, 112; Award, 20
Marshall Plan, 49, 52, 68, 92, 103, 109-111, 319, 346
Martí, 141
Marx, Karl, 9, 132, 322
Marxism, 16, 243-244, 349
Mediterranean, 141; eastern, 23
Mekong River, 180
Melanesia, 199
Menzies, Robert G., 197
Merrow, Congressman, 147
Mexico, 152-153, 259
Military, 109-110, 121, 188, 231, 236, 262, 343-344
Ministerial Council, 229

Montesquieu, 333
Moon, 292
Moratorium: and China, 217-218; and nuclear testing, 277, 278, 287, 297
Morrill, Senator, 53
Morse, Senator, 147
Moscow, 26, 27, 140, 162, 173, 175, 194, 244, 249, 305-306
Mount Victoria (New Zealand), 206
Multilateral Security Trade Control System, 248
Murrow, Edward R., 291
Mussolini, Benito, 37

National Gallery, 330
nations: free, 44-59; industrialized, 49-51, 53, 117; uncommitted, 11-12, 16, 247; underdeveloped, 347-348, see also: Development
nationalism, 14
Netherlands, the, 49, 174
New Delhi, 209
New York City, 333
New Zealand, address at parliamentary dinner, 1962, 205-212; 51, 103-106, 177, 197, 199, 201, 205-212
Nigeria, 118-119, 259
North Atlantic Council, statement on arrival at Athens, 1962, 175-176
North Atlantic Treaty Organization (NATO), news conference, 1961, 174; 17, 53, 98, 109, 119, 159-176, 231, 241, 254, 346; signatories, 174
North Carolina, 89, 95
Norway, 173
nuclear: energy, 236; monopoly (U.S.), 22; testing, statement to Geneva Disarmament Conference, 1962, 277-288; 208-211,

231, 233, 250, 259-300, 345;
weapons, 30, 37, 58, 135, 258,
262, 263, 291, 292

officials, public, 12-13
Operation Deepfreeze, 206
Operations Coordinating Board,
63
Organization of American States
(OAS), 55, 127, 135-149; reso-
lutions, quotes, 127, 136-137
Organization for Economic Coop-
eration and Development
(OECD), 89, 95, 98, 113, 120, 243
Orientale (the Congo), 221
Ottawa, 175
Oxford Union, 37
Oxford University, 198

Pacific, 327-329; Islands, 207-208;
Northwest (U.S.), 289; Ocean,
195; South, 199
Pak, General Chung Hee, 216
Pakistan, 117, 118-120, 228
Palestine, 303
Palestine Refugee Program, 125
Paris, 168, 169, 174
Pasternak, Boris, 7
Pathet Lao, 31
Peace Corps, 38, 52
Peiping, 194
Permanent Council, 176
Perth, 205
Peru, 152
Philippines, the, 51, 93, 177, 327-
329
"Point Four," 93, 109
Poland, 235, 242, 244-246, 251, 278
Policy, foreign, 302
Portugal, 174, 226
Powers, colonial, 6
Preparatory Commission, 285, 311
press, the, 12-13
Princeton University, 337-338

Privy Council, Judicial Committee,
198
Project Mercury, 204-205
Punta del Este, Uruguay, Conference at, 118, 120, 123, 127-149

ROTC, high school, 19
Reconstruction Finance Corpora-
tion, 113
Reed, Stanley Forman, 332
revolution: American, 8; Bolshe-
vik, 8; of freedom, 41-42; of
progress, 43-44
Roa, Raúl, quote, 136
Rockefeller, John D., III, 80, 82
Rockefeller Foundation, 198, 319
Rockefeller Public Service Awards,
82
Rome, 89
Rome, Treaty of, 49-50
Roosevelt, Franklin D., 130, 324;
quote, 212
Rousseau, Jean Jacques, 333
Rumania, 278
Rusk, Dean, quotes, 127-128, 350-
351; political philosophy, arti-
cle from Saturday Evening Post,
1962, 1-10

Samoa: American, 207; Western,
207-208
San José (Costa Rica), 135, 144
San Martín, José, 141
Santiago, Declaration of, 137
Science, scientists, address at Seat-
tle World's Fair, 1962, 289-294;
38, 41, 251-252, 289-292, 315-
317
Selden, Congressman, 147
Sihanouk, Prince, 178, 183, 184
Sino-Soviet bloc, 16, 24, 99-100,
114, 124, 246-248. See also: Com-
munism; U.S.S.R.
Song, Yo Chan, General, 215
South Pacific Commission, 208

Southeast Asia Treaty Organization (SEATO), address at SEATO, 1961, 177-181; statement on return to U.S., 1961, 181-182; 55, 109, 177-194, 207; signatories and protectorates, 177

Souvanna Phouma, Prince, 177, 191, 193

space, outer, 262, 263, 292-294

Space Needle, 289

Special Fund, 124

Stalin, Joseph, 37, 133, 160, 322

Stanleyville, 224

Stevenson, Adlai, 18

Suez, 303

Supreme Council for National Reconstruction, 216

Sweden, 259

Tanganyika, 119

Tennessee, University of, 52

Tennessee Valley Authority, 46-47, 130

Thailand, 177

Thompson, Llewellyn, 168

Tito, Marshall, 243

Tocqueville, Alexis de, 38; quote, 206

Tokyo, 35

Totalitarian system, 35-36

trade, address before Conference on Trade Policy, 1962, 97-102, address at Official State Reception, New Zealand, 1962, 102-106, testimony before House Select Committee on Export Control, 1961, 235-255

Trade Expansion Act of 1962, 86, 89-91, 97-102

troika, statement for the press, 1961, 305-307; 314

Truman, Harry S., 218; quote, 68

Truman Doctrine, 109

Tshombe, Moise, 223-227

Tunisia, 118

Turkey, 23, 109, 174, 228

United Arab Republic, 259

United Kingdom, 119, 163-165, 174, 177, 178, 182-191, 202, 228, 238, 259-300. See also: Britain

United Nations and United Nations Charter, *passim*; address at Assembly of United Church Women, 1961, 301-305, remarks at Foreign Press Association Luncheon, 1961, 307-314. General Assembly, 22, 28, 79, 168, 217-219, 307-314. Secretary-General, 310-314. Security Council, 307, 311.

United Nations Children's Fund (UNICEF), 125

United Nations Relief and Rehabilitation Administration (UNRRA), 92, 109

Union of Soviet Socialist Republics, *passim*. See also: Communism; Sino-Soviet bloc

United States of America, *passim*. Department of Commerce, 86, 101, 241. Department of State, 20, 28, 38, 61-70, 86, 101, 162, 250, 302, 321, 331, 341; Secretary of State, 27-29, 34, 338, 345; assistant, 74-76. Department of the Treasury, 164. Aid, address at Chamber of Commerce, 1961, 107-115, statement to Senate Foreign Relations Committee, 1962, 115-126. Industry, 90-91. Policy, address at University of Tennessee, 1962, 41-59; foreign, remarks to U.S. Department of State policy-making officers, 61-70; 11, 13, 18-19, 41-59, 61-70; economic, address at Charlotte, North Carolina, 1962, 85-97

U.S. Army, Association of, 19

U.S. General Staff, 22
U.S. foreign service, remarks at luncheon of American Foreign Service Association, 1961, 70-80, talk before Advertising Council, Inc., 1962, 83; 101
U.S. Information Agency, 325
U.S. Office of War Information, 324
U.S. public service, remarks made at Rockefeller Public Service Awards Luncheon, 1961, 80-82
U.S. Strategic Air Command, 38
U Thant, 314

Venezuela, 5, 152, 348
Venus, 292
Vienna, 160-161, 249, 344
Viet-Nam, news conference, 1962, 194-195; 120, 142, 194-195, 201; North, 4, 9, 131-132, 181, 194, 233-235, 247, 350; Republic of (South), 3-4, 31, 32, 177, 180, 182, 202, 233, 247, 343, 344
Viet Minh, 201
Voice of America, remarks at 20th anniversary of, 1962, 245, 324-325

Wainwright, General Jonathan, 328
war, by accident, 29-30, 262-263; cold, address at Memorial Dinner, George Catlett Marshall, 1961, 19-27, 140, 243, 259; Korean, 248

Warsaw, 219
Warsaw Pact, 143, 244
Washington, George, 4, 29, 96-97
Washington, D.C., remarks at Bataan Day, 1961, 327-329; 96-97, 140, 168-170, 212, 232, 309, 327-329, 333
Washington (State), 289, 291
Wellington, 203
Whitehead, Alfred North, quote, 80-81
Wilkins, Sir Hubert, 205
Wilson, Woodrow, quote, 45
Woodrow Wilson School, 82
World: Northern Hemisphere, 30-33, 38, 54-56, 103, 303; Southern Hemisphere, 30-33, 38, 54-56, 303; Western Hemisphere, addresses at Punta del Este Conference, 1962, 127-143, report to U.S. people, 1962, 144-149; 155, 304
World Bank, 120, 125, 303
World War: I, 103, 305, 324; II, 2, 13, 21, 28, 31, 32, 34-35, 75, 86, 92, 96, 140, 150, 163, 198, 258, 269, 305, 324, 345, 349

Xieng Khouang (Laos), 183

Yalta, 16
Yugoslavia, 235, 242-244

Zorin, Valerian A., 266, 300